DATE DUE

	MAY 2 4 1995
UPI 261-2505	PRINTED IN U.S.A.

NERVOUS LAUGHTER

Media and Society Series

J. Fred MacDonald, General Editor

NERVOUS LAUGHTER

Television Situation Comedy
and
Liberal Democratic Ideology

Darrell Y. Hamamoto

PRAEGER

New York
Westport, Connecticut
London

Library of Congress Cataloging-in-Publication Data

Hamamoto, Darrell Y.
    Nervous laughter : television situation comedy and liberal
democratic ideology / Darrell Y. Hamamoto.
       p. cm. — (Media and society series)
    Bibliography: p.
    Includes index.
    ISBN 0–275–92861–6 (alk. paper)
    1. Comedy programs—United States. 2. Television politics—United
States. 3. Liberalism—United States I. Title. II. Series.
PN1992.8.C66H3 1989
791.43′09′0917—dc19   88–30279

Library of Congress Catalog Card Number: 88–30279
ISBN: 0–275–92861–6

First published in 1989

Praeger Publishers, One Madison Avenue, New York, NY 10010
A division of Greenwood Press, Inc.

Printed in the United States of America

The paper used in this book complies with the
Permanent Paper Standard issued by the National
Information Standards Organization (Z39.48–1984).

10 9 8 7 6 5 4 3 2 1

For June Kurata and Gena Hamamoto

Contents

Preface

Like most of my cohorts who grew up in the 1950s and 1960s, life without television is impossible to imagine. As I remember it, the luminescent presence of our Zenith set dominated almost every aspect of our family life. Its hours of operation, who got to see what, when, and for how long was endlessly negotiated among two parents and four children. Back then, having more than one television set in order to satisfy conflicting tastes was inconceivable. Compromise in program selection was born of necessity rather than choice. As a result, each family member spent a good deal of time watching programs not of his or her own choosing.

The immediate, unrehearsed world of talk shows, for instance, would have been lost on me had not my mother insisted on watching them. Long before Morton Downey, Jr., or Wally George, the late Joe Pyne took sport in baiting audience members who might dare stand in the "Beef Box" to disagree with Pyne's social philosophy, which was somewhere to the right of Attila the Hun. Pyne had a wooden leg to replace the one he had lost in World War II. Sometimes he would invoke the leg to justify his patriotism and rabid defense of all things American. Pyne's hurt somehow took the edge off his meanspirited aggressiveness, but it was in watching the local *Joe Pyne Show* that I learned of TV's power to evoke visceral reaction and foster intolerance.

Quite at the other end of the emotional spectrum was a local talk show hosted by one of television's few eccentrics and certified geniuses, Oscar Levant. Both the hunger for a life of the mind and the nicotine habit I later developed (and kicked) probably began with watching Levant, forever enveloped in sensuous volumes of cigarette smoke, ramble on about any topic at all that flitted through his tormented mind. Oscar Levant demonstrated TV's capacity for intimacy, intelligence, and kindness.

We kids rose early on Saturday and Sunday to watch hours on end of cartoons from Warner Bros., Terrytoons, Hanna-Barbera, and Walter Lantz. When school was out, summer days were occupied by the bountiful supply of vintage Hollywood films from the 1930s and 1940s. All through the year evenings were reserved for television Westerns in deference to the household patriarch who daily battled foes considerably more intractable than those seen on the horse operas.

Despite our varied tastes, there was one form of television that we could enjoy together—situation comedy. Unlike the other forms of television, the sitcom seemed best able to convey the lived experience of everyday American people left alone to enjoy unparalleled prosperity and global dominance. The sitcom was about *us*. Americans who were otherwise divided by ethnicity, geography, levels of educational attainment, age, and gender could gather equally around the TV to share in the physical comedy of Lucille Ball, the pathos of the Anderson family, or the angst of Dobie Gillis. The better situation comedies never failed to hit home.

What at first appeared to be only innocuously funny, the bohemianism of Maynard G. Krebs in *The Many Loves of Dobie Gillis* foreshadowed the social and political turmoil that began to build throughout the 1960s and early 1970s. Before too long, problems of racism, inequality, and war began to clash with images of peaceable sitcom communities like Central City, Mayfield, Mayberry, Hilldale, and Springfield. We did not know it at the time, but Zelda Gilroy hinted at the revival of feminism in the 1960s.

As America slipped into a host of related crises precipitated by the war in Vietnam, sitcoms became further removed from reality. Flying nuns, scantily clad genies, angels, ghosts, Martians, and talking cars began to populate the sitcom universe. It was at this point that I abandoned television for books and the cinema, not to return until the sitcoms of Tandem Productions and MTM Enterprises revived my interest in the form during the 1970s.

About this time, my interest in the meaning of significance of mass-mediated popular culture began to take root. Theories of media "manipulation" were still in vogue at the time, yet they seemed one-sided and more than slightly condescending to the viewing public. Such theories also tended to denigrate cultural workmen—actors, writers, producers, and directors—who were not given enough credit for the art of smuggling incisive social truths aboard such conventional TV forms as the sitcom. I remained intrigued by the way mass-mediated popular art had helped to democratize American society even as it left alone the mechanisms of social repression and domination. It is this duality that I have sought to explore in this book. Toward that end, I have borrowed freely from a number of related disciplines in an attempt to explain the curious grip the television situation comedy has had on its audience for over four decades.

Social, cultural, and economic crises deepened in the 1980s. By the end of Ronald Reagan's two-term presidency, Americans seemed poised to renew their commitment to the liberal democratic legacy of progressive social change after having learned many sobering lessons in the years following the Great Society. The strong showing of Jesse Jackson in the 1988 Democratic primaries was a glimmer of hope amidst persistent divisions among the electorate. The subsequent triumph of George Bush in the general election revealed America's continuing collective uncertainty in the face of mounting international challenges. In keeping with recent trends, a sizable percentage of the electorate stated their preference in presidential candidates by simply staying at home rather than venturing forth to cast a vote at the neighborhood polling place.

Like American society itself, the situation comedy has undergone much change even as it maintained continuity with its historical past. In the pilot for *The New Leave It to Beaver Show*, Beaver Cleaver returned to Mayfield a divorced parent of two. His big brother Wally lived next door with the girl of his dreams: middle-American keeper of the genetic material, Mary Ellen Rogers. That Wally Cleaver now suffered from impotence in his maturity paralleled America's waning powers since the time the original program first aired.

Oddly, what began as a personal interest in television began to take a vocational direction after I received a graduate fellowship to study at the Center for the Study of Popular Culture at Bowling Green State University. It was there that my interest in popular culture as a legitimate area of academic inquiry was validated. I must thank Ray Browne for his pioneering efforts in building this unique program. Michael Marsden and Joseph Arpad were especially helpful in setting me on the trail. Thanks also to Rosemary Johnson and Bruce Kurek for keeping me nourished with kielbasa, Lake Erie turtle soup, and Perrysburg powie.

My studies in mass media and popular culture took me next to the Program in Comparative Culture at the University of California, Irvine. While my research interests were not necessarily well received, they were at least tolerated. I should like to express my gratitude to both the department and the University of California for providing me with several quarters of employment as a teaching assistant. Thanks to former department chairman Joseph Jorgensen for developing an innovative approach to the study of culture and society. I owe an enormous intellectual debt to Pete Clecak, who has supported my work from the beginning. Karen Leonard and the late John Leonard were both very generous with their time at an early stage of this project and for this I am grateful. Carlton Moss, whose professional commitment and excellence as a filmmaker, writer, and educator continues to be a source of inspiration.

This book would not have been possible without the unwavering support of Anne-Marie Feenberg, dean of the School of Arts and Sciences at National University. I am grateful to her for having given me a chance to work.

The person responsible for having this book see the light of day is Fred MacDonald, who rescued me from obscurity. His valuable observations, critical comments, and factual corrections have been indispensable in the writing of this book. Of course, all errors of fact or interpretation are mine alone.

One of the more gratifying aspects of a project such as this is that it can be shared freely with friends who have listened, willingly or not, to bits and pieces of the arguments developed herein. I extend thanks to Carl Boggs, the best blues-harp-playing social theorist that I know. Dave Williams of Double Veteran and Formosa Studios deserves a medal for serving as a sometimes reluctant sounding board. Thanks also to Bob Ahart for supplying me with the freshest of trends in popular culture. To Charles Igawa, I give thanks both for his friendship and the intellectual imprint he has left on me, and his wife, Yuko Igawa, who has always warmly received me in their home.

I should like to express my gratitude to Joel K. Hamamoto, Joan Hamamoto, Henry Kurata, and Nancy Kurata for providing assistance to a family trying to live in the highly inflated Orange County real estate market. Where went Mayfield?

To June Kurata and Gena Hamamoto, my heartfelt appreciation for their understanding and tolerance in matters related to this undertaking.

1
Introduction

PERSISTENCE OF VISION

The television situation comedy has been a staple of commercial television entertainment for over forty years. In only a few TV seasons have situation comedies not dominated the network ratings. Certainly other television entertainment forms have outdistanced the sitcom in the ratings sweepstakes, in the short run at least. Throughout much of the 1950s, for example, TV Westerns regularly rode roughshod over most other dramatic genres. But the adult Western peaked in 1959 with fully 28 programs (which represented almost 25% of all evening programing) and by the 1970s had all but faded.[1] For a time, during the early 1970s, crime shows placed very high in the ratings as well. Nevertheless, it has been the situation comedy that has proven to be the most enduring and resilient of all television entertainment forms.[2]

To explain the durability of the sitcom form at its simplest, both intrinsic (aesthetic) and extrinsic (social) modes or categories of analysis might be brought to bear on the question. By this reduction, the enduring popularity of the television situation comedy can be attributed to two complementary characteristics of the form: (1) its multivalent social ideologies and mores that function within the larger framework of liberal democratic ideology and (2) the commercial system that produces and distributes the product for private profit alone. The former characteristic has tended toward emancipation, the latter, repression.

In the first category, the plural and indeterminate interplay of ideologies within the sitcom have drawn directly from the conflicts and accommodations that have arisen from the transformation of postwar American society, a transformation that has included unprecedented economic growth, increased social entitlements administered by a vastly enlarged state, the struggles of the equality revolution, and the rise of the new middle class. The situation comedy, as an aesthetic form grounded in realism and contemporaneity, has remarked upon almost every major development of postwar American history.

In tandem with the political struggles of the postwar era that have led to greater democracy, the situation comedy has supported and extended what has been described by Douglas Kellner as "emancipatory popular culture."[3] To a greater degree than perhaps any other popular art, the situation comedy has offered oppositional ideas, depicted oppression and struggle, and reflected a critical consciousness that stops just short of political mobilization. More than the simple reflection of hegemonic class interests, reduced to the "dominant ideology" of the corporate capitalist order, the situation comedy has embodied emancipatory beliefs proven to have had deep resonance with its diverse audience.[4]

In the second category, the commercial system that produces and distributes the situation comedy proceeds from an altogether different set of premises. Against the emancipatory tendencies of the situation comedy, the logic of the commercial media and communications industries admits only the "profitability factor, not the viewer/listener's wants and needs," which tends to repress the full development of democratic culture and society.[5] Although emancipatory democratic values have always informed the situation comedy, the realization of such values in actual practice has been woefully restricted by the commercial system of television. Since the beginning of the postwar era, the commercial system of television has successfully packaged and marketed the affirmative aspects of democratic culture such as freedom, equality, community, autonomy, self-determination, planning, and popular control. Unfortunately, the commercial system of television has helped to confine the affirmative aspects of domestic culture to the private sphere organized around domestic life.

The false separation between private living space and public forum has allowed for the relatively free expression of liberal democratic values, but stripped of its political implications. The domestication, that is, containment of liberal democratic ideals, has minimized the risk emancipatory ideals might pose to undemocratic economic and political structures of domination. To add to the dilemma, the model of learning and action taught by television drama is based on individualistic and private approaches to social problems. This model of social action has forestalled the many challenges to the legitimacy of network oligopolies, which reap substantial private profit and exercise tremendous power through the exclusive control of a social resource.

As for what constitutes the proper "wants" and "needs" of the audience, this has been a question that has been endlessly debated by critics and advocates of the commercial networks. So far, however, the debate has not truly touched at the core issue: How can decision making and democratic control of a social resource effectively take place within undemocratic social institutions, specifically, the network oligopolies? The expansion of democratic principles and concomitant growth of the welfare state in the postwar era has highlighted with increasing intensity the contradiction between democracy and capitalism. This has been especially true during the difficult economic times of the Reagan presidency, during which the political rights of subsistence and social welfare (democracy) have been sacrificed to the higher cause of preserving the historic inequalities within the economic system (capitalism).[6] The symbolic means of overcoming this fundamental division within liberal democratic thought has remained a crucial problem addressed by the situation comedy.

NEW DEAL LIBERALISM

The social and cultural ideologies found in the television situation comedy have constituted a relatively consistent and coherent common discourse referred to in these pages as "liberal democratic ideology." This dominant model of social knowledge, organization, action, and political power emerged from the New Deal liberalism of the 1930s. Liberalism represented a break in the conservative laissez-faire doctrine of the minimalist state. According to John Kenneth Galbraith, the state under the New Deal became "active and interventionist on an unprecedented and previously unimagined scale."[7]

With the advent of the New Deal, no longer were the vagaries of the national economy to be guided by impersonal market forces free from government intervention. Beginning with the New Deal and continuing until the mid–1970s, the governmental activism of "practical liberalism" had "irreversibly established the terms and limits of debate for U.S. domestic national politics."[8] The political and economic objectives and policies of the New Deal were accepted as inevitable by traditional conservatives, Republicans, and Democrats. As Theda Skocpol has observed, "arguments were not over *whether* the government should undertake basic "positive" programs, but over the details of *how* government should act. . .*who should benefit*. . .and *how federal expenditures should be financed*."[9]

It is important to note that by this description, the ideological consensus wrought during the time of the New Deal bridges the common distinction made between "liberal" versus "conservative" politics. Since the time of the New Deal both liberals and conservatives have shared the same basic set of assumptions concerning politics and society. They have differed primarily in the specific methods and means of achieving common goals.

Rhetorical distortions and variations in terminology have often confused what is meant by "conservatism" or "liberalism," especially when treating distinct but related spheres of activity such as the economy, the polity, and culture. It is possible, therefore, for someone like Daniel Bell to describe himself in the foreword to *The Cultural Contradictions of Capitalism* as at once a socialist in matters of the economy, a liberal in politics, and a cultural conservative.[10]

What is referred to, then, in these pages as the dominant liberal democratic ideology is far from being simply the monolithic, univocal expression of a capitalist social order that seeks to directly control the process of its own ongoing legitimation.[11] Rather, the dominant liberal democratic ideology is itself cross-hatched by a variety of contradictory and oppositional thought, aspects of which find their way into the television text. John Fiske made the following observation: "Despite the homogenizing force of the dominant ideology, the subordinate groups in capitalism have retained a remarkable diversity of social identities, and this has required capitalism to produce an equivalent variety of voices. The diversity of capitalist voices is evidence of the comparative intransigence of the subordinate."[12] Mass-mediated popular culture such as the situation comedy is popular with its diverse audience to the extent that it validates and renews the three "generic values" of liberal democracy: freedom, equality, and democracy.[13]

RADIO PRECURSORS

The situation comedy, prior to its introduction to television, developed in a milieu of rapid social change brought about by a fundamental transformation of the American economy. The transition of American society from a rural agricultural economy to an urban industrial economy was not without fitful dislocations of peoples separated by geography, language, and culture. As such, the situation comedy as popular art was born amidst labor and capital conflict, interracial hostility, regional and sectional rivalries, and the pressures of Americanization faced by millions of immigrants working in a harsh, competitive environment during worldwide economic depression. Radio assisted in building a popular, uniquely American political culture. Radio comedy in particular helped mediate the clashes of immigrant cultures and eased the sense of deprivation inflicted by the Great Depression.[14]

The radio situation comedy was the aesthetic site upon which the inconsistencies, clashes, and conflicts of the larger social system were argued and settled. As in the liberal pluralist model of power in society, radio situation comedy provided piecemeal, ameliorative, and conciliatory solutions to structural problems. In this, the radio sitcom bore striking similarity to the liberal pluralist model of intergroup conflict—the "race relations cycle"—advanced by Chicago school sociologist Robert E. Park.

For Park, race relations progressed first from initial contact between groups, to competition, to accommodation, and finally to assimilation. In its denial of class conflict and teleological hopes for gradual reform, the race relations cycle was the liberal social science analogue of the situation comedy in the early stage of its development. This similarity between popular and social scientific models of understanding also shows the degree to which liberal pluralism, not conflict theory, has informed seemingly unrelated spheres of liberal democratic society.

The television situation comedy form grew out of such network radio programs as *Amos 'n' Andy* and *The Rise of the Goldbergs*. Shows such as these were enormously popular during the late 1920s at the onset of the Great Depression. Radio through much of the 1930s still drew heavily from the rich legacy of vaudeville. It was not until the 1940s that the situation comedy reached its maturity as an aesthetic and social form as its vaudevillian traces faded. Over this fairly short span of time, the portrayal of the hardscrabble existence of the ethnic underclass in *Amos 'n' Andy* and *The Goldbergs* and the hillbilly or "rube" humor of *Lum and Abner, Fibber McGee and Molly*, and *The Judy Canova Show* gave way to white "middle-class morality tales" the likes of *The Aldrich Family, The Adventures of Ozzie and Harriet*, and *The Great Gildersleeve*.[15]

The ethnic and hillbilly humor heard on the radio comedy of the 1930s dramatized the dislocations and strains caused by the rapid urbanization of American society. The Southern Appalachian coal boom that took place between 1912 and 1927 saw the coal extraction industry help transform a relatively autonomous regional economy, society, and culture into one composed of workers dependent on either the corporate wage or "company store" system of (unequal) exchange. Once the Depression ended the coal boom, a large number of the white rural underclass fled to the "little Kentuckies" of midwestern cities and incurred the hostility of the native population. Similarly, the large urban centers of the Northeast were arenas for economic competition between European immigrant labor and blacks, who fled the devastated agricultural economy of the South in large numbers. Radio situation comedy humor doubtless served the twin function of easing the pain of economic depression and venting interethnic tensions.[16]

Typically 15 minutes long, early radio situation comedies were often produced entirely by advertising agencies working for corporate advertisers. The shift from strongly drawn portrayals of underclass life to that of the middle class roughly paralleled the growing power and influence of advertising agencies, a key institution that brokered the growth of the consumer economy. By 1929, advertisers spent $3.4 billion annually, equivalent to 3 percent of the gross national product. Audience rating and measurement services, such as the early Crossley and Hooper ratings services, reached a level of sophistication that enabled them to provide advertisers with relatively detailed analysis of the radio audience. By the late 1940s to early 1950s, the A. C. Nielsen Company and the Arbitron Company were able to supply advertisers reliable audience data on a national basis.

The length of the radio sitcom was the result of the segmentation of the broadcast hour, parts of which were dedicated to the selling of commercial advertising time. This segmentation of time followed the overall pattern of increased rationality and commodification of life that attended the transformation of an advanced industrial form of production into a consumer economy. Rather than having arisen from Aristotelian imperatives or transhistorical aesthetic ideals, the structure of the sitcom owed much to the limits imposed by the needs of commerce.[17] In television, sole sponsorship of programs was eventually replaced by the "magazine concept" of selling advertising, whereby shows were further subdivided—like real estate—into segments that could be sold more profitably to a number of advertisers.

In early television situation comedies, commercials were often part of the dramatic flow, especially when they were broadcast live. This posed no problem in the case of single sponsorship, since strong viewer identification with products, personalities, and programs was desired. The magazine concept of advertising, however, dictated that the situation comedy be made amenable to the insertion of commercial messages at precise moments during the course of a 30-minute program. In time, innovations such as canned laughter and applause, videotape technology, and electronic editing further refined the exacting technique of building a program around commercial interruptions.

SIGNAL ENCLOSURES

The poetics of the television situation comedy have been defined in part by governmental regulatory power exercised by the Federal Communications Commission (FCC). The FCC was created by Congress through the Communications Act of 1934, which replaced its institutional predecessor, the Federal Radio Commission (FRC). The FRC, created by Congress through the Radio Act of 1927, was meant to impose order on the chaos created by the scramble among broadcasters for position and strategic advantage during the wildcatting phase of early radio.

In accordance with its congressional mandate, the FCC has been entrusted with the allocation of a scarce public resource, radio frequencies, to commercial broadcasters for the purpose of private profit taking. The expropriation of social resources for the benefit of a few has not been without historical precedent. By way of example, in Great Britain the "enclosure" of agricultural land once held in common occurred at a pivotal moment in its transformation from an agriculturally based economy to an industrial empire.[18] Similarly, the enclosure of the airwaves in the United States took place at a crucial juncture during its transformation from an industrial to a consumer political economy. As an agency of the state, the FCC has been charged with the responsibility of reconciling corporate profit-seeking behavior with public needs. As a result, a certain minimum level of public service has been required of broadcasters in order to maintain licenses granted by the FCC.

The commercial nature of broadcasting as established by the FCC and business interests was further validated by Congress in 1967, when it created a parallel but significantly less powerful agency, the Corporation for Public Broadcasting (CPB). A private, nonprofit corporation, the Corporation for Public Broadcasting was created to assist in financing educational programs. The formation of the CPB was a tacit admission of the priority of capital over the public interest. In effect, a dual market of private and public spheres was formally institutionalized. However, the relationship has been hardly one of equals. As late as 1986, the amount of federal money spent on public broadcasting totaled a meager $200 million. At the same time, contrary to its mandate, the CPB has been subjected to intense government pressure and control.[19]

NAB-BING THE AIRWAVES

The television situation comedy also owes much to institutionalized inequalities within the broadcasting industry. Even as late as 1977, a study of women and minorities in television conducted by the United States Commission on Civil Rights was highly critical of broadcasters, the FCC, and the National Association of Broadcasters (NAB). The report chided these three bodies for their failure to provide equality of employment opportunity for women and minorities, and for perpetuating gender and ethnic stereotypes. The study concluded that the "failure of industry self-regulation" was responsible for the institutionalized inequalities and distortions that characterized television.[20]

The report was especially critical of the FCC and its reliance upon network self-regulation to protect against the possible abuse of a public trust. The reluctance of the FCC to fulfill its regulatory mandate and the inability of the NAB to hold its members accountable has had no small impact on the television situation comedy. The relative lack of regulatory accountability has often resulted in demeaning portrayals of women and minorities in television drama and has restricted their representation within the broadcasting industry. The institutional role of the NAB is worth brief mention in this context.

The National Association of Broadcasters was established in 1922 to represent the interests of commercial radio broadcasters and licensees. By the time television became a national medium of communication in the late 1940s, the NAB had assumed the mantle of institutional legitimacy. As a broadcasting industry self-regulatory organization, the NAB acted as a lightning rod for criticism directed at commercial broadcasting interests by religious groups, government, and the public at large. As an advocate for industry interests, the NAB did much to help justify the maintenance of a system that guaranteed monopolistic control of a public resource used for private profit.

In its preamble, the "NAB Television Code" established the joint "responsibilities" of broadcaster, advertiser, and viewer. Responsibility toward children, animals, community, and family has been stressed by the code. Program standards also governed the depiction of violence, obscenity, sex, controversial issues, and religion.[21] At the same time, unchallenged assumptions about the "free, competitive American system of broadcasting" have left intact a business and governmental relationship that has permitted the systematic extraction of private profit from the public domain. The code's veneer of moral probity and responsibility has hidden the fundamentally unequal relationship between broadcasters, advertisers, and viewers.

Since its founding, the NAB has been aggressive in promoting the use of broadcast television for advertising purposes. In the past, for example, it has opposed alternative mass media such as "pay" TV, which would have posed a competitive threat to "free" programing. Indeed, the activities of the NAB Radio Advertising Bureau and Television Bureau of Advertising have reflected an overriding interest in preserving broadcast television as a medium for advertising above all else. However, the NAB has responded on occasion to public pressure and criticism. In one such instance, in 1967 the NAB made a virtue of necessity by restricting the number of commercial interruptions that were to be "allowed" during the course of a given program. The public interest sometimes even has prevailed over the needs of advertisers and the networks. Such was the case when Congress banned cigarette advertising from television, which took effect in 1971.

TELEVISION AND THE AMERICAN CENTURY

The technology of television broadcasting and reception existed by the 1930s, but regulatory and industry disputes delayed the development of television into a national commercial system until after World War II. Material and labor resources commanded by the war effort also slowed the introduction of network television. Importantly, by the time network television was introduced, the radio broadcasting industry had established the legal and regulatory precedents that similarly would allow a public resource to be maintained for private profit. In sum, the democratizing potential of the new medium—its potential "radically to disrupt pre-existing social formations"—went largely unfulfilled.[22]

The rise of television in the 1950s as a national medium of communication coincided with the notion of "abundance" that was advanced to explain postwar American economic supremacy. As articulated by historian David M. Potter, the material prosperity of the postwar American economic system held the promise of blurring, if not obliterating ethnic, regional, and most importantly, class differences in the United States.[23] The new medium of television was to become an important instrument in heralding the new order of postwar society.

The notion of beneficent abundance also fueled Cold War ideology. The underlying assumption held by many cold warriors was that capitalism was an innately superior system of politico-economic organization. Unlike communist or socialist (the two were often confused) systems, the U.S. economy "delivered the goods" as advertised. Abiding by the aesthetic conventions of "capitalist realism," the American advertising industry employed the "tube of plenty" to entertain postwar America with visions of unabated prosperity and security.[24] It was a vision of society that overlooked flaws that later became painfully evident.

The dynamism of the U.S. economy in the immediate postwar years was not sufficient to hide deeply ingrained problems. Beginning in the mid–1950s and through the 1960s, the unfulfilled promise of full equality raised by the growing civil rights movement, the war in Vietnam, and the youth-oriented culture of opposition portended trouble in paradise for the people of plenty. The secular ideology of "democratic consumerism" had no moral center, nothing to bind citizens together save its existence as a universal market for advertised goods.[25] The monumental cost of waging war in Vietnam without attendant income tax increases launched the United States economy into the twin orbits of inflation and chronic high unemployment. Added to this was the economic ascent of Japan and West Germany, whose budgets allowed little in the way of wasteful military spending. The belief in the capacity of the economic system to sustain the high level of growth enjoyed earlier began to falter as the country experienced severe fiscal crises moving into the 1970s.

By the end of the 1970s, middle-class Americans began to fear for their financial well-being as they became unwilling foot soldiers in the "revolution of falling expectations."[26] Victims of inflation-fed income tax bracket creep, middle-Americans became less interested in questions of social welfare and more involved with concerns of the self.[27] The sadly ineffectual presidency of Jimmy Carter scored high on honesty and believability in the wake of the Watergate scandals that swamped the Nixon administration. However, not only did President Carter fail to stem the tide of economic recession, he had the misfortune of presiding over the Iranian hostage crisis, a crisis that seemed to symbolize America's waning international power. It was into this desolate setting that Ronald Reagan rode, armed with a rusty but serviceable mythos and an economic battle plan that promised to recapture the high ground in the face of tough foreign competition and a weakened domestic economy.

REAGAN KNOWS BEST

Beyond the specific institutional and programmatic changes brought about by the Reagan regime, the Reaganites sought to restore the mythic laissez-faire ideology of the self-regulating market, minimalist state, and promise of American capitalism's pastoral bounty.[28] It perhaps came as no surprise when President Reagan revealed, in a speech to the Boy Scouts of America, that *Family Ties* was his favorite television program.[29] The premise of *Family Ties*—generational conflict between parents who came of age during the countercultural 1960s and their yuppie son—captured the mood of a country that had retreated out of necessity to a preoccupation with materialistic concerns.

By playing on the American sense of freedom, adventure, opportunity, optimism, and exploration, the social nostalgia of Reaganism brought back into fashion greed, jingoism, catchpenny opportunism, and excessive personal ambition. In promising to lead America back to the golden age of limited government and small-town life, the Reaganites further legitimized the expanding power of the most conspicuously nondemocratic institution, the transnational corporation. And as an unprecedented number of corporations played "grab-assets" in the free-for-all inspired by "deregulation," quick paper profits became a favorite method of avoiding problems associated with slow economic growth.[30]

CRITICAL SITUATION

Study of the television situation comedy is an exercise in examining the relationship of popular art to its historically specific setting. The present study has taken care in properly representing the sweep of thought and critical opinion concerning the culture and politics of American society over the past four decades. The television situation comedy—the most popular American art form— is a virtual textbook that can be "read" to help lay bare the mores, images, ideals, prejudices, and ideologies shared—whether by fiat or default—by the majority of the American public. How this ensemble of ideologies becomes transformed into political action or inactivity is a question of no small importance. There is much history that can and must be rescued from the sitcom.

The study of television has in the past been marked by a brand of empiricism that imitates the scope and methods of the natural sciences.[31] The empiricist tradition of American media and communications studies has been marked by a built-in inconclusiveness that forestalls linkage with larger social theory, the proper goal of all research in the social sciences.[32] The pseudo-scientific behavioralist fascination with media "effects" has become an end in itself, standing in the way of explaining and understanding television and its forms through more comprehensive means.[33]

As an antidote to the elegant but inconclusive empiricism of such media scholarship, the television situation comedy might be better served by being studied through qualitative methods that eschew both scientific pretensions and purely aesthetic exercises. Rather, by examining television texts as part of a polysemic signifying system that "contain within them unresolved contradictions," certain theoretical questions can be addressed that do not even exist for those working exclusively within research traditions marked by abstracted empiricism.[34] The ideologically loaded question of realism in television situation comedy, for example, is lost on empirically oriented studies. As the dominant mode of representation and apprehension (especially in popular art) in Western culture, the notion of realism itself becomes problematic once the myth of its universality is exposed.[35]

Like abstracted empiricism, aesthetic approaches that would minimize the concrete social settings in which art is produced are inadequate as well. Aestheticism often takes the form of specious cross-cultural, sometimes transhistorical, comparisons of superficial similarities between art works.[36] The effect of liberal humanist aestheticism is to depoliticize what are at bottom, thoroughly politicized art works. For at bottom, as Terry Eagleton reminds, signifying practices of all kinds (including the television situation comedy) have the "most intimate relations to questions of social power."[37]

SITCOM SOCIOLOGICAL POETICS

The primary insight of Saussurean linguistics—that meaning in discourse is generated by the binary opposition of phonemes, the smallest possible units of language—has acted as the motor for formalist, structuralist, and poststructuralist criticism.[38] Broadly stated, anthropologist Claude Lévi-Strauss extended this linguistic model and applied it in his structural study of myth and the expressive forms of premodern societies such as the seemingly inexplicable facial adornment practices of Caduveo in Brazil. Lévi-Strauss observed that such practices were the symbolic resolution of real power conflicts found to exist even within this relatively simple social system.[39] Similarly, in the western United States, the Ute and Shoshone peoples created the "Sun Dance Religion" to mediate the contradiction between the "corporate collectivism" and "Protestant ethic individualism" of the dominant white society and the tribal values of "Indian collectivism" and "hedonic individualism."[40]

The structural anthropology of Lévi-Strauss made no hierarchical distinction between the "savage" mind and the "civilized mind" as it pertains to the processes of the imaginery, the expressive capacity of man in society. This innovative conflation of primitive and modern mind paved the way for critics such as Roland Barthes to interrogate the meaning of "myths" in modern society.[41] More recently, Fredric Jameson by way of Bakhtin has extended these insights by asserting that all narrative and formal structure" is to be grasped as the imaginary resolution of a real contradiction."[42] As in the facial art of the Caduveo or the Sun Dance of the Utes and Shoshones, the art of the television situation comedy embodies the uneasy truce between the many contradictions of postwar American society.

Postformalist schools of literary criticism such as the so-called Bakhtin circle have established that both form and content of the aesthetic object are informed by the "ideological horizon" of its time.[43] In his study of Dostoevsky, for example, Bakhtin sought to demonstrate the ideological character of literary style, technique, and formal devices. This stands in contrast to the Russian formalists and their methodologically close American cousins, the New Critics. As a starting point, both argued for the hermetic integrity of the cultural artifact free from the taint of history and politics. The Russian formalists viewed the proper function of criticism to be no more than the close examination of literary texts, without reference to the social world, to arrive at its poetics. The Bakhtin circle in its modification of Saussurean linguistics reintroduced history and society and redefined the use of words and language as being "a primarily class-based struggle for the terms in which reality is to be signified."[44] Bakhtin/Medvedev referred to this object, task, and method of study as being a "sociological poetics."[45]

What follows, then, is an extended look at liberal democratic ideology in postwar American society and the ways in which it has informed one specific cultural form, the television situation comedy. The television situation comedy as a historically specific expression of social and political struggle, has proven to be infinitely adaptable to shifting power relations in postwar American society.[46] As new political subjects such as women and minorities have emerged, for example, so the democratic tendencies of the sitcom have expanded. For the core values of freedom and equality inhere in the sitcom just as these selfsame values form the basis of liberal democratic society itself.

The persistence of liberal democratic thought in the situation comedy ultimately forces the issue of its incomplete expression in the structure of American society, its political institutions, and in the distribution of social wealth. In modern democratic societies, as Bryan Turner points out, the "progressive expansion of egalitarian citizenship" has continued along with "de facto inequalities in terms of class, status, and power."[47] Nowhere is this paradox of liberal democratic society more apparent than in the popular culture represented by the situation comedy. This is the point where the discussion of the situation comedy— of media and society in general—necessarily shades over into the realm of politics.

NOTES

1. J. Fred MacDonald, *Who Shot the Sheriff? The Rise and Fall of the Television Western* (New York: Praeger, 1987), p. 55.

2. For a premature postmortem, see Julianne Hastings, "Sitcoms' Decline No Laughing Matter," *Los Angeles Times*, May 28, 1984, p. 10. See also Susan Horowitz, "Sitcom Domesticus—A Species Endangered by Social Change," in *Television: The Critical View*, 4th ed., ed. Horace Newcomb (New York: Oxford University Press, 1987), pp. 106–111.

3. See Douglas Kellner, "TV, Ideology, and Emancipatory Popular Culture," in *Television: The Critical View*, 4th ed., ed. Horace Newcomb (New York: Oxford University Press, 1987), pp. 471–503.

4. Stuart Hall, "Signification, Representation, Ideology: Althusser and the Post-Structuralist Debates," *Critical Studies in Mass Communication*, 2 (1985):91–114.

5. Herbert I. Schiller, *Information and the Crisis Economy* (New York: Oxford University Press, 1986), p. 115.

6. See Frances Fox Piven and Richard Cloward, *The New Class War: Reagan's Attack on the Welfare State and Its Consequences* (New York: Pantheon Books, 1982).

7. John Kenneth Galbraith, *Economics in Perspective: A Critical History* (Boston: Houghton Mifflin Co., 1987), p. 248.

8. Theda Skocpol, "Legacies of New Deal Liberalism," *Dissent*, 30 (1983):33.

9. Skocpol, p. 34.

10. Daniel Bell, *The Cultural Contradictions of Capitalism* (New York: Basic Books, 1978), pp. xi–xxix.

11. See Ralph Miliband, *The State in Capitalist Society: An Analysis of the Western System of Power* (New York: Basic Books, 1969), pp. 219–264.

12. John Fiske, *Television Culture* (New York: Methuen, 1987), pp. 309–310.

13. Frank Cunningham, *Democratic Theory and Socialism* (Cambridge: Cambridge University Press, 1987), p. 145.

14. See Arthur Frank Wertheim, *Radio Comedy* (New York: Oxford University Press, 1979).

15. J. Fred MacDonald, *Don't Touch That Dial! Radio Programming in American Life from 1920 to 1960* (Chicago: Nelson-Hall, 1979), p. 141.

16. See Joseph Boskin and Joseph Dorinson, "Ethnic Humor: Subversion and Survival," *American Quarterly*, 33 (1985):81–97.

17. See David Antin, "Video: The Distinctive Features of the Medium," in *Video*

Culture: A Critical Investigation, ed. John Hanhardt (New York: Visual Studies Workshop Press, 1986), pp. 56–57.

18. Writes E. J. Hobsbawm: "Enclosures meant the rearrangement of formerly common or open fields into self-contained private land-units, or the division of formerly common but uncultivated land. . .into private property." E. J. Hobsbawm, *Industry and Empire: From 1750 to the Present Day* (New York: Penguin Books, 1969), p. 100.

19. David Crook, "CPB President Resigns in Dispute Over Policy," *Los Angeles Times*, November 15, 1986, pt. IV, pp. 1, 12.

20. U.S. Commission on Civil Rights, *Window Dressing on the Set: Women and Minorities in Television* (Washington, D.C.: A Report of the United States Commission on Civil Rights, 1977), p. 148.

21. Craig T. Norback, Peter G. Norback, and the editors of *TV Guide* Magazine, *TV Guide Almanac* (New York: Ballantine Books, 1980), pp. 484–496.

22. Brian Winston, *Misunderstanding Media* (Cambridge: Harvard University Press, 1986), p. 23. See also A. Frank Reel, *The Networks: How They Stole the Show* (New York: Charles Scribner's Sons, 1979); and Stanley M. Besen et al., *Misregulating Television: Network Dominance and the FCC* (Chicago: University of Chicago Press, 1984).

23. David M. Potter, *People of Plenty: Economic Abundance and the American Character* (Chicago: University of Chicago Press, 1954).

24. Michael Schudson, *Advertising, the Uneasy Persuasion: Its Dubious Impact on American Society* (New York: Basic Books, 1984), p. 214. See also Erik Barnouw, *Tube of Plenty: The Evolution of American Television*, rev. ed. (New York: Oxford University Press, 1982).

25. Russell L. Hanson, *The Democratic Imagination in America: Conversations with Our Past* (Princeton, N.J.: Princeton University Press, 1985), pp. 257–292.

26. Irving Louis Horowitz, *Ideology and Utopia in the United States: 1956–1976* (New York: Oxford University Press, 1977), pp. 427–438.

27. See Christopher Lasch, *The Culture of Narcissism: American Life in an Age of Diminishing Expectations* (New York: W. W. Norton & Co., 1979) and Peter Clecak, *America's Quest for the Ideal Self: Dissent and Fulfillment in the 60s and 70s* (New York: Oxford University Press, 1983).

28. See Irving Howe, "The Spirit of the Times: Greed, Nostalgia, Ideology and War Whoops," *Dissent*, 33 (1986):413–425.

29. Ellen Levy, "The Packaging of America: Politics as Entertainment, Entertainment as Politics," *Dissent*, 33 (1986):441–446.

30. In recent years, the broadcasting networks themselves became targets for corporate takeovers. Capital Cities Communications acquired ABC in 1985 for $3.5 billion. That same year, General Electric Company announced that it would pay $6.3 billion for the RCA Corporation, which included its NBC subsidiary. In 1985, CBS staved off a hostile takeover attempt by media baron Ted Turner. See Thomas Moore, "Culture Shock Rattles the TV Networks," *Fortune*, April 14, 1986, pp. 22–27; Marilyn A. Harris et al., "Not Just Another Takeover—Or Is It," *Business Week*, December 30, 1985, pp. 48–51; and Stratford P. Sherman, "Ted Turner: Back From the Brink," *Fortune* July 7, 1986, pp. 24–31.

31. See George Comstock et al., *Television and Human Behavior* (New York: Columbia University Press, 1978). This Rand Corporation volume is a compilation of empirically oriented studies of television "effects." More recent is Shearon Lowery and

Melvin L. DeFleur, *Milestones in Mass Communication Research: Media Effects* (New York: Longman, 1983).

32. See Peter Golding and Graham Murdock, "Theories of Communication and Theories of Society," *Communication Research*, 5 (1978):339–356.

33. For a survey and critique of current research approaches, see Conrad Lodziak, *The Power of Television: A Critical Appraisal* (London: Frances Pinter, 1986).

34. John Fiske, "Television: Polysemy and Popularity," *Critical Studies in Mass Communication* 3 (1986):392.

35. On the varieties and limitations of film and television realism, see John Ellis, *Visible Fictions: Cinema, Television, Video* (London: Routledge & Kegan Paul, 1982), pp. 6–10.

36. The argument for aestheticism is made by David Thorburn, "Television as an Aesthetic Medium," *Critical Studies in Mass Communication* 4 (1987):161–173.

37. Terry Eagleton, *Literary Theory: An Introduction* (Minneapolis: University of Minnesota Press, 1983), p. 22.

38. See Terence Hawkes, *Structuralism and Semiotics* (Berkeley and Los Angeles: University of California Press, 1977).

39. Claude Lévi-Strauss, *Structural Anthropology*, trans. Claire Jacobson and Brooke Grundfest Schoepf (New York: Basic Books, 1963); Claude Lévi-Strauss, *Tristes Tropiques*, trans. John Russell (New York: Atheneum, 1971).

40. Joseph G. Jorgensen, *The Sun Dance Religion: Power for the Powerless* (Chicago: University of Chicago Press, 1972), p. 232.

41. Roland Barthes, *Elements of Semiology*, trans. Annette Lavers and Colin Smith (New York: Hill & Wang, 1968); Roland Barthes, *Mythologies*, trans. Annette Lavers (New York: Hill & Wang, 1972).

42. Fredric Jameson, *The Political Unconscious: Narrative as a Socially Symbolic Act* (Ithaca, N.Y.: Cornell University Press, 1981), p. 77.

43. No attempt will be made to survey the contributions of the Bakhtin circle here. See Joseph Frank, "The Voices of Mikhail Bakhtin," *New York Review of Books*, October 23, 1986, pp. 56–60. Tzvetan Todorov, *Mikhail Bakhtin: The Dialogical Principle*, trans. Wlad Godzich (Minneapolis: University of Minnesota Press, 1984).

44. Tony Bennett, *Formalism and Marxism* (London and New York: Methuen, 1979), p. 80.

45. M. M. Bakhtin/P. N. Medvedev, *The Formal Method in Literary Scholarship: A Critical Introduction to Sociological Poetics*, trans. Albert J. Wehrle (Cambridge: Harvard University Press, 1986).

46. According to Poulantzas, "power relations do not constitute a simple expressive totality, any more than structures or practices do; but they are complex and dislocated relations, determined in the last instance by economic power. Political or ideological power is not the simple expression of economic power." Nicos Poulantzas, *Political Power and Social Classes*, trans. Timothy O'Hagan (London: Verso Editions, 1978), p. 113.

47. Bryan Turner, *Equality* (New York: Tavistock Publications, 1986), p. 119.

2
A Strained Consensus

ALL QUIET ON THE DOMESTIC FRONT

The United States emerged from World War II as the preeminent global military and economic power. Compared to the Soviet Union, the closest political rival of the United States in the postwar era, the United States emerged from the war relatively unscathed. U.S. war dead numbered 322,000, while the Soviet Union lost approximately 22 to 24 million. Germany suffered 4.2 million dead. Furthermore, the war years were an economic boon to the United States. Vexing problems of the Great Depression—high rates of unemployment, deflation, and lackluster industrial performance—were overcome as government and industry combined to increase greatly the total wealth of the nation. The gross national product rose from $91 billion in 1939 to $212 billion in 1945.[1]

The severe economic and social crises wrought by the Great Depression were temporarily assuaged during the war through the intense mobilization of industry required by the war effort. Women and black Americans assumed an unaccustomed role by filling the labor vacuum created by the conscription of 13 million civilians. In a show of national unity, major labor unions informally pledged not to hamper the wartime production. For its part, the Roosevelt administration established the National War Labor Board in 1942 to keep labor strife to a minimum. Even so, there were nearly 15,000 recorded work stoppages during the war.

While labor bore the economic brunt of the war by having wages frozen during an inflationary cycle and through the rationing of scarce items, corporate profits actually increased. Between 1940 and 1944 after-tax profits of American corporations rose from $6.4 billion to $10.8 billion. Industrial expansion during

World War II resulted in the triumph of corporate liberalism as business oligopolies consolidated their power with the assistance of the federal government.[2]

The war years also precipitated the tremendous expansion of federal spending. The government spent $321 billion during the war, or twice as much as the previous 150 years of its existence. The vastly expanded role of the state and the close ties forged with the corporate sector set the stage for the worldwide economic dominance of the United States in the postwar era.[3] These advances in politico-economic growth, however, did not come without first winning public approval of government goals. The means by which political economic goals were to be met required management of consensus.

The management of public consensus during wartime was an important function of both mass media oligopolies and government. Although not so blatant as during the war, this was a relationship that continued once peace was restored. Both the film and radio industries were enlisted to support wartime policies on the domestic front by means of various promotional campaigns. On radio, popular comedians such as Bob Hope, George Burns and Gracie Allen, Jack Benny, and Fred Allen made frequent patriotic appeals to the American public. Popular radio programs such as *Amos 'n' Andy* and *Fibber McGee and Molly* worked references to the war into their shows to help bolster morale. The corporate elite in the media industry, as in other large industries, were enlisted to help wage the war to win the hearts and minds of the American public. Chairman of CBS William Paley helped by serving in the Office of War Information as deputy chief of the Psychological Warfare Division. President of NBC David Sarnoff served as a reservist in the U.S. Army Signal Corps and was promoted to the rank of brigadier general for his contribution to the war effort.

The cessation of hostilities, however, meant a return to unresolved issues suspended by the war. Just as the economy had to go through a period of reconversion, so too did social relations. The peacetime constitution of social and political relations had to be renegotiated, especially in light of the brief economic empowerment experienced by previously dispossessed groups such as women and blacks. Of even more weight were the claims of G.I.'s reentering the civilian economy. Most G.I.'s rendered military service under conditions set by the first peacetime draft registration and conscription in American history. Draft legislation had not been popular in the first place; when the draft law came up for renewal in 1941 it passed by only a single vote. Patriotic duty notwithstanding, it was understood that this population of young men would require some form of compensation after having made the world safe for American liberal democracy.

The Servicemen's Readjustment Act of 1944, better known as the G.I. Bill of Rights, was the single most important government move to grant returning veterans a share in postwar prosperity. The G.I. Bill provided financial assistance for education, housing, and health care. Other government agencies joined in assisting returning veterans as well. The Federal Housing Administration (FHA) help "put the federal government firmly in the housing business" by subsidizing purchases by making available low interest loans.[4] Veterans Administration programs provided the model for later federal entitlement programs that would come to include others identified as being disadvantaged. The concept of "compensatory action"—a pathbreaking admission of government responsibility in redressing inequality—was later expanded in the nonmilitary sector to include minorities and women.[5] The participation of black Americans in World War II helped motivate President Truman in his Fair Deal proposals to acknowledge their demands for social and economic equality. The creation of both the federal Civil Rights Commission in 1946 and the Fair Employment Practices Commission was intended to eliminate racial discrimination in governmental hiring practices. The belated desegregation of the armed forces under the Truman administration reaffirmed that the war fought in the name of democracy was a victory for all Americans.

Among the groups hardest hit by the civilian reconversion process were women. The war years saw a 60 percent increase of women in the workplace. Many took nontraditional jobs in heavy industry and for this brief moment in time viewed as civilian heroines. The "Rosie the Riveter" image, popular during the war, made it acceptable for women to assume "men's work" in vital war industries. Once former G.I.s returned to the workplace, however, the presence of female labor became problematic. The displacement of this significant percentage of the work force was negotiated somewhat amicably in the postwar era by the cult of domesticity that centered around mom, pop, and family. Nowhere was this more evident than in the family television situation comedies of the 1950s.

ALL IN THE NUCLEAR FAMILY

The fundamental unit of social organization in urban industrial America has been the nuclear family. As a cultural ideal arising from the material imperatives of capitalist production and consumption practices, the nuclear family minimizes the importance of wider, "outside" social ties. Primary emphasis here is placed upon affective bonds between parents and children in the absence of a larger network of economic and emotional sustenance. The nuclear family ideal places overriding importance on the individual breadwinner, the father, whose relative success or failure in the labor marketplace decides the family's status vis-à-vis the "outside" world of business, politics, and society. This cultural ideal also determines the degree of influence the paterfamilias wields "inside," in the world of domestic life. Such was the basic tension of domestic situation comedies as they mediated the civilian reconversion process.

Sitcom fathers of the 1950s were either bumbling fools or wise patriarchs depending upon how they represented their families to the world through occupational status. Occupational prestige was divided roughly along class lines: white collar professionals were the wise patriarchs, blue collar workers or newly arrived mid-level managers were the bumbling "dads." Due to the real economic growth of the postwar era, which enlarged the middle class in absolute numbers, the dimension of class politics was obscured and became transcoded into a mere question of "status politics."[6] Class tension and conflict, exacerbated during the Great Depression and temporarily suspended during World War II, reemerged as questions of professionalism, technocratic advantage, and administrative (i.e. managerial) competence.

THE LIFE OF STATUS ANXIETY

In *The Life of Riley* (October 4, 1949, to August 22, 1958), William Bendix played Chester Riley, a harried television dad who suffered acutely from the psychic wounds inflicted by postwar status politics.[7] He was not so apparently self-conscious of his white ethnic, Irish-American identity as were the tormented "bogmen" depicted in the drama of Eugene O'Neill. Still, he seemed a long-suffering victim of status anxiety who, to compensate, always tried his best to "look good" in the eyes of friends and family. Somehow, Riley's attempts at becoming a big shot always fell short of the mark. His children Babs (Lugene Sanders) and Junior (Wesley Morgan) were tolerant of their father's ineptitude, while Riley's wife Peg (Marjorie Reynolds) bailed him out of one "revoltin' development" after another.

Chester Riley was one of the many anxious blue collar aristocrats created by the postwar economic boom. The Rileys lived in one of the newly developed Southern California suburban neighborhoods that accommodated veterans buying into the American dream with a little help from mortgage money provided by the FHA. He was a slightly disoriented settler of the great "crabgrass frontier," an updated version of the Jeffersonian yeoman carrying forth the suburbanization process. The tract home in the suburbs rather than the self-sufficient family farm became the indivisible unit of consumption, with its glorification of automobility as one of the new means of enforcing racial and politico-economic segregation.[8] The automobile also conferred immediate status on its owner according to a commonly accepted hierarchy based on make and model year.

Chester worked with his sarcastic friend, neighbor, and fellow Irishman Gillis (Tom D'Andrea) in one of the aerospace factories that absorbed excess wartime industrial capacity once normal civilian economic activity resumed. Gillis's wife Honeybee (Gloria Blondell), like her counterpart Peg, tended to domestic matters with a seriousness of purpose that resisted encroachment by the male breadwinners. In *The Life of Riley*, the postwar pact between husband and wife concerning the social divison of labor was strictly observed. Problems most often arose when Riley intervened in affairs and concerns implicitly conceded to Peg. The problems caused by Riley were endless, for Peg's sphere of influence encompassed the entire household including Babs and Junior.

The Life of Riley served as an entertaining reminder to newly expanded middle-class America of its humbler, working-class and immigrant origins. It was a muted celebration of the postwar prosperity that allowed a hardworking man like Chester Riley to own a nice home in pleasant surroundings among people like himself, while supporting a wife and children on a single paycheck. At the same time, however, the program enforced the new rules adopted by white middle-class Americans as part of the suburban compact. Working-class behavior such as the penchant for betting in games of chance, for example, was punished in one episode after Riley and Gillis won a baseball pool at the plant.[9] Threatened with the loss of Gillis's friendship after a series of complications, Riley withdrew his claim on half of the winnings rather than risk alienating his buddy. "This'll teach me to never let an evil thought in my head," said a chastened Riley. "From now on I'm keeping it empty."

THE HONEYMOON'S OVER

Less fortunate than Chester Riley was Ralph Kramden, played by Jackie Gleason, in *The Honeymooners* (October 1, 1955, to September 1956).[10] Unlike his suburban counterpart Chester Riley, Ralph Kramden had not yet raised himself into the middle class. The program hinged upon Kramden's thwarted quest to better his position in life. For Ralph Kramden, the root of his ceaseless frustrations was blocked access to big money. Whether opening a hot dog stand ("Howard Johnson's" is due to open down the road), mass marketing "Handy Housewife Helpers" on television (Ralph suffers from camera fright), or currying favor with his boss to earn a promotion by bragging about his golfing prowess (he cannot golf), Ralph would try virtually anything to gain the necessary advantage that would bring success.

Kramden's job as a bus driver barely kept him and his homemaker-wife, Alice (Audrey Meadows), installed in their sparsely furnished walk-up in Brooklyn. They made do with an ancient icebox, not a refrigerator, and communicated with the Nortons—Ed (Art Carney) and Trixie (Joyce Randolph)—by shouting up the airshaft, since they were without a telephone. There were few furnishings in the apartment and even fewer appliances. The Nortons were not much better off. The Nortons and the Kramdens even tried sharing an apartment once during an especially severe financial crunch. There was a neat symmetry in that Ralph's subterranean counterpart Norton worked the sewers of New York while Ralph drove the streets overhead. As for Trixie, she was a former burlesque queen turned housewife. Despite their squalid lives, the Kramdens and the Nortons were bound together by friendship, love, and the promise of advancement that never quite came about.

Like *The Life of Riley*, *The Honeymooners* is best understood as the dramatic confirmation of a way of life made possible by the surge in material well-being for most Americans during the 1950s. By deliberately withholding the appurtenances of middle-class prosperity from the set of *The Honeymooners* and by making financial struggle its very premise, the program provided a quaint memento of a mean style of life that had faded into memory for most television viewers of the day. There was no other plausible reason for the Kramdens' apartment to look so pitiably shabby considering that the production costs for the first (1955) recorded episode of *The Honeymooners* totaled $75,000. *I Love Lucy* in comparison cost half as much to produce.[11]

It is more likely that Jackie Gleason, whose authorial influence on *The Honeymooners* was undeniably strong, well understood the dreams and aspirations of a national audience that had suffered through not only economic depression but world war as well. Gleason, like most of his contemporaries, did not have an easy time of it while growing up. Gleason rose from his tough Bushwick neighborhood in Depression-era Brooklyn to become one of the highest paid performers in television history.[12] Gleason's rise to the top conformed to the common myth of the individual who succeeds, in spite of adversity, to become someone who matters. As for the underside of the myth, forgotten were the institutionalized structures of inequality that kept Ralph Kramden in Bensonhurst and Gleason's mates in Bushwick, struggling to break free.

DARK SHADOWS

Film actor and radio performer Stu Erwin starred in the eponymous *Stu Erwin Show* (October 21, 1950, to April 13, 1955), yet another program cast from the inept father mold. As principal of Hamilton High School, Stu Erwin was slightly more respectable than his blue collar brethren Chester A. Riley and Ralph Kramden. But like them, Erwin always seemed to find a way of bungling even the simplest of tasks. Erwin's real-life wife, June Collyer, played his television wife, also named June. (In the 1950s, only professional women—those with identities apart from their husbands—were given special dispensation by not having to take the family name of their spouses.) The Erwin household was completed by two dutiful daughters, Jackie (Sheila James) and Joyce (Ann Todd, later, Merry Anders). Sheila James later went on to costar in *The Many Loves of Dobie Gillis* (September 29, 1959, to September 18, 1963) as Zelda Gilroy, a brainy but homely proto-feminist.

Another historical curiosity within the Erwin household was black handyman Willie (Willie Best). Willie, as a sign of his historically rooted subordination, had no last name in the show. The character of Willie was an extension of the roles popularized in the movies by black actor Stepin Fetchit. Willie Best himself worked for a time under contract to RKO and was "one of several Negro actors who played Fetchit-type roles."[13] Willie Best also served a similar function in *My Little Margie* (June 16, 1952, to August 24, 1955) as Charlie the elevator operator. Such demeaning characterizations of blacks became less evident in television situation comedy as their irrepressible presence—often tinged with controversy—increased in entertainment and sports programs. Just as Jackie Robinson in 1947 had broken the major league baseball color line to compete on an equal footing with whites, Nat Cole's shortlived *The Nat "King" Cole*

Show (November 5, 1956, to December 17, 1957) had the similar effect of revealing blacks in their full humanity, live, immediate, and uncensored.

Since the situation comedy is a dramatic form grounded in aesthetic and social realism, caricatures as performed by a Willie Best or an Eddie "Rochester" Anderson were eventually rendered obsolete because they ceased to be realistically credible to an audience who were gradually exposed to undistorted images of ethnic minorities through nonfiction television forms such as live sports events, news programs, and variety shows. This is not to state that the black presence in American society ceased to be problematic. The opposite is more the case. Rather, from the mid–1950s to the end of the 1960s, the situation comedy displaced the problem of politically marginal peoples by retreating into fantasy. It would not be until the 1970s that American blacks returned to the situation comedy, not as secondary characters but as subjects.

The dark shadows cast by the seemingly benign dramatis personae of *The Stu Erwin Show*—June Collyer, Sheila James, Willie Best—obscured the very real social contradictions of the time. Amidst the gags and guffaws, the program portrayed gender and ethnic minority subordination by a white patriarch trying, ineptly, to maintain the ongoing system of power and privilege. If the characters in the show embodied larger, deep-seated social contradictions, then its dramatic content attempted an aesthetic reconciliation of conflicting demands as well. Stu Erwin's seriocomical effort in mediating conflicting imperatives was shown in the episode, "The Soft Touch," aired during late 1954.[14]

In "The Soft Touch," fundamental anthropological facts including kinship, economic exchange, regulation of sexuality, and parental authority came into conflict with the relatively modern notions of romantic love and individual autonomy. Kinship linkages in societies that espouse egalitarian ideology, as in the United States, are problematic since courtship patterns based on the ideal of romantic love confuse the overriding function of marriage as a primary means of economic exchange.[15] Romantic individualism, another core American value, in turn diminishes the role of the parent in negotiating the terms of marriage.

Since Erwin had no formal power in enforcing his personal will in the question of marriage, he was forced into spying on Joyce's suitor, Jimmy Clark (Martin Milner), to learn his true intentions. He was especially interested in finding out whether Jimmy Clark had pursued Joyce strictly for the sake of her family's money. Erwin devised an elaborate ruse whereby Jimmy Clark would think that he was marrying into an impoverished family. After Jimmy offered to lend his future father-in-law money, Stu realized that he had been overly suspicious.

By the end of the episode, however, the extreme caution exercised by Erwin in protecting the family wealth was played down as Joyce's personal happiness and fulfillment once more gained foreground as the "true" issue after all. Thus what at the subtextual level was a question concerning the possible dangerous economic consequences of marriage in an open-market system subtly reverted to the romance of spurious individual autonomy. The family's dual existence as both a place of emotional refuge and a basic economic unit was also intertwined, with the former given priority over the latter in the final analysis.

MANAGERIAL PATRIARCHY

Complementing the many bumbling father portrayals in the television sitcoms of the 1950s were programs that featured patriarchs who were decidedly more authoritarian in personal style. Three of the more well-known shows of this sort included *Father Knows Best* (October 3, 1954, to April 5, 1963), *Leave It to Beaver* (October 4, 1957, to September 12, 1963), and *The Donna Reed Show* (September 24, 1958, to September 3, 1966). Predating these programs, however was *Life with Father* (November 22, 1953, to July 5, 1955). *Life with Father* was developed from a series of articles authored by Clarence Day, Jr., for the *New Yorker* during the 1920s. A bestselling novel, play, and film were also adapted from the original material. By means of nostalgic remembrance, the show portrayed the domestic relations of an upper-middle-class American household in the Victorian era.

The device of narrative reminiscence in *Life with Father* allowed for the worst excesses of historicism. The program was guilty of having imposed contemporary ideologies on a historically dissimilar, fictive past. This distorted reinterpretation of the past in terms of the present meant the revision of history to suit 1950s social ideologies, thereby legitimizing then current social practices. As such, *Life with Father* pertained more to the role of the American paterfamilias of the 1950s than his late nineteenth-century predecessor. A large part of the curious appeal of the program was found in its contrasting portrayal of the Victorian family patriarch as "boss" versus the fact of the middle-class modern father as organization man or "manager."[16] Jim Anderson, Ward Cleaver, and Dr. Carl Stone represented this latter category of patriarch.

As an exercise in nostalgia, *Life with Father* also offered a soothing retreat to an age predating the postwar rise of the "new class," of which professional managers composed a significant part. It was a social grouping that, since World War II, came to occupy an increasingly ambiguous position between labor and capital up until the present day.[17] The Day family, in *Life with Father*, inhabited a world of capitalist owners whose influence, prestige, and power were to eventually give way to the present system of corporate oligopoly in postwar America.[18] The program dramatized the once invaluable lessons that would guide the lives of the four redheaded offspring of Clarence Day, Sr., the next generation of capitalist owners. These lessons, of course, were made obsolete by virtue of the ascendancy of corporate oligopolies and the attendant change in the social relations of production: Family run businesses that once operated by a "value system that's an extension of *family* values" were replaced by the abstracted professionalism of professionally trained managers.[19] The individual capitalist ethos espoused by the likes of Clarence Day, Sr., was a quaint reminder of a bygone era that, while not perfect, at least offered a core of belief lacking in the new post-industrial corporate environment.

The rigid, hierarchic roles within the Day household were markedly at variance with the "prefigurative" family relations of the postwar family.[20] Clarence, Sr., was shown as decisive and in command. He needed neither reassurance nor approval from his wife, and least of all his children. His paternal control extended to his social inferiors, which included a maid, Margaret, and an alcoholic coachman, Michael. The tippling coachman might be censured for his intemperance— a lower-class trait antithetical to the puritanical abstemiousness of the master class—but he was nonetheless tolerated by his employer. In *Life with Father*, the family patriarch held himself aloof from the rest of the household. By contrast, most other family situation comedies of the 1950s valued intimacy and open displays of affection. Unlike the autocratic "boss" in *Life with Father*, the middle-class heads of TV households were "managed" by nice guys whose amiability was in perfect alignment with the needs of the managerial revolution.

Life with Father also shed light on the transformation of childhood in postwar American society. Prior to the late 1940s and 1950s, most children had a quite different relationship to the larger political economy in that they were directly contributing, productive members of households that depended upon the labor output of its children. By the 1950s, children ceased to have this direct, productive function. Rather, one of the primary functions of the child in the postwar political economy was to consume. A system of related industries thrived on this altered relationship between parents and children, resulting in a new cultural configuration based on the family. In particular, the radio, film, television, recording, magazine and book publishing, cosmetics, clothing, and incipient fast food industries catered to the needs created by the postwar consumer economy.

Such a revolutionary changeover in the social role of the child was not affected without somehow managing the tension created by residual values fostered by an economy based on production versus the emergent values of an economy based on consumption. In an episode entitled "Father and the Dress Suit," Clarence, Jr., learned what it meant to forego immediate needs in favor of long-term, character-building investments in the future.[21] In this episode, Clarence, Jr., struggled through the dilemma of wanting a new suit of clothes to impress his lady friend, but being reluctant to ask his frugal father for the money. Unlike the kids of the 1950s who received "allowances" and had lavished upon them a bounty of products aimed at the new teen market, Clarence, Jr., did not take his wealth for granted. Even his mother Vinnie was reluctant to intercede, lest she incur the wrath of her husband. When asked by her son whether he should ask Clarence, Sr., for the $22.00 that would buy the suit, Vinnie replied, "That's hard to say. It all depends on how your father feels about the country's economy at the moment. If he thinks we're headed for prosperity, he might buy you one. On the other hand, if he thinks the country is going to the dogs. . . ."

Vinnie and Clarence, Jr., were eventually to solve the problem by having one of his father's suits temporarily altered. Clarence, Sr., did eventually discover the ruse. Unlike most other television sitcom fathers, however, Clarence Day, Sr., withheld direct expression of caring and in general dealt with his sons with the detached, impersonal air of the levelheaded businessman. By not buying a suit for Clarence, Jr., until he was off at college, for example, Clarence, Sr., hoped to "build character" in his son so that he could one day "fill his shoes." This anachronistic sentiment was by the 1950s vastly at odds with the transformed occupational structure of the postwar new middle class, a class formation mostly dependent upon the corporation or government—no longer the family—for employment.

Part of the nostalgia appeal of *Life with Father* for its television audience no doubt stemmed from its "old-fashioned" attitudes toward work, money, and family. Children viewing the program could be amused by all the elaborate machinations of Vinnie and young Clarence just to get a suit. For their part, most of the adult audience would have had direct experience with the material deprivations of the Depression. For adult viewers, the years of want and painful necessity could be entertainingly relived, but within a much improved zone of comfort removed in time.

As the direct beneficiaries of postwar economic abundance, the baby-boom generation simply assumed that such favorable material circumstances would last in perpetuity. It was a delusion suffered by most Americans until the nation entered its current period of decline beginning in the late 1960s. But unlike their parents, who had been directly touched by the deprivations imposed by the Great Depression and World War II, the children of the 1950s developed values that were an outgrowth of the postwar consumerist economic push that placed children at its center. *Life with Father*, then, managed to symbolically mediate that clash of values that arose from two discrepant politico-economic orders.

"SOMETHING'S WRONG WITH THE BEAVER"

Insurance man Jim Anderson of *Father Knows Best* (October 3, 1954, to April 5, 1963), Ozzie Nelson (exact occupation unknown) of *The Adventures of Ozzie and Harriet* (October 3, 1952, to September 3, 1966), pediatrician Dr. Alex Stone in *The Donna Reed Show* (September 24, 1958, to September 3, 1966), and even night club entertainer Danny Williams in *Make Room for Daddy/The Danny Thomas Show* (September 29, 1953, to September 14, 1964) were each charged with the responsibility of enforcing the values of "family culture" in the television situation comedies of the 1950s.[22] As they administered the needs of their respective families, the notions of togetherness, responsibility, maturity, adjustment, and enlightened permissiveness in the raising of children commingled in an eerily silent political vacuum. Yet the decade of the 1950s was highly politicized, if politics is defined as the ongoing contestation of power relations that determine the control or allocation of scarce economic resources.

The family-centered television situation comedies of the 1950s were similar in the way they *seemed* to escape the intrusion of the state. The state, civil society, even the common world of work were alien activities existing somewhere "out there," beyond the pleasantly manicured suburban lawns. Politics, by its telling absence, was a contaminating force to be kept beyond the threshold of the private home. Yet these households were themselves liberal democratic models of procedural justice. Grounded as they were in the first principles and premises of the larger liberal democratic society, sitcom homes also realized justice, fairness, and equality through pluralistic decision-making procedure. Mediated by the controlling authority of the family patriarch, group consensus was always realized by the conclusion of a given episode as stability was restored.

Ward Cleaver (Hugh Beaumont) in *Leave It to Beaver* (October 4, 1957, to September 12, 1963) occupied one of those multipurpose managerial positions held by TV dads of the 1950s. The relationship Ward enjoyed with his sons Wally (Tony Dow) and Beaver (Jerry Mathers) was like that of a senior executive to junior colleagues, unlike the stern Victorian patriarch portrayed in *Life with Father*. Ward Cleaver, in consultation with wife June (Barbara Billingsley), allowed Wally and the Beaver to work through carefully controlled personal problems that would result in the revitalization of values and beliefs cast only temporarily in doubt.

The brainchild of two former advertising men who once worked for the J. Walter Thompson agency, Bob Mosher and Joe Connelly, *Leave It to Beaver* did not feature provocative or particularly uproariously funny storylines during the course of its six-year run of 234 episodes.[23] Rather, what distinguished the program and those similar to it, such as *Father Knows Best*, was the vision of micro-social harmony arrived at through the piecemeal solution of mundane problems. Show after show, disrupting problems ("Ward, something's wrong with the Beaver.") were neutralized. Ward Cleaver, like any leader possessing even a modicum of political savvy, was careful not to permanently alienate the losers—usually, Wally or the Beaver—in a zero-sum game. The family situation comedies, then, reproduced liberal reformist approaches to handling social contradictions and conflict. Whether they lived in the homogenous hamlets of Mayfield, Springfield, or Hilldale, the family was offered as the one institution wherein the problems of the wider society could be controlled and managed.

An idealized community though it was, Mayfield was not fully insulated from the more unseemly aspects of life. Not so pleasant reminders of the real world were often leaked into episodes of *Leave It to Beaver* by the cynical teenage realist, Eddie Haskell (Ken Osmond). Whenever the Beaver or Wally were faced with a vexing predicament, Eddie Haskell could be counted on to advocate the expedient, adult way out. Haskell would never fail to press an advantage, however dubious. Eddie Haskell in "Wally's Orchid" once advised Wally Cleaver to make a date with a vulnerable young woman who was suffering from a romance that had just "busted up":

EDDIE: The thing to do is move in and take advantage of it before they make up.
WALLY: You think it'll work?

EDDIE: Sure—that's the way my Pop picks up houses cheap. He watches the divorce notices in the paper and then calls the people up.[24]

Eddie Haskell's perspective on the world was drawn directly from his observations of adult behavior, particularly that of his oft-mentioned but never-seen father. Eddie Haskell was acutely aware of adult hypocrisy. When Wally told his friend about a lecture he had received from Ward about "values," Eddie remarked, "My Pop's always givin' me that line. And all the while he's sittin' there puffin' them eighty-five-cent cigars." By his introduction of real-life behavior, the character Eddie Haskell satisfied an aesthetic requirement of all drama, including the situation comedy. Aesthetically, the values held by Haskell served as the necessary dramatic foil to the pure and noble sentiments of the Cleaver household. But in meeting a purely aesthetic requirement, Eddie Haskell could not help but disclose the underside of 1950s domestic tranquility. His casual mention of divorce, for example, was shocking for a time when open discussion of marital dissolution was cause for shame. As a recognizable social type, Eddie Haskell embodied in concentrated form the worst excesses of individualism that could have—if unchecked—led to a brand of opportunism destructive to the community. Far from being a passive receptacle for the dominant liberal ideology, then, even a program such as *Leave It to Beaver* can be seen to have contained the seeds of discord and opposition.

EMPTY HUTS

In retrospect, the self-satisfied, romanticized depictions of the American family on television situation comedies of the 1950s seemed the swan song for a moribund way of life. To be sure, the simple virtues of caring, understanding, and closeness in programs such as *Leave It to Beaver* held undeniable appeal for the audience; but it was an audience already caught in the tightening grip of forces that otherwise militated against such wistful visions of domestic tranquility. For as the post-industrial state expanded the scope of its politico-economic activity and influence, the family became targeted as little more than the smallest calculable unit of consumption. Or, in the perversely apt parlance of the advertising business, households were reconceptualized as "Homes Using Television" or "HUT."

In effect, the self-flattering television situation comedy portrayals of the family attempted to balance two not always compatible imperatives: the family as a commodified unit of private consumption and the family as an autonomous unit of personal fulfillment. The distinction between the two imperatives did become blurred at times: personal fulfillment seemed sometimes to be gained only through private consumption. In the family sitcoms, however, the fulfillment of personal desires would never take precedence over the needs of the family or community. The family was depicted as the one pure institution that allowed for the full flowering of the individual, but only within the rules and procedures set by society. The delicate task of balancing the sometimes contradictory imperatives of the family fell to the sitcom character of the mother/housewife.

It was the housewife who guided the family's habits of consumption. It was she who was responsible for cooking, shopping, and cleaning for her family. Mass marketers such as Procter & Gamble understood this relationship perfectly and exploited it accordingly. At the same time, the ideal mother took responsibility for the emotional well-being and "adjustment" of her young charges. If responsibility for the establishment and enforcement of proper procedure and law fell to the patriarch, then it was the mother's prerogative to humanize the domestic sphere of the family. By virtue of her vital, but noneconomic (but nonetheless productive) role within the family, the sitcom housewife/mother was in most cases granted compensatory symbolic dominance in exchange for the lack of power wielded by women in the larger social arena.

The fetishization of the American housewife in the immediate postwar period stemmed from the tenuous compromise struck between male breadwinners and their spouses. The relatively high rate of divorce during World War II, which rose to about 14 percent at its peak, served as a reminder of the fragility of hearth and home. In 1946, fully 18.3 percent of existing marriages terminated in divorce. Not until 1968 did divorce rates again increase after two decades of stability.[25] The greater degree of economic independence enjoyed by women during the war made it at least financially feasible for divorce to take place, although the degree of social opprobrium cast upon the divorce was strong. It is no surprise, then, that programs such as *Father Knows Best, The Adventures of Ozzie and Harriet, Leave It to Beaver*, and *The Donna Reed Show* raised motherhood to such exalted heights, for it was mother's unpaid, alienated labor in the domestic workplace that quietly hummed along as one of the engines of economic growth during the 1950s.

LOYAL OPPOSITION

It would be mistaken to interpret the 1950s sitcom cult of domesticity and motherhood as symptomatic of total female subjugation in the larger society. The cult of domesticity was not entirely without a self-consciously critical edge even as it seemed to embrace its premises. Alice Kramden might have been consigned to the socially restricted role of housewife, but she never fully gave in to the role either, much to the chagrin of Ralph Kramden. Even the saintly Donna Stone suffered momentary lapses of belief. Further, the exaggerated attention that the mother/housewife character devoted to her family and home could in itself be construed as an implicit criticism of a threatening, hostile world beyond the domestic threshold. Within the mother/housewife sitcom character lay hidden an oppositional stance taken against the dehumanizing forces of the dominant society. It was a stance that built upon the strength of kinship ties kept tightly bound by the family matriarch.

Even so venerable a program as *I Love Lucy* (October 15, 1951, to September

24, 1961) was based upon the premise of a restless, dissatisfied housewife who continually tested the limits imposed upon her by a moderately domineering husband. No matter how often she failed to subvert his authority, Lucy always seemed ready for a new challenge that would establish her own self-worth. Lucy was particularly persistent in trying to launch herself into a show business career such that her husband Ricky Ricardo (Desi Arnaz) enjoyed as a popular nightclub entertainer. Lucy often tried to work her way into Ricky's acts, which would invariably result in her humiliation. Failing this, Lucy went to extremes in placing herself near greatness, whether it be Cornel Wilde, John Wayne, Orson Welles, or other celebrities she hounded over the course of the program's 180 episodes.

That Lucy Ricardo (Lucille Ball) could count on the complicity of her neighbor Ethel Mertz (Vivian Vance) in all manner of wild schemes implied a more generalized sympathy among viewers for Lucy's thwarted attempts at personal success. Both Lucy's and Ethel's small-scale acts of rebellion hinted at the ongoing power contest based on gender being waged in the larger society. On occasion, the battle lines would be explicitly drawn as in the episode "Equal Rights." Having demanded full equality from their spouses, Ricky and Fred (William Frawley) promptly made Lucy and Ethel pay their half of a dinner check.[26]

FIRELESS COOKING

One of the more obvious examples of the affirmative aspects of the mother/housewife character was to be found in the long-running program *Mama* (July 1, 1949, to July 27, 1956). The program, produced by Carol Irwin and directed by Ralph Nelson (who also on occasion doubled as a writer), was based upon a best-selling novel that was later adapted into a Broadway play. In 1948, the play in turn was made into an RKO film. Each episode was prefaced by the fond remembrance of the now grown-up daughter, Katrin (Rosemary Rice). Mama Marta Hansen (Peggy Wood) was the quietly forceful matriarch of a Norwegian-American family that lived in San Francisco. Her husband Lars (Judson Laire) was a skilled craftsman, a carpenter by trade. Through his skill, Lars was able to provide his family with life's necessities but not much more than that.

Although sponsored by General Foods and its Maxwell House brand coffee, certain episodes of *Mama* surprisingly dealt with politically sensitive topics. Certain scripts included Katrin's falling in love with a Jack London-styled radical poet and Nels's (Dick Van Patten) invitation to a high society Nob Hill party. Yet another script "dealt quite subtly with the problems of capital versus labor."[27] Both writer Frank Gabrielson and director Ralph Nelson were of Scandinavian heritage, and through their empathy for the fictive Hansen family, they expressed a persistent ambivalence toward American class society and its indignities. But by employing the dramatic device of nostalgic narrative, the writers of *Mama* were able to transport such touchy subjects back to a time and place beyond the grasp of the sponsor.

An episode of *Mama* entitled, "Mama's Birthday" (or "The Fireless Cooker") deserves extended analysis as a case study in the sociological poetics of the 1950s television situation comedy.[28] The episode is particularly worth the retelling for two reasons: (1) Specifically, it establishes both the aesthetic and sociological truth of the mother/housewife character as engaging in oppositional as well as acquiescent forms of behavior; (2) more generally, this episode illustrates the process by which social contradictions are symbolically (via dramatic art) resolved in the television situation comedy. It can be seen that a seemingly simple sentimental tale of a birthday gift is motivated by deeper thematic conflicts and conflicts in values that lay at the heart of American society, conflicts that are "married" by the end of the episode.

The story began with the Hansen children, Katrin, Nels, and Dagmar, trying to decide on a birthday gift for Mama. They want the gift to be special but not frivolous; the Hansens lived in a time not as yet engulfed by the consumerist ethic. A "fireless cooker" is decided on by the children, but after visiting a showroom displaying a cooker, the children find its price of $15.75 to be too dear. Mr. Snow, a salesman, couched his sales spiel in the rhetoric of democracy. Said Mr. Snow, "The fireless cooker is a new Emancipation Proclamation. . .settin' housewives free from their old kitchen range." Not having enough money to complete the purchase, the children took on odd jobs. For this part, Lars decided to build a fireless cooker on his own. In one particular scene, however, Lars expressed to his wife the doubts he had about being able to compete on the same footing as an entire factory. Not knowing that the cooker was meant for her, Mama encouraged Lars to do his best in spite of this disadvantage.

The salesman Mr. Snow was described in the script as being a "Yankee trader," or one who is presumably motivated by the penurious, freebooting values of an earlier stage of capitalist development. When, for example, the children had difficulty in meeting the advance payments stipulated by the terms of the installment contract, Mr. Snow insisted that they hold to the agreement. When Mama finally learns of the deal, she persuades Mr. Snow to return the money to her children. In exchange, Mama gives Mr. Snow a wedding present of hers, a cherished silver coffee urn. The coffee (Maxwell House?) urn later figures prominently in the reconciliation of Mr. Snow's hardnosed business values and the values held by the family.

Having perhaps wrestled with his conscience, Mr. Snow finally allowed sentiment to prevail over commerce. He drops by the Hansen household to give Mama a birthday present—her silver coffee urn nestled in a bed of American Beauty roses. It seems that the more intimate precapitalist social relations evoked by the memory of his grandfather induced Mr. Snow into an uncharacteristic show of generosity. "Kinda felt 'twould make a nice present. . .for a fine lady!" said Mr. Snow. "Yes siree! Figgered it's the sort've thing Grandpa Snow might have done.. . ." By the end of the tale, each of the principal parties had realized their respective goals: The children were able to present Mama a practical gift, a set of dishes; Lars maintains his status as a craftsman by presenting Mama with a handmade fireless cooker; and Mr. Snow had been given the chance to regain his humanity.

Beyond the manifest sentimentality of this episode of *Mama*, there were a number of curious thematic operations taking place. Strongly implied is a critique of contemporary society as represented in its early form by Mr. Snow. For one, the heartless, anonymously commercial, and impersonal social relations based upon the legalisms of contract law embodied in the installment contract signed by the Hansen children is abandoned for the system of obligation implied by the gift, the silver coffee urn. Further, the coffee urn mediates two opposed systems of economic exchange. It is a valued object of economic exchange that occupies an intermediate position between the all-purpose money used in the impersonal market economy of Mr. Snow and the reciprocal system of exchange based upon strong kinship ties.

The voiding of the installment contract and acceptance of the wedding coffee urn (an object that in itself symbolizes kinship) by Mr. Snow is a clear violation of the cultural codes governing anonymous market economic activity. Mr. Snow's act of altruism, then, stands as an implicit critique of the abstract, impersonal social relations of production characteristic of market economies. Also at play are two closely related oppositions: (1) Mr. Snow is a trader while Lars is a craftsman. Mr. Snow is in the business of trading for profit, while Lars is engaged in building products for use; (2) the rationalized, mass production capabilities of the factory are pitted against the handicraft tradition as maintained by Lars.

Finally, most noteworthy of all is Mama's pivotal role in mediating two contradictory imperatives. It is she who brings the two sides together in a symbolic "wedding" of sorts. Viewed from one perspective, the socially restricted role of the housewife/mother character in *Mama* might be interpreted as a form of powerlessness. But it is also seen that the half-hidden oppositional stance taken against the dominant society (represented by Mr. Snow) builds upon the strength of kinship ties kept tightly bound by the family matriarch. Far from being just a reactionary social institution that replicates in miniature the oppressive power relations of the wider society, this story hints at how the family could function as the wellspring of social change.

BEYOND FAMILY

Romanticized portrayals of family culture in 1950s vintage television situation comedies notwithstanding, the times were not entirely free of despair over the viability of the family as a politically insular and economically privatized social institution within liberal democratic society. The twin themes of generational conflict and alienation were explored in theatrical films featuring James Dean and Marlon Brando, while the paradoxes of Cold War America were given expression by writers such as John Updike, Norman Mailer, and John Cheever.

Figure 2.1
Symbolic Resolution of Social Contradictions in *Mama*

Mama Hansen

mediator

wedding coffee urn

Mr. Snow	Papa Lars
Yankee trader	craftsman
commodity relations	kinship ties
market exchange	reciprocity
legal coercion	personal obligation
mass production	handicraft

Ethnic and regional writers similarly voiced reservations about the rise of the new middle class. The countercultural opposition was adumbrated by literary artists such as Jack Kerouac, William Burroughs, Allen Ginsberg, and others identified with the "Beat" movement. Despite the luminescent image, the world beyond family-centered television sitcoms was considerably more fraught with tension and contradictions than otherwise depicted.

There were any number of sitcoms that appeared in the 1950s that featured men and women who lived outside the comfortable confines of the family. Ann Sothern, for example, played unmarried business helpmate to male superiors in both *Private Secretary* (February 1, 1953, to September 10, 1957) and *The Ann Sothern Show* (October 6, 1958, to September 25, 1961). Both programs obliquely approached the theme of thwarted female professional ambition. Ironically, Sothern was, apart from her television personae, a capable and shrewd businessperson who amassed great personal wealth. In both programs, the professional discontent suffered by Sothern's characters Susie McNamera and later Katy O'Connor was implied to originate in matters of the heart. Impeding the occupational rise of the characters played by Sothern was their ability to keep separate their personal and professional lives in a working world dominated by men.

Sometimes resistance to this general pattern of dominance was shown, however slight. In a 1953 episode of *My Friend Irma* (January 8, 1952, to June 25, 1964), the issue of discrimination provides the conflictive impetus for an otherwise inert story line.[29] Irma Peterson (Marie Wilson), a "dumb blonde" whose gender-specific illogic provided the laughs for the program, roomed with an intelligent and ambitious woman named Kay Foster (Mary Shipp). In contrast to Irma, Kay was a college-bred woman who aspired to work as a journalist. Kay expressed her frustration at being kept in a dead-end job in the classified advertising department of the New York newspaper for which she worked:

KAY: Four years of journalism in college, two years working on the paper back home—and here I am selling classified ads at eight cents a line!

IRMA: Oh, don't worry, the price is bound to go up.

KAY: All my life I wanted a career as a newspaper woman. I just can't stand being stuck behind a desk and being completely uncreative.

In the episode, Kay's desperate desire to become a reporter pushed her to enlist the aid of Irma to get a news scoop on a certain cosmetics tycoon's impending divorce. Despite Irma's masquerade as an eavesdropping French maid, the scoop did not pan out and Kay for the time being was left selling ad space.

THOSE WHO CAN'T

Unmarried men and women seemed to be overrepresented in "classroom" situation comedies of the 1950s. It was as if their anomalous social role as single, nonprocreative adults had a parallel in the ambiguous relationship that has existed between intellectual labor and the forces of production. That is, teachers were not exactly social parasites, but neither did they seem to *produce* anything tangible. The teaching profession had traditionally provided single women with a respectable paid occupational role and independent income relatively free of social censure. Even so, the teaching profession was often assumed to be simply a way station on the road to connubial bliss as in the case of Miss Landers in *Leave It to Beaver*. As for male teachers, they were often viewed as individuals not equipped to survive in a highly competitive, pragmatic, can-do society that has been long distrustful of intellect.[30]

The different standards applied to unmarried men and to unmarried women can be observed by a comparison of two classroom sitcoms, *Our Miss Brooks* and *Mr. Peepers*, both of which aired over roughly the same span of time. Whereas the unmarried teacher Connie Brooks (Eve Arden) in *Our Miss Brooks* (October 3, 1952, to September 21, 1956) aggressively but unsuccessfully pursued the eligible biology teacher Philip Boynton (Robert Rockwell), myopic and meek Robinson Peepers (Wally Cox) in *Mr. Peepers* (July 3, 1952, to June 12, 1955) was tentative in his low-key romance with school nurse Nancy Remington (Patricia Benoit). The program ended its run the year following the on-air wedding of Robinson Peepers and Nancy Remington at the end of the 1953–54 season.

For her part, Miss Brooks presumably never managed to corral Mr. Boynton, much to her frustration. As a running gag in the program, Connie Brooks's failed overtures to Boynton dramatized perhaps a countertendency within 1950s family culture, a tendency Barbara Ehrenreich has expressed as the male "flight from commitment."[31] For men such as Philip Boynton, the flight from commitment meant an implicit repudiation of the single income "breadwinner ethic." It was the breadwinner ethic of the 1950s that established men as heads of households by rationalizing the discriminatory advantage they exercised over women in the labor market. For women in the position of a Connie Brooks, the failure to land a male breadwinner seemed to negate the benefits of autonomy and financial independence won through the pursuit of a profession. In *Our Miss Brooks*, Boynton's retreat from intimacy and family culture was implicitly affirmed. Conversely, being denied love seemed almost a form of "punishment" for Connie Brooks, a cautionary warning perhaps to women intrigued by the notion of independence.

BACHELOR SOCIETY

The male flight from commitment was seen at its more extreme in the form of the narcissistic character Bob Collins in *The Bob Cummings Show* (January 2, 1955, to September 15, 1959). As a ladies' man and a professional photographer treated to an unending parade of beautiful models, Bob Collins seemed the personification of the "playboy philosophy," a loosely articulated set of iconoclastic ideas that sought to carve out an autonomous social space free from the constraints of postwar family culture. Founded by Hugh Hefner in Chicago, *Playboy* made its first appearance in October 1953 and featured a nude photograph of the then-unknown Marilyn Monroe. Whether the Bob Collins character was modeled after Hugh Hefner is uncertain. There did, however, seem to be more than superficial similarities between the two figures.[32]

Beyond the guffaws and titters, *The Bob Cummings Show* was an exercise in male supremacy. In the broadest sense, the premise of the program hinged upon the maintenance of the swinging single life-style—implicitly understood to be the sole prerogative of men—against the domestic tradition represented by Bob Collins's widowed sister Margaret (Rosemary DeCamp) and to some extent by his homely secretary Schultzy (Ann B. Davis). Schultzy had a long-standing crush on her boss but was of course outdone by the beauteous competition that Collins kept around his studio. Although Collins's special way with women might have given the male audience vicarious thrills, the program did not go so far as to repudiate the desirability of family life headed by a male breadwinner.

In *Bachelor Father* (September 15, 1957, to September 25, 1962), successful Beverly Hills attorney Bentley Gregg (John Forsythe) enjoyed the best of both worlds. Not only was he single, wealthy, and the object of ceaseless female attention, but he had a niece to whom he could dispense fatherly advice when called upon to do so. Not to be overtaxed, the more mundane aspects of Gregg's single parenthood—cooking, cleaning, shopping, laundry—were left to his Chinese houseboy, Peter Tong (Sammee Tong).

Freedom from family culture, however, was not absolute in either the *Bob Cummings Show* or in *Bachelor Father*. The family as the primary, irreducible element of liberal society persisted. Both male lead characters were integrated into extended families by virtue of their caretaker responsibilities of either a nephew or niece. Bob Collins tutored his teenage nephew Chuck MacDonald (Dwayne Hickman) in the mysteries of manhood, especially that of bachelor society.[33] Bob Collins's modern twist on the story of Antony and Cleopatra, for example, served as a lesson in male dominance for Chuck in one episode.[34] Bentley Gregg in *Bachelor Father* was assisted by his servant Peter Tong in raising his niece Kelly Gregg (Noreen Corcoran). Peter would often throw "hysterical" tantrums over the often inscrutable behavior of the teenage Kelly. What gaps there were left by the inadequate "mothering" of Peter were filled by Kelly's girlfriends or other female acquaintances.

Although sometimes absent in its conventional nuclear form, the family has served as the model of all social formations short of political organization in the television situation comedy. With the erosion of its central function as a productive unit within the postwar political economy, the family became the "institution in which the search for personal happiness, love, and fulfillment takes place."[35] Within the family, the cultivation of subjectivity, concern with self-hood, and pursuit of personal life apart from politics reflect the inability of liberal democratic society to adequately provide the polity with meaning outside the family. The television situation comedy, even as it promulgates dominant social ideologies, exposes the failure of liberal democratic society to argue conclusively the case for its long-term legitimacy.

SCHOOL DAYS

Rivaled perhaps only by television as the preeminent agent of socialization and cultural integration in postwar American society, schools have historically functioned as a crucial means of perpetuating the dominant liberal ideology.[36] The classroom, then, would seem the ideal forum for the regular renewal, reinforcement, and sometimes renegotiation of the tenets of liberal democratic society. It is no wonder that the classroom sitcom has remained one of the more enduring subtypes of the genre. It can be seen that Mr. Peepers, Miss Brooks, and their fellow television teachers often conducted lessons in substantive issues of liberal democracy. No less a weighty topic than First Amendment rights is the object of study in one specific episode of *Mr. Peepers*.[37] In the episode, Mr. Peepers managed to satisfy the freedom of speech claims of his journalism students against the Jefferson High School administration without subverting the interests of the larger institution.

As exercises in liberal pluralist conflict resolution, classroom sitcoms have had a close analogue in courtroom dramas such as *The Defenders* (September

16, 1961, to September 9, 1965), *The Young Lawyers* (September 21, 1970, to May 5, 1971), and *Storefront Lawyers* (September 1970, to September 1, 1971). Although intended more to elicit laughs than provoke deep thought, the situation comedy is no less "serious" a genre than the courtroom drama for the ideological burden it carries. Like Robinson Peepers, Connie Brooks often found herself solving substantive problems translated into the rhetoric of comedy. In an episode entitled "The Embezzled Dress," Miss Brooks found herself having to reconcile the traditional values of thrift and saving with the new economic order based upon consumption.[38]

The unstated premise of this episode of *Our Miss Brooks* was the question of how to protect the traditional virtues of forbearance and delayed gratification (which had their basis in an earlier economy of scarcity) against the onslaught of the new postwar political economy based on the assumption of unlimited growth fueled by ever-increasing levels of consumption. In this episode, principal Osgood Conklin's (Gale Gordon) desire to establish a "students' savings fund" at school was artfully contrasted with Miss Brooks's illegitimate "purchase" of a new dress on credit. A clash of values stood for what at a deeper level was a clash of economic imperatives.

Efforts such as that of Mr. Conklin were overwhelmed and rendered obsolete by the advertising and consumer credit industries that aggressively stimulated consumer demand for a wide array of goods, resulting in the precipitous rise in consumer debt. Between the years 1954 and 1960 consumer credit increased from $4 billion to $43 billion.[39] Seen in this light, the students' savings fund— described by Mr. Conklin as a "sacred trust"—could be viewed as an amusing anachronism. The artful genius of "The Embezzled Dress," however, was the implication that Miss Brooks's purchase of a dress on credit could be understood as a form of "embezzlement"; that the larger credit economy might merely be a "Ponzi" scheme writ large, a matter of robbing Peter to pay Paul.

MAKING AMERICANS

The history of labor immigration to the United States is of central importance to the American experience. Contrary to textbook explanations, labor migration to the United States was both international in scope and systematic rather than simply fortuitous in nature. The creation of the reserve pool of immigrant labor grew out of the logic of capitalist development whereby the tendency of profits to fall could be temporarily counteracted by exploiting cheaper sources of labor.[40] The need to recruit precapitalist workers from less developed countries to fuel the expansion of American industrial capital stood at the center of the so-called open door policy. Between the years 1820 and 1920 about 33 million immigrants entered the United States.[41] In addition, the internal migration of blacks from the rural South to the urban centers of the North beginning in 1915 created added pressure on social resources. The dislocation of black Americans and the rapidity with which it occurred seriously strained intergroup relations.

The entrance of cheaper sources of labor into the marketplace caused severe hardships for native-born members of the underclass. Interethnic conflict took its most pathological forms in various nativist movements and was often officially institutionalized through exclusionary legislation such as the Dillingham Act (1921), which imposed quotas on southern and eastern European immigrants and the National Origins Act (1924), that favored Northern Europeans. Hostility in the West against Chinese labor resulted in a series of Asian exclusion acts applied first to Chinese and later to Japanese immigrants.

Although there have been many examples of spontaneous and institutional violence directed against immigrant groups throughout American history, interethnic relations have nonetheless been guided by the liberal "dominant American legend" symbolized by the image of the melting pot.[42] For the immigrant to America, the push toward assimilation into the dominant society was tempered by the need to maintain ethnic ties not only for the sake of cultural continuity but out of economic necessity as well. Often excluded from certain jobs and professions, immigrants relied upon ethnic subeconomies for survival.[43]

The years following World War I saw vigorous Americanization campaigns mounted by organizations such as the Daughters of the American Revolution, Knights of Columbus, American Legion, Boy Scouts, National Security League, and other agencies concerned about the large foreign-born population in their midst. Employers were especially anxious that Americanization succeed in "making immigrants into productive and compliant workers."[44] Informally, lessons in Americanization took place in the cinema. Founded by men of immigrant origins for the most part, the film industry was anxious to advance the ideals of the dominant social order.[45]

Radio also assisted in the Americanization campaign albeit on a more subtle, perhaps more effective, level. The radio program *Abie's Irish Rose* (January 1942, to September 1944) had as its premise the intermarriage of a Catholic and Jewish family. While conflict was invariably soothed by romantic love, the subtext of the program concerned the issues of amalgamation and assimilation in American life. The sponsors of *Abie's Irish Rose*, Procter & Gamble, dedicated the show to the "spirit of freedom and equality which gives to this nation the greatness that is America."[46] Implied by this tribute was the notion that all people are equal in that all people are equally consumers.

LIFE WITH "SOCIOLINGUINE"

If cinema and radio were important agents of socialization for the working class immigrant generation, then television served the same function for their American-born progeny who held middle-class aspirations. The immigration experience, now one generation removed, became the subject of television situation comedy sociodrama by which Americans could better comprehend the contours of power and conflict in liberal democratic society. Ethnic situation comedies of the 1950s like *Life with Luigi* (September 22, 1952, to December 22, 1952) were revisionist explorations of the immigration experience as seen through the lens of a middle class not quite sure of its location within the status hierarchy, yet distantly secure enough to laugh about its origins.

The program focused on the travails of an Italian immigrant, Luigi Basco (J. Carroll Naish), who arrived in America under the sponsorship of his cousin Pasquale (Alan Reed). Both actors used dialect humor to great effect, playing with the plastic and transformative qualities of language to produce comedic effects. The malapropism, the out of kilter homily, the spoonerism, syntactic errors, and folk expressions that had no relevance to the new social environment provided virtually inexhaustible sources of humor.

Dialect humor is only possible when placed in opposition to the "official" language of a given speech community. The use of dialect humor in *Life with Luigi* had a twofold thrust: It heralded the triumph of the assimilative strategies of the second generation in American society as represented and mediated by language. At the same time it gave a nod and wink to the restricted sociolinguistic world of their fathers. The sons and daughters of the "new immigration" were full-fledged Americans now; there was no need to be defensive, no need to be as careful about ethnic identity.[47] The cacophony of clashing alien tongues had been reorchestrated into the symbolic structural harmony of the liberal democratic state in its penultimate form. A common tongue implied cultural coherence, social stability, political conformity, and the furtherance of an equitable economic system whose agents of ordered change and continuity would be the great middle class.

Luigi received a crash course in American identity in an episode entitled "Boy Scouts."[48] He was made to pass muster not only as a Boy Scout leader, but as an American as well. For lack of proper identification, Luigi was not allowed to cash a check at a drugstore. Luigi had needed the cash to buy his troop hot dogs for a cookout. When asked for identification at the drugstore, Luigi opened his shirt and exposed his birthmark, but he was sent away nonetheless. Luigi managed to obtain $40 in cash after a chair is sold at his antique store. Too late to have gone on the planned hike, the troop led by Luigi erected their pup tents at "Pasquale's Spaghetti Palace" and had their "cookout" there.

The poignant humor in this vignette stemmed from Luigi's utter incomprehension of an impersonal economy and the way in which it left no room for social identity. From his untutored standpoint, all the fuss at establishing his identity was unwarranted. Luigi was utterly at odds with a system of exchange that judged individuals on the basis of credit ratings rather than on character and reputation within the community. Luigi had mistakenly assumed his innate goodness to be self-evident simply because people in his former village had known him and trusted him. But Luigi had been transplanted to America. He would no longer enjoy the familiarity and personal ties maintained in the village society of the old country. Most noteworthy, although Luigi probably understood the psychic costs of his decision to become an American, Luigi more than willingly accepted the trade-off. For Luigi Basco and his countrymen, despite its flaws, America still was considered to be superior to any other country.

ALIENS AND THE AMERICAN DREAM

Hey Jeannie! (September 8, 1956, to September 30, 1960), like *Life with Luigi*, was a program that dramatized the new world predicaments of recent arrivals. Although set in contemporary times, the pilot script for *Hey Jeannie!* in effect revised the history of American immigration by editing out its sordid aspects and highlighting its implied grandeur.[49] The script described such visual clichés as a stock shot of a passenger liner moving past the Statue of Liberty. Harried immigration officials performed their duties amidst the babel of foreign tongues, a scene evocative of the well-worn melting-pot metaphor. Scottish immigrant Jeannie MacLennan (Jeannie Carson) was shown mediating a petty squabble between two people of different nationalities, wresting peace and unity out of conflict and diversity.

Jeannie discovered that no matter how willing she might be, becoming an American required an extended socialization process. It was during that probationary period in which dominant social ideologies were to be internalized by the immigrant. The point was made clear to her by an immigration official at the conclusion of her initial immigration interview. At the interview, Jeannie asked the official whether she was now an American citizen. Jeannie drew a humorous parallel, with serious social overtones, between the world renowned American system of mass industrial production and the immigration process itself:

OFFICIAL: You can't become an American over night. It takes months to get you citizenship papers.

JEANNIE: Months? But I understand you make five thousand automobiles a day.

OFFICIAL: Miss MacLennan, we can't turn out citizens on an assembly line like automobiles.

JEANNIE: (resigned) It's too bad—the cars are getting so much prettier than the people.

Unlike the manufacture of automobiles, the ideological formation and maintenance of Americans is a much more prolonged, intensive procedure. In Jeannie's case, as it developed in the episode, part of her socialization required being properly schooled in fundamental American values rooted in economic self-sufficiency. Jeannie's plans were almost dashed when her original sponsor was discovered to be on the public dole but thanks to a sympathetic cab driver Al Murray (Allen Jenkins) and his sister Liz (Jane Dulo), Jeannie was able to pursue her dreams.

In *Hey Jeannie!*, liberal values based on personal achievement, self-help, equality of opportunity, and possessive individualism were linked to the pursuit of the American dream. That an immigrant such as Jeannie McLennan would dare leave her homeland in search of a better life and economic freedom served as testimony to the essential goodness of the social order for those citizens fortunate enough to be American by birth. *Hey Jeannie!* was a dramatic reminder that the majority of Americans are a self-chosen people and that they are unique in this regard. Further, the ideology of self-selection has a built-in safeguard that suppresses dissent, for if Americans are a self-chosen people, then they have *voluntarily* submitted to a system that by implication stands at the apex of all other social experiments. The "gratitude factor" of immigrant peoples, even to the present, has functioned in a way that enforces ideological conformity throughout American society.

There was, however, a central contradiction in this episode of *Hey Jeannie!* That is, values associated with liberal individualism came into conflict with the realities of the modern welfare state. In this episode, an immigration official made it clear that only productive people such as Jeannie were to be admitted into American society. Jeannie had run into a problem when her original sponsor fell from the economic tightrope into the welfare state's social safety net. Had not Al Murray interceded, Jeannie would have been sent home. The net risk to the state was minimized by involving third-party sponsors, Al Murray and his sister Liz. In this liberal sociodrama, then, each party came away a winner: The state increased its productive potential by one human soul, Jeannie got her try at the brass ring, and the Murray siblings had their mean lives reinvigorated by the presence of a spirited immigrant go-getter.

MAKE ROOM FOR ETHNICS

Danny Thomas began his television career as one of the alternating hosts for the comedy variety program, *All Star Revue* (October 4, 1950, to April 18, 1953). Thomas started in show business as a night club entertainer whose self-deprecating ethnic humor was an important part of his lounge act. Like many American ethnics, Thomas used the entertainment field to overcome blocked access to economic resources. The show *Make Room for Daddy*, later called *The Danny Thomas Show*, marked Thomas's rise to middle-class respectability as a successful entertainer. In the program, Thomas played the role of Danny Williams, a night club performer whose professional commitments sometimes kept him away from a strongly valued homelife.

The ethnic dimension of Danny Williams's life was minimized but not absent from the program. Occasional visits from Uncle Tonoose (Hans Conried) were a reminder of the old country and Williams would often tell stories using dialect humor in his nightclub act. Thomas, however, never surrendered the memory of his ethnic past. As a skilled comedian, an artist who succeeds or fails by his intuitive grasp of the subterranean passions of the audience, Danny Thomas understood the deeper meaning of ethnicity and its centrality to the American dream. In his act, Thomas often told amusing anecdotes that showed pride in his Lebanese heritage. Through his humor, Danny Thomas reminded the public of past immigrants' struggles and reaffirmed that it was the promise of America that allowed for the full flowering of the human soul.

The centrality of ethnicity in American life was seen in the episode "Pardon My Accent."[50] In it, Danny Thomas/Williams paid homage to his immigrant father and, by extension, to American society at large. A cross-generational rift had developed between Peter Lorenzo, a classmate of Rusty Williams (Rusty Hamer), and his father, an immigrant shoemaker. The gap in language and socialization between father and son was brought to the fore when Peter won an award for elocution at school. Since Rusty Williams had won an award for neatness, both boys were invited to a father and son banquet. After having heard that Mr. Lorenzo declined to attend the banquet, Williams visited the shoemaker at his shop. Mr. Lorenzo, as it turned out, was self-conscious about his ability to speak English. As Lorenzo explained, "My boy win a-prize to speak good English. And me go up and tell how I help him. That's a-crazy." "It doesn't matter the *way* you talk," Williams responded, "it's *what* you talk." Lorenzo finally agreed to attend the banquet if Williams would make an acceptance speech in his stead.

In accepting the award on his son's behalf at the banquet, Danny Williams held forth with captivating eloquence. Williams's monologue, couched in the rhetoric of democratic liberalism, recounted the romance of immigration as experienced by his own father:

He was quite a man. A man who had the humblest of beginnings. Born of an immigrant father. A sheepherder, he saw life on the most famous hills on earth, the slopes of Lebanon. A man who came to this country a young fellow and married and raised a family of ten against tremendous odds. It wasn't only the problem of providing for his family. He had to adjust himself to new customs and a strange language.. . .But one thing was certain: when my father had something to say, he said it. And when he said it, people listened. My dad was never ashamed of his dialect because if he were, it would be as though he were ashamed of his heritage. And that, my friends, he definitely was not. Many times in the early days of my career, and I would tell stories about him and his dialect, and the audience would laugh and applaud, and I'd look over and see his face beaming with pride. Because he knew that that laughter and applause was a tribute to him and his kind. The men who helped make America great. The immigrants who sought freedom—and had the courage to come to a strange land and earn it. I know I was supposed to talk about my son tonight. I wound up paying tribute to my father. I assure you fellas, this tribute is fitting and proper. For were it not for our fathers, we their sons, should never have been blessed with having been born in these great United States of America. And our sons, would not be here in this auditorium tonight, honored by the PTA, clutching character awards in their hot hands. Here you are, son. (To Rusty).

Moved by Danny's rhapsody, Mr. Lorenzo forgot his self-consciousness and decided to present the acceptance speech himself. He recited the Pledge of

Allegiance. "And if you don't think that's a fine speech," he exclaimed, "you can take your shoes somewhere else."

The tag scene had Mr. Lorenzo in his shop thanking Danny Williams for his help: "You do for me what Garibaldi do for Sicily—you make me free inside." In a curious if not implausible turnabout, Mr. Lorenzo was shown having reversed roles with his son. Mr. Lorenzo had somehow become articulate, while his son spoke in Italo-American dialect. Williams, through the force of his panegyric on the greatness of America civilization, enabled Mr. Lorenzo to miraculously overcome his position of disadvantage. Thus were generational, political, and cultural contradictions put ceremoniously to rest through sitcom humor.

INTERNAL IMMIGRANTS

There was a shadow figure in *The Danny Thomas Show* who hinted at a presence confined to the margins of society, that of black Americans. Louise (Amanda Randolph) faithfully served the Williams family as its maid. The program *Beulah* (October 3, 1950, to September 22, 1953) had already fore-grounded the sociodramatic role of the black maid on television after having appeared as a radio program spun off from the radio version of *Fibber McGee and Molly*. Like Beulah (Ethel Waters, then Louise Beavers), the character Louise represented the occupational structure of domestic work segmented according to both gender and color. While 60 percent of black working women were employed as domestics by 1950, only 16 percent of white working women were so employed.[51] As an internal immigrant, people such as Louise were no less problematic to the larger society than the foreign-born immigrants similarly forced to undergo the assimilation process. As such, it remained equally important to hold in check internal immigrants such as Louise and José Jiminez (the Latino elevator operator played by comedian Bill Dana) by relegating them to subservient roles.

Armaments manufacturing during World War I provided the original impetus for the "Great Migration" of blacks out of the agrarian South as they were recruited, resettled in the North, and recast in the role of the industrial proletariat. The Great Migration was slowed by the Depression until the pull of industry gearing up for World War II transformed a formerly southern and rural people into a significant population in northern urban centers. About 1.7 million blacks moved North in the 1940s, 1.5 million in the 1950s, and 1.4 million in the 1960s.[52] The demographic shift of this massive internal immigration was attended by the ambivalent manner in which black Americans were presented on television: they were accepted as entertainers but not as legitimate economic actors. The Great Migration had placed blacks in direct economic competition with not only older-stock Americans, but with white ethnics as well. As a result, the regulatory function of ethnic humor was never more in evidence than in the television situation comedy of the 1950s.

After a short-lived period of hope that television would help fulfill the promise of democracy, it became evident that the relative political powerlessness and economic subordination of the black population would not be altered by the introduction of a novel communications technology. There was a black American presence on the television of the 1950s, but only in "familiar or stereotyped situations" admitting them as entertainers, supporting actors, or as "impersonal competitors in some sports."[53] Singular strides were made in showcasing black singers, dancers, musicians, and sports heroes. Less fortunate were Paul Robeson and Nat King Cole, both entertainers who did not toe the invisible line of economic segregation by straying past the perimeters of political dominance maintained by the majority society. The acceptance of Afro-American artistic forms on the part of the dominant society signaled a willingness to accept blackness as an *aesthetic* experience, but only through the simultaneous rejection of blackness as a *political* reality.

GOSDEN 'N' CORRELL

The all-black situation comedy *Amos 'n' Andy* (June 28, 1951, to June 11, 1953) stirred controversy from its first appearance on television. Created and first performed on radio by white actors, Freeman Gosden and Charles Correll, the program stands as a prime example of the curiously split relationship of blacks in relation to American society: Their exploited labor has throughout history been a vital, productive driver of the economic system; yet the rhetoric of liberal democracy based on civil liberties and individual freedom has been contradicted by the presence of structured social inequality that has kept the majority of black Americans in a subordinate position. Gunnar Myrdal referred to this contradictory clash between social reality and official ideology as the "American dilemma."[54]

The aesthetic pleasure derived from the sociodrama *Amos 'n' Andy* stemmed from its adherence to liberal democratic rhetoric while leaving the structure of inequality unquestioned and intact. George "Kingfish" Stevens (Tim Moore) was "free" to hatch as many doomed money-making schemes as he liked, even as it was humorously obvious that his avenue to success was permanently blocked by forces larger than himself. After each personal failure, Kingfish would rally his friends and fellow members of the Mystic Knights of the Sea Lodge to have another go at the brass ring. Fraternal secret orders like the Mystic Knights of the Sea Lodge have functioned in host societies as a means of carving out an autonomous realm of economic activity in highly stratified systems characterized by the differential access to basic resources. As such, each personal failure of Kingfish—leader of the Mystic Knights—represented the collective failure of an ethnic-based parallel economic institution formed to provide for the well-being of a membership excluded from mainstream participation.

The most vehement critic of *Amos 'n' Andy* was the National Association of Colored People (NAACP). The NAACP represented the black middle class in its fight to have *Amos 'n' Andy* removed from the air, arguing that the program was demeaning to blacks who had successfully escaped the cultural and economic backwardness of their underclass brethren. Both the NAACP and their opponents in the controversy were in agreement by assuming that the future of blacks meant a "benignly liberal drift toward an eventually painless, fully integrated place in the American social order."[55] Kingfish, Amos Jones (Alvin Childress), and Andy Brown (Spencer Williams) were an all-too-painful embarrassment to the black middle class: they wore outlandish clothes, were often aggressive or "pushy," and spoke a white rendition of Afro-American rural dialect. Their black bourgeois betters who appeared often in the show, however, were accorded the outward speech, manner, and dress of the dominant northern white society. This culturally kept Kingfish and his cronies in their place. By holding up his failed money-making schemes for ridicule, the program also kept Kingfish's economic drive in check.

The furor over *Amos 'n' Andy* was not over the issue of racism alone. It was not a simple matter of blacks versus whites. Rather, the conflict revolved around the anxiety of the newly arrived black middle class and its ambiguous relationship to the upstart black underclass. That is, they were members of the same ethnic group, but not members of the same "ethclass."[56] The NAACP's case against *Amos 'n' Andy*—which, ironically, was middle class and affirmative in its system of values—arose out of the common confusion over the concepts of ethnicity and social class in liberal democratic discourse. The conflation of the two terms, ethnicity and class, paved the way for the accommodationist black sitcoms of the 1970s and for later programs of the 1980s based on the bizarre premise of permanently stunted black children living with white "parents."

Immigration and ethnicity in American life as mediated by the television situation comedy has managed to divert attention from the central contradiction of society, its class character. American liberal democratic ideology in the sitcom has denied the existence of class society and repressed it to the point where it reemerges as the more easily understood category of ethnicity. The concept of ethnicity itself and its political manifestation, interest group politics, implies a liberal pluralist conception of power relations in society rather than one based on antagonistic class interests. The liberal pluralist model of power relations in turn suggests the existence of an open social system that holds out upward mobility as a realistically attainable reward for individual effort, talent, and initiative. To admit the existence of a rigid American class structure would be to admit how narrowly channeled and limited are opportunities save for those who have already won the lottery of birth.

U.S. DEPARTMENT OF CONSCIOUSNESS

Commercial network television had by the end of the 1950s established itself as an unofficial for-profit branch of the federal government. By its appropriation of public resources for private gain, the structure of network television followed the logic of capitalism in which basic necessities such as food, housing, transportation, and medical care are subject to profit-maximizing market forces alone. Equally as important, the institution of commercial network television helped to consolidate a vision of American society that claimed to have overcome the political controversies of the past. Overt political conflict had been rendered obsolete, or so the new anti-ideological orthodoxy contended.[57] The United States had discovered the secret of sustained economic growth making it possible for all American citizens to benefit equally from its bounty. While on the surface overt conflict seemed blandly pasted over during the not-so-silent 1950s, democratic liberal ideology based on the primacy of private property rights, individualism, materialism, and the acceptance of economic inequality remained intact and was reproduced daily by network television, pushed downward and repressed into the content of its programs.

Television situation comedy came of age during a time when American society was straining to realize ideological consensus. The case of Alger Hiss, the execution of the Rosenbergs, the detonation of nuclear weapons by the Soviet Union, the fall of China to communist rule, and the protracted war in Korea cast a pall upon the politics and culture of the 1950s as America retreated into the metapolitics of domesticity. In its most pathological form, the strain toward consensus eased the rise to prominence of the senator from Wisconsin, Joe McCarthy. His ill-fated purge of heterodox belief from political, educational, religious, and media institutions presupposed the objective existence of a fictive social order known loosely as the "American way of life."

In the television industry, the practice of blacklisting put a lid on dissenting views of American society. Jean Muir, hired to play the mother in *The Aldrich Family* (October 2, 1949, to May 29, 1953) and Philip Loeb, who played the first Jake Goldberg in *The Goldbergs*, were two of the more prominent television actors who fell victim to the inquisition.[58] Although later cleared by the House Committee on Un-American Activities, no more sacred a personage than Lucille Ball herself came under suspicion. In a direct appeal to a studio audience awaiting the filming of a show, the beleaguered Desi Arnaz claimed that there was nothing "red" about Lucy except her hair, and "even *that's* not legitimate."[59] Anticommunist themes ran consistently through television programs that had to do with spies, law enforcement, and espionage. Neither religious nor children's programing were held sacred as Cold War ideology was served up as television entertainment.[60]

The television situation comedy of the 1950s reproduced fairly consistently the dominant social ideologies of the times. This is not to imply that ideological discourse was ever uniform or completely closed off. Close examination of such popular programs as *The Honeymooners* or *Mama* make it evident that social contradictions actually *supply* the premises for sitcom sociodrama. As power relations shift among competing groups in the liberal model of politics, so do the dramatic premises. As social roles undergo the process of renegotiation, so personal identities become transformed. Robin Morgan, who played the dutiful daughter Dagmar in *Mama*, later became a leading proponent of the feminist movement. She edited the seminal feminist anthology *Sisterhood Is Powerful* and later proclaimed herself to be a radical lesbian.[61] Sheila James (later Sheila Kuehl), Zelda Gilroy in *The Many Loves of Dobie Gillis*, later attended Harvard to earn a law degree and went on to a teaching career. Astonishing as these real-life turnabouts may be, even the seemingly innocuous programs like *Father Knows Best* or *The Donna Reed Show* disclose in part the secret contradictions of American life, for no program can escape reference to the wider contemporary society without sacrificing the dramatic realism that stands at its core.

The television situation comedy of the 1960s would further flee from reality until later in the decade, when relevance was found to be marketable. For a while sitcoms escaped to talking horses (*Mr. Ed*), suburban witches (*Bewitched*), wayward extraterrestrials (*My Favorite Martian*), mothers reincarnated as automobiles (*My Mother the Car*), and flying nuns (*The Flying Nun*). Despite their collective flight from reality, the fantasy-based sitcoms of the 1960s are useful documents for understanding the intense political and cultural ferment of the times. Like the de facto rules regulating power relations in America, the fantasy sitcoms could symbolically exclude but not long deny the obtrusion of competing political and cultural truth-claims. By mid-decade, the pajama-clad children exposed to the most powerful socializing agent of the modern era found themselves suffering the cognitive dissonance created by afterimages that did not square with distorted, mass-mediated representations of the social world.

NOTES

1. James Gilbert, *Another Chance: Postwar America, 1945–1985*, 2d ed. (Chicago: Dorsey Press, 1986), p. 8.

2. The rise of "corporate liberalism" in the postwar period is traced in Marty Jezer, *The Dark Ages: Life in the United States 1945–1960* (Boston: South End Press, 1982). The phrase refers to the historically unique intervention of the federal government in regulatory, labor, and social welfare matters not adequately dealt with by business.

3. Gar Alperovitz and Jeff Faux, *Rebuilding America* (New York: Pantheon Books, 1984), pp. 17–18.

4. William Issel, *Social Change in the United States, 1945–1983* (New York: Schocken Books, 1987), p. 89.

5. Frederick F. Siegel, *Troubled Journey: From Pearl Harbor to Ronald Reagan* (New York: Hill & Wang, 1984), p. 92.

6. T. B. Bottomore, *Classes in Modern Society* (New York: Vintage Books, 1966), p. 105.

7. *The Life of Riley* first appeared on radio with William Bendix in the starring role. Jackie Gleason played the role of Chester Riley in the first television version, which lasted only one season. Bendix resumed the role on television three years later.

8. Kenneth T. Jackson, *Crabgrass Frontier: The Suburbanization of the United States* (New York: Oxford University Press, 1985), p. 41.

9. Written by Dick Conway and Roland McLane and directed by Jean Yarborough.

10. *The Honeymooners* began as a sketch on *Cavalcade of Stars* on the DuMont

network in 1951 and went through various incarnations before the final, more commonly known version.

11. Donna McCrohan, *The Honeymooner's Companion: The Kramdens and the Nortons Revisited* (New York: Workman, 1978), p. 34. Shortly before his death in 1987, Jackie Gleason released "lost episodes" of *The Honeymooners* that he had kept in his personal possession.

12. For a brief survey of Jackie Gleason's career, see David Marc, *Demographic Vistas: Television in American Culture* (Philadelphia: University of Pennsylvania Press, 1984), pp. 99–128.

13. Thomas Cripps, *Slow Fade to Black: The Negro in American Film, 1900–1942* (New York: Oxford University Press, 1977), p. 106.

14. "The Soft Touch," written by Warren Wilson and Emerson Treacy with a revised script dated September 24, 1954. An almost identical story is used in an episode of *The Adventures of Ozzie and Harriet* almost two years later, suggesting the salience of the theme. The latter script was written by Don Nelson, Jay Sommers, and Ozzie Nelson, adapted from a story by Dick Bensfield and Perry Grant.

15. See Edward Shorter, *The Making of the Modern Family* (New York: Basic Books, 1975), pp. 148–167. The author discusses the shifting relationship between romantic love and community control in courtship.

16. See Richard Sennett, *Authority* (New York: Alfred A. Knopf, 1980), p. 51.

17. For an update on the concept of the "new class," see Dennis Wrong, "Skeptical Thoughts About a Fashionable Theory," *Dissent*, 30 (1983):491–499.

18. This transformation in capitalist enterprise is outlined in Harry Braverman, *Labor and Monopoly Capital: The Degradation of Work in the Twentieth Century* (New York: Monthly Review Press, 1974), pp. 257–270.

19. Laurence Shames, *The Big Time: The Harvard Business School's Most Successful Class—And How It Shaped America* (New York: Harper & Row, 1986), p. 101.

20. Margaret Mead, *Culture and Commitment: The New Relationship Between the Generations in the 1970s*, rev. ed. (Garden City, N.Y.: Anchor Books, 1978), p. 83. This observation had been made many years earlier in David Riesman et al., *The Lonely Crowd: A Study of the Changing American Character*, abridged ed. with a new foreword (New Haven, Conn.: Yale University Press, 1961), pp. 38–55.

21. "Father and the Dress Suit," written by Bob Ross and Dave Schwartz, produced by Fletcher Markle, Vincent McConnor, associate producer, directed by John Claar. The revised script is dated September 16, 1953. Interestingly, John Cheever, the "Chekov of the Suburbs," wrote a few scripts for *Life with Father* before returning fulltime to the writing of fiction.

22. See Gilbert, pp. 54–75 on "family culture" of the 1950s. "Togetherness," an idea popularized by McCall's "set a moral requirement that family members do things together or else not at all." Paul A. Carter, *Another Part of the Fifties* (New York: Columbia University Press, 1983), p. 95.

23. See Irwyn Applebaum, *The World According to Beaver* (New York: Bantam Books, 1984) for other episode plots.

24. "Wally's Orchid," written by Bob Ross, Joe Connelly, and Bob Mosher. The script bears production number 13230 and is dated February 15, 1960.

25. Gilbert, p. 57.

26. Vince Waldron, *Classic Sitcoms: A Celebration of the Best Prime-Time Comedy* (New York: Collier Books, 1987), p. 28.

27. Max Wilk, *The Golden Age of Television: Notes from the Survivors* (New York: Dell, 1976), p. 50.

28. This episode aired September 10, 1954. The script is dated August 30, 1954. Written by Bradford Ropes and Elizabeth Meehan, produced by Carol Irwin, directed by Ralph Nelson.

29. "The French Maid" is dated December 4, 1953. Written by Frank Galen and Joel Kaner, produced by Nat Perrin, directed by George Cahan, executive producer Ben Feiner, Jr.

30. See Richard Hofstadter, *Anti-Intellectualism in American Life* (New York: Vintage Books, 1963), pp. 299–322. Hofstadter discusses the historical and cultural bases of the teaching profession in the United States.

31. Barbara Ehrenreich, *The Hearts of Men: American Dreams and the Flight from Commitment* (Garden City, N.Y.: Anchor Press/Doubleday, 1983), p. 178. For Ehrenreich the family had been a "private-sector welfare system, in which a woman's only 'entitlement' was her share of her husband's wage."

32. Later, less successful bachelor sitcoms included *The Tab Hunter Show* (September 1960, to September 1961) and *Bringing Up Buddy* (October 10, 1960, to September 25, 1961).

33. As of this writing, Dwayne Hickman works as a CBS programing executive.

34. "Bob Tangles with Ruthie," no. 84. Written by Paul Hennig, Shirl Gordon, Phil Shuken, Dick Wesson, directed by Bob Cummings. Filmed December 13 and 14, 1956, released February 14, 1957, produced by Paul Hennig.

35. Eli Zaretsky, *Capitalism, the Family and Personal Life* (New York: Harper & Row, 1976), p. 65.

36. See Samuel Bowles and Herbert Gintis, *Schooling in Capitalist America* (New York: Basic Books, 1976).

37. Written by Jim Fritzell and Everett Greenbaum, produced by Fred Coe, directed by Hal Keith, created by David Swift. The episode is dated April 12, 1953.

38. "The Embezzled Dress," written by Al Lewis. n.d.

39. Jezer, p. 126. For a historical survey of this fundamental change in the political economy, see E. K. Hunt, *History of Economic Thought: A Critical Perspective* (Belmont, Calif.: Wadsworth, 1979), pp. 393–394. See also Paul A. Baran and Paul M. Sweezy, *Monopoly Capital: An Essay on the American Economic and Social Order* (New York: Modern Reader Paperbacks, 1966), pp. 112–141.

40. Lucie Cheng and Edna Bonacich, eds. *Labor Immigration Under Capitalism: Asian Workers in the United States Before World War II* (Berkeley: University of California Press, 1984), p. 46.

41. Alice Kessler-Harris and Virginia Yans-McLaughlin, "European Immigrant Groups," in *Essays and Data on American Ethnic Groups*, ed. Thomas Sowell (Washington, D.C.: Urban Institute, 1978), p. 107.

42. John Higham, *Send These to Me: Jews and Other Immigrants in Urban America* (New York: Atheneum, 1975), p. 199.

43. See Edna Bonacich and John Modell, *The Economic Basis of Ethnic Solidarity: Small Business in the Japanese American Community* (Berkeley: University of California Press, 1980).

44. Gary Gerstle, "The Politics of Patriotism: Americanization and the Formation of the CIO," *Dissent*, 33 (1986):84–92.

45. See Robert Sklar, *Movie-Made America: A Cultural History of American Movies* (New York: Vintage Books, 1975).

46. John Dunning, *Tune in Yesterday: The Ultimate Encyclopedia of Old-Time Radio 1925–1976* (Englewood Cliffs, N.J.: Prentice-Hall, 1976), p. 4.

47. See Irving Howe, *World of Our Fathers: The Journey of the East European Jews to America and the Life They Found and Made* (New York: Touchstone, 1976), p. 569.

48. "Boy Scouts," #15. Script dated December 29, 1952.

49. "Jeannie's Here!" Pilot script. Created and written by Charles Isaacs.

50. "Pardon My Accent," dated February 17, 1958.

51. Jacqueline Jones, *Labor of Love, Labor of Sorrow: Black Women, Work, and the Family from Slavery to the Present* (New York: Vintage Books, 1986), pp. 234–235.

52. Charles R. Morris, *A Time of Passion: America 1960–1980* (New York: Penguin Books, 1986), p. 68.

53. J. Fred MacDonald, *Blacks and White TV: Afro-Americans in Television since 1948* (Chicago: Nelson-Hall, 1983), p. 49.

54. See Gunnar Myrdal, *An American Dilemma: The Negro Problem and Modern Democracy* (New York: Harper & Row, 1944).

55. Thomas Cripps, "'Amos 'n' Andy' and the Debate Over American Racial Integration," in *American History/American Television: Interpreting the Video Past*, ed. John E. O'Connor (New York: Frederick Ungar, 1983), p. 43.

56. See Milton Gordon, *Assimilation in American Life: The Role of Race, Religion, and National Origins* (New York: Oxford University Press, 1964). Gordon in this classic text pointed out the analytic confusion between the concepts of ethnicity and class in discussions of American ethnic groups.

57. Primary texts of the Cold War "end of ideology" orthodoxy include Daniel Bell, *The End of Ideology: On the Exhaustion of Political Ideas in the Fifties*, rev. ed. (New York: Free Press, 1962) and Sidney Hook, *Political Power and Personal Freedom: Critical Studies in Democracy, Communism, and Civil Rights* (New York: Criterion Books, 1958).

58. See John Cogley, *Report on Blacklisting, II: Radio-Television* (New York: Fund for the Republic, 1956), pp. 67–88. See also Merle Miller, *The Judges and the Judged* (Garden City, N.Y.: Doubleday, 1952), p. 30.

59. Bart Andrews, *The "I Love Lucy" Book* (Garden City, N.Y.: Doubleday, 1985), p. 127.

60. See J. Fred MacDonald, *Television and the Red Menace: The Video Road to Vietnam* (New York: Praeger, 1985), pp. 101–145.

61. Robin Morgan, *Going Too Far: The Personal Chronicle of a Feminist* (New York: Vintage Books, 1978), p. 174.

3
Quiescent Changes

FINE TUNING A CONSENSUS

The gentle television situation comedies of the immediate postwar period were a soothingly entertaining balm for a nation aching from years of grappling with crises both foreign and domestic. The American nation had been rocked by one profound challenge after another since 1929 and yet, a scant twenty years later, the United States had emerged as a country of unparalleled wealth, resources, and military might. Two generations of adult Americans also held in common the memory of no less than three dislocating "social traumas"; the Depression, World War II, and the demise of the extended family.[1] The overall conservative mood of the age, then, perhaps had both a psychosocial as well as a politico-economic basis. Still, postwar American society was not without its structurally ingrained contradictions.

The nostalgic yearning in the Reagan era for the cultural styles of the 1950s has had the unfortunate effect of glossing over the substantial problems and conflicts that surfaced in the immediate postwar period. Once peace had been restored internationally, for example, there was a renewal of the strife between capital and labor that had been suspended for the duration of the war. The new militancy of the trade unions, however, was ultimately blunted by the "capital-labor accord" that culminated with the Taft-Hartley Act (1947).[2] With labor finally subdued, postwar corporate oligarchies—the communications industry included—were left relatively free to expand the scope of operations and quest for profit with the assistance of the liberal state. To a large extent then, the television situation comedies of the 1950s reflected corporate America's push for a placidly idealized way of life presented to a fairly receptive audience unaccustomed to the new affluence. Even so, it could also be seen that select situation comedy plots often cut against the grain of the dominant ideology. As has already been discussed, kernels of counterhegemonic thought and critical outlook have always informed the content of television situation comedy. To reiterate, conflict—social conflict—is one of the defining characteristics of sitcom drama.[3]

As the American public settled back in its easy chair to enjoy the spoils of the victory over fascism, the larger world remained in turmoil. Debate over the political destiny of Eastern Europe turned a former ally, the Soviet Union, into a feared enemy. In 1949, China was "lost" to communist leadership, which further added to the pervasive sense of postwar anxiety. In June of 1950, South Korea was invaded by North Korea, setting in motion a war that dragged on for three years until an armistice was brought about in 1953. America nevertheless maintained a substitute presence in Southeast Asia by helping France prop up its Asian colonial outpost in Indochina. By 1954, the United States was financing over 50 percent of the war waged by France against the Vietminh.

Embattled abroad, Americans domestically arrived at a high degree of ideological consensus, in part enforced by the myth of monolithic world communism threatening to overrun the tight circle of wagons pulled together in collective security. Television Westerns divided the world into a Manichean battle between good and evil, with the frontier homesteaders (suburbanites?) invariably prevailing over the abstract menace represented by the North American "Asiatic Mongol Hordes."[4] Unlike the television Western, the situation comedy could not pretend to solve all crises, foreign or domestic. But like the popular, benign citizen-soldier President Dwight D. Eisenhower, the television situation comedy reassuringly made problems at least *appear* less serious. In doing so, the sitcom perhaps partially fulfilled an objective need for order and stability after years of uncommon disorder.[5]

QUIZZICAL ATTITUDES

Moving into the decade of the 1960s, commercial television went through a brief period of self-assessment after having borne the brunt of much criticism from conservative and liberal quarters alike. The quiz show scandal of 1959 seemed to confirm some critics' displeasure with what they viewed as the manipulative and deceitful nature of American commercial television. The intelligentsia, never well-disposed toward the new medium anyway, seemed particularly humiliated by having one of their own, an English instructor at Columbia University by the name of Mark Van Doren, confess to having been provided correct answers in advance for the quiz show *Twenty-One*. The networks seized upon the scandal as an opportunity to consolidate their already imposing financial power by wresting control over program production from commercial sponsors. The networks went about polishing their tarnished image by investing heavily in news and informational programing.

Out of the many controversies surrounding television in its second full decade, an important study was conducted that attempted to answer questions on the transformation of cultural and political values and social practices as a result of commercial television. *The People Look at Television: A Study of Audience Attitudes* by Gary A. Steiner was a work of social science research that sought to legitimate the established for-profit structure of mass-mediated culture and politics.[6]

The study was financed by CBS pursuant to a proposal made by the president of CBS, Frank Stanton, in 1955. The research was conducted under the aegis of the Bureau of Applied Social Research at Columbia University. Among those affiliated at one time or another with the bureau were such luminaries of communications research as Paul F. Lazarsfeld, Bernard Berelson, and Frank Stanton himself.[7] Frank Stanton had gone to work for CBS in 1935 after having earned a Ph.D. in industrial psychology. Stanton and Lazarsfeld had also developed an ingenious device nicknamed "Little Annie" as a scientific means of testing audience response to new radio programing in the late 1930s. The Lazersfeld-Stanton Program Analyzer was later enlisted during World War II to study the effects of indoctrination films made for G.I.s.[8]

The 1961 "vast wasteland" speech of FCC chairman Newton Minow had given special urgency to the findings of the Bureau of Applied Social Research. An appointee of the culturally minded, intellectually inclined, and image-conscious New Frontier administration of the newly elected President John F. Kennedy, Minow strongly stated that commercial television broadcasters were not meeting their obligations to the public. In his speech, given before the 39th annual convention of the National Association of Broadcasters, Minow put the broadcast industry on notice that license renewal would not be a pro forma exercise. Rather, renewal would be contingent upon programing practices that best served the public interest. "The squandering of our airwaves," said Minow, "is no less important than the lavish waste of any precious natural resource."[9]

After having polled about 2,500 adults across the country with the assistance of the National Opinion Research Center at the University of Chicago and Elmo Roper and Associates, Steiner came to the conclusion that the interests of the viewing public were indeed being properly served by arguing that "good, enriching entertainment should be recognized *as* public service, perhaps the most important public service performed by TV."[10] Steiner rejected the distinction made by the FCC between "public service" and "entertainment" programing. He reasoned that if the widest audience sought entertainment fare, then this would be justification enough for the networks to provide it. Steiner implied that the differences in the levels of viewers' cultural attainment (class position) were resolved through what he referred to as "cultural democracy." Accordingly, viewers voted their preferences with a simple turn of the channel selector. The report combined an argument heavily laden with populist and democratic rhetoric ("The People") with a snow of social scientific data assembled to counter the threats of the FCC. In any case, the mild push for reform ended after Newton Minow left the FCC in 1965 to return to a private law practice. CBS later became one of his major clients.

CORN MEAL TICKET

Just prior to the publication of the CBS-sponsored *The People Look at Television*, *The Beverly Hillbillies* appeared (September 26, 1962, to September 7, 1971) on the selfsame network. The immediate success of *The Beverly Hillbillies* perversely confirmed Steiner's self-validating populist logic arguing for the commensurability of entertainment in commercial television programing with public service. No other new program (*The $64,000 Question* began as a summer series) had ever gained such rapid popularity, as it held the number one position in the Nielsen ratings for the first two years of its nine-year run. With the later appearance of *Gomer Pyle, U.S.M.C.* (September 25, 1964, to September 9, 1970), *Petticoat Junction* (September 24, 1963, to September 12, 1970), and *Green Acres* (September 15, 1965, to September 7, 1971), the rural situation comedy declined from incisive satire to mere farce.

Although critics generally disliked *The Beverly Hillbillies*, the show was a sitcom breakthrough of sorts. The conventional false romanticizing of rural life in modern mass-mediated lore (as in the earlier *Andy Griffith Show*) was challenged by the use of corny stereotypes that had obviously long outlived their usefulness in an urbanized, white collar world. By sheer dumb luck, the Clampetts had bypassed the invisible social gauntlet that has kept most Americans from accumulating wealth. Not only did they escape having to play by the standard rules of attaining worldly success, the Clampetts because of their wealth unwittingly got away with mocking the lifestyles of their upper-class "friends," who but for a simple twist of fate would have been their social antagonists.

Mr. Drysdale (Raymond Bailey), who ran the Commerce Bank in Beverly Hills, had to put up with all manner of outré hillbilly behavior to ensure that the Clampett fortune remained in his bank. His wife Margaret (Harriet Mac-Gibbon) suffered inordinately from indignities innocently inflicted by parvenues too rich to risk offending. No better was Mrs. Drysdale's personal and class-based dilemma dramatized than the time her prized purebred dog was impregnated by the Clampett's mutt. The pollution of upper-crust society by mangey vectors was the premise of *The Beverly Hillbillies*.

The mutt stood as a symbol of the easy physicality and unrepressed sexuality attributed to marginal peoples such as blacks, Latinos, and mountain people— unbound sexual prowess being one of the few sources of selectively exercised personal power that commands respect in all sectors of society. The nubile Elly May (Donna Douglas) in her tight jeans and bursting midriff blouses (as Granny was wont to observe) never acknowledged a man to be her physical equal, challenging their superiority at every opportunity much to the detriment of her romantic life. The unbridled sexuality of Elly May's weak-minded cousin Jethro

Bodine (Max Baer, Jr.) had a riveting effect on Drysdale's Eastern-educated, highly cultivated assistant Jane Hathaway (Nancy Kulp). Miss Hathaway's civilizing mission was undone by base passions roused by Jethro. A one-dimensional reading the *The Beverly Hillbillies* would have it dismissed as a denatured product of the consciousness industry. But if viewed through an ironic lens, *The Beverly Hillbillies* was close in substance and in spirit to the irreverence of Al Capp's "Li'l Abner" cartoon strip.

RURAL ROUTES

The rural situation comedy on television originated with *The Real McCoys* on ABC (October 3, 1957). The show was subsequently bought by rival CBS where it joined its consistently popular country cousin, *The Andy Griffith Show* (October 3, 1960, to September 16, 1968). Both *The Real McCoys* and *The Andy Griffith Show* featured likeable characters who might well have existed in a distant, idealized time when members of an organic community were linked by deep bonds of affection rather than by the impersonal forces of the marketplace. Even the Mexican hired hand in *The Real McCoys*, Pepino Garcia (Tony Martinez), possessed a dignity based on his indispensibility to the daily operations of the family farm.

The Andy Griffith Show began as a spin-off from *The Danny Thomas Show*. General Foods, sponsor of *The Danny Thomas Show*, responded favorably to an episode featuring Andy Griffith and consequently supported the proposed new program.[11] After an auspicious start in films, theater, and recordings, Andy Griffith only reluctantly entered episodic television with *The Andy Griffith Show*. Despite his reservations about the artistic merits of television comedy, Griffith and his agent negotiated a favorable equity position giving them over half ownership of the show. The other owners included Sheldon Leonard, director and producer of *The Danny Thomas Show*, and Danny Thomas himself.

The fictional hamlet of Mayberry might have been the Winesburg, Ohio, of Sherwood Anderson without the undercurrent of morbidity. Like Winesburg, the citizens of Mayberry were generally distrustful of strangers and discouraged even mild forms of deviance. The community placed great faith in the unwritten rules of society, transgressions of which were handled by the good-natured brand of procedural justice administered by Sheriff Andy Taylor (Andy Griffith). Rarely did Sheriff Taylor have to use force majeure to keep order; he did not even carry a gun. The slightly skittish deputy Barney Fife (Don Knotts) was allotted only one bullet (which he carried in his shirt pocket) for his service revolver. Instead, conflict was handled through good old-fashioned moral persuasion. If Andy's son Opie (Ronny Howard) wanted to join a rock band or the town pharmacist Ellie Walker (Elinor Donahue)—a woman, and independent to boot—ran for a seat on the town council, their personal rebellion was always channeled toward more constructive ends by the conclusion of the episode. In the all-white, presumably segregated, town of Mayberry there was no need for police dogs or fire hoses à la "Bull" Conner to quell civil disturbances. There was no danger of four black college students ever sitting down at the lunch counter at Woolworth's demanding service. That was reserved for life outside the peaceable kingdom Mayberry.

Rural situation comedies were not created with the intention of offering critiques of the excesses of urbanism and consumer culture in favor of a society and way of life that had all but disappeared. Rather, the overriding motive was to tap the growing audience in rural areas of the country as the number of local television stations rose and the price of TV sets fell. The rural sitcom served as a meal ticket of sorts for CBS. The strategy must have worked, for CBS television under the leadership of James Aubrey doubled its net profits from $25 million to $49 million between the high-yield corn comedy years of 1959 to 1964.[12] Once, however, it was determined that such programs were no longer delivering the right type of demographics to advertisers, the rural sitcom subgenre would cease to dominate network programing to the same extent it had during the 1960s.

MILITARY COMPLEX

As a social institution, the rise of the military establishment accompanied the precipitous growth of the state in the postwar era. The increase in spending on the military budget since World War II created the contradictory situation whereby American supremacy was ensured internationally while high military expenditures degraded the quality of life at home. The closely forged links between government, the military, and large defense contractors such as Lockheed, General Dynamics, and Rockwell has made civilian labor dependent on the permanent war economy.[13]

Critics of the "military-industrial complex" claimed that high military expenditures solved the problems of underconsumption and unemployment and were therefore functionally necessary for the stability of capitalism. More recent studies have shown, however, the permanent war economy to have been inadequate fiscal policy at best, dysfunctional at worst. While succeeding perhaps in temporarily deferring economic problems in the immediate postwar period, the military economy eventually served to limit growth and lower social wealth through high inflation and low rates of investment.[14] It has also been observed that American defense policy has only "served to preserve the nation's outmoded industrial base, instead of adapting it to international competition."[15]

Beyond the structural contradictions of the military-industrial economy, on the personal level the military model of organization stood as antithetical to the traditional, Emersonian belief in the inviolability of the individual, which elevates the "*I* to semidivine status."[16] Bureaucratic routinization, the attenuation of individual liberties, rank-ordered hierarchies, and extraconstitutional military justice went very much against the grain of the "American Creed."[17] Yet for veterans of World War II and Korea, military service was probably the most important socializing force in their lives, giving them a first hand look at the absurdities of bureaucratic "rationality" in postindustrial society. The politico-economic contradictions and personal dilemmas of the military-industrial complex were well-suited to comedy.

STAND-IN WAR

Individual rebellion against inflexible bureaucratic structures was the prevailing theme of *The Phil Silvers Show/You'll Never Get Rich* (September 20, 1955, to September 11, 1959). Sgt. Bilko (Phil Silvers) spent most of his enlistment time devising ways to "jerk" the system with the help of his crew of noncoms. Like his white collar managerial counterparts in the civilian world, Sgt. Bilko went about his business according to the same sound fundamental management principle of maximizing gain while incurring minimum risk. He intuitively understood that no one ever got rich on take-home pay alone. Making money on the side was the only way anyone could ever even hope to come out ahead in a game where the odds always favored the house. After having put in his twenty years of service, Bilko could retire at a relatively young age with a military pension and embark on a second career, double dipping his way into the middle class.

One of the more insidious effects of *The Phil Silvers Show* was to normalize the historically novel circumstance of maintaining during peacetime an enormous standing army used to support a greatly expanded military machine. Despite the vision of domestic bliss and suburban placidity rendered by many of the 1950s sitcoms, the civilian reconversion process was less than complete. The peacetime military was to be instrumental in the new strategy of containment stated in the Truman Doctrine in March 1947. The titanic struggle between the two global superpowers—the United States and the Soviet Union—would be stalemated by a permanent American military presence in every part of the world where Soviet expansion was feared.

Although never explicitly stated, the soldiers serving under Sgt. Bilko were somewhat unwilling participants in a peacetime military draft. In 1948, Congress restored the Selective Service System, which made universal military training compulsory. The original title of *The Phil Silvers Show, You'll Never Get Rich*, was a phrase taken from a popular ditty expressing resignation and perhaps resistance to being conscripted into the U.S. Army. Nonetheless, the program never alluded to the 23,000 Americans killed and over 100,000 wounded during the three years of the Korean War (June 1950 to July 1953). The Korean War as a setting for a situation comedy would not come about until *M*A*S*H* appeared in 1972 during the Vietnam War. As early as 1955, the year *The Phil Silvers Show* first aired, Vietnam had become part of the American mission to save the world from international communism.

The Vietnam era lasted approximately twenty years—from 1955 to 1975—with American combat forces present between 1961 and 1973. Nearly two dozen military situation comedies appeared on television during this span of time. Of these programs, not a single one used Vietnam as a dramatic backdrop. The only program that came close to violating this unofficial code of silence was *M*A*S*H*, set in a medical outpost during the Korean War. More representative of the subgenre were programs such as *McKeever & the Colonel* (September 23, 1962, to June 16, 1963), *F Troop* (September 14, 1965, to August 31, 1967), *McHale's Navy* (October 11, 1962, to August 30, 1966), *Hogan's Heroes* (September 17, 1965, to July 4, 1971), *Mr. Roberts* (September 17, 1965, to September 2, 1966), and *The Wackiest Ship in the Army* (September 19, 1965, to September 4, 1966).

Each of these programs was set in the remote past or in "safe" locations far beyond the disturbing reach of the Vietnam War. *Hogan's Heroes*, for example, went so far as to burlesque life in a Nazi concentration camp.[18] CBS News, which had once covered the signal events of World War II by employing such exceptional journalists as Edward R. Murrow and William Shirer, had by the 1960s acceded to competitive market forces and offered the television public "an almost obscenely comic view of the Third Reich" during the height of American involvement in Vietnam.[19] Although the major networks kept news of the Vietnam debacle before the American public in what critic Michael Arlen dubbed the "living room war," there was no similar objective acknowledgement in the television situation comedies of the 1960s. By the time *Gomer Pyle, U.S.M.C.* (September 25, 1964, to September 9, 1970) appeared on CBS, military life in general and specifically American militarism, as depicted on television, had been rendered innocent of its maleficent international consequences. It seemed as if the horror of war had been transformed into the laughter of controlled hysteria.

ROOKED PAWN

Gomer Pyle, U.S.M.C. began as a spin-off from *The Andy Griffith Show*. In *The Andy Griffith Show*, Gomer Pyle (Jim Nabors) was a simple gas station attendant who later went on to join the Marine Corps. The new show retained the folkiness of its progenitor and pitted the caring, good nature of the country bumpkin against the rigors of military life. Gomer's friendly nemesis was Sgt. Carter (Frank Sutton), a tough career Marine who would brook no deviation from the rules. In practice, when faced with the childlike truth of Gomer's observations, Sgt. Carter would more often than not slightly bend the rules to accommodate the new recruit. Gomer's gentle sincerity and work ethic seemed to touch the ordinarily hard-bitten sergeant.

A reworking of the fabulist La Fontaine's tale of the country mouse and his city cousin provided the dramatic armature for the episode "Survival of the Fattest."[20] Like the original tale, the show implied that specific survival skills in one setting did not necessarily equip one to deal with a different set of realities. In this episode, Sgt. Carter and his men were subjected to a field survival test.

The sergeant had not been sure whether Gomer would be able to pass the test, which was designed to push each man to the limit of his endurance. Sgt. Carter took precautions to protect Gomer from harm, but discovered Gomer to possess the field skills of a "Daniel Boone." Once Gomer found out that Sgt. Carter had been needlessly trying to protect him, he made the sergeant feel better by building him up, lying that he would not have made it without the sergeant's help. Unlike the predatory, anti-establishment scams of a Sgt. Bilko during an earlier phase of the war economy, Sgt. Carter's relationship to his men—Gomer Pyle in particular—was one of therapeutic adjustment to an institution whose presence had become nonproblematic.

Having left the mythic town of Mayberry to join the Marines, Gomer Pyle was thrust abruptly into a vastly expanded and bewildering world. His passage through discrepant social worlds was a story familiar to most Americans, given both the role of immigration in the history of the nation and the existence of somewhat indistinct social class lines that nonetheless structure society. Gomer's personal predicaments and their homely resolution served as a palliative for the faltering belief of all who might have once naively believed the world to operate by the principles of unconditional generosity, fairness, and equality. Instead, as Gomer indirectly observed, such hurdles as an individual's class affiliation, regional origins, gender, and ethnicity stood in the way of success. Even in *Gomer Pyle, U.S.M.C.*, the situation comedy served as the symbolic means for the reconciliation of the official ideology of equality with the hard realities of inequality as seen by the presence of rank, and, by extension, class distinctions.

By way of example, in "A Date for the Colonel's Daughter," the class nature of civilian society was echoed by the structural similarities of the military hierarchy.[21] Social class differences were explained away in purely personal terms by the end of the episode. The story opened with the base commander Colonel Harper looking for a date for his daughter Jane. Jane was home from college for a visit. The occasion was an enlisted men's dance to be held on the base. Jane was described in the script as being plain in appearance to the point where none of the officers wanted to be seen with her. Col. Harper's aide suggested that an enlisted man would make a more appropriate date anyway. The pairing would make the affair seem more equalitarian, since it was after all an enlisted men's dance.

Gomer Pyle was selected as the date for the Colonel's daughter after Sgt. Carter had submitted his name for consideration. Upon hearing the news, Gomer began to experience acute status anxiety:

GOMER: The Colonel's daughter? Gosh, even if I didn't have plans, I just couldn't take her.

SGT. CARTER: Why not?

GOMER: Well, gosh. . .she's. . .golly, a colonel's daughter.. . .

SGT. CARTER: You've taken out girls before. . .or have you?

GOMER: Shucks, yes. But nobody this important. The most important girl I ever took out back home was the County Assessor's daughter. And that's as high as I ever wanna go. . .the daughter of a Civil Service man.. . .

Sgt. Carter tried to convince Gomer that it did not matter whether Jane Harper was the daughter of a colonel. In doing so, two latent meanings were communicated by Carter (1) that since the colonel's daughter is a "girl," class differences were not as important and (2) that Gomer might have been perceived as "gay" were he not interested ("You've taken out girls before. . .or have you?"). In this short exchange, two modes of subordinate social existence—the female and the homosexual—were worked into the calculus of class domination and used as a form of "logical" leverage against the defenseless Gomer.

The problem was of course that it really *did* matter that an enlisted man, an unschooled rustic, was to date the daughter of a U.S. Marine Corps colonel. The Colonel's wife, Mrs. Harper, made precisely that point when she questioned her husband's judgment in permitting the couple to date. While Col. Harper imputed purity and innocence to country folk, Mrs. Harper took the opposite position: "They're the worst kind. Those quiet country boys. . .they're the ones who turn into howling wolves." For his part, Gomer remained doubtful of his ability to keep pace with a big-city sophisticate. Sgt. Carter tried his best to put him at ease, but Gomer insisted that he and the young woman were "from different worlds." Gomer assumed that co-ed Jane Harper was accustomed to high society life, having "probably even been to New York."

Upon meeting Gomer, Mrs. Harper's fears seemed to have been confirmed. Gomer's small talk about his hometown Mayberry was construed by her in the worst possible ways. Throughout the evening Mrs. Harper kept the couple under close observation. At Jane's insistence, the couple fled the dance unnoticed and finally escaped the close scrutiny of her parents. Mrs. Harper became alarmed when she could not locate the couple and sent her husband to find them.

At the conclusion of the episode, a crafty but important switch in emphasis was pulled: Instead of this tale taking the theme of class differences to its proper destination, it was diverted into a question of parental authority over an intractable child. After Gomer and an unmolested Jane were found by a small detachment of Marines, Jane boldly kissed Gomer as a gesture of defiance directed against her mother.

By means of this code-switching maneuver, the story at once satisfied the objective demand of the plot to properly resolve and displace the full implications of the original problem, the clash of class differences. The shy, retiring subject of democratic liberal society—class antagonism (personified by the character Gomer Pyle)—was repressed only to reemerge as a simple disagreement between individuals. In accordance with the liberal pluralist model of social relations, such personal disagreement would pass into a higher order of group consensus once all competing claims for power or autonomy had been satisfied. By the end of the episode, Gomer Pyle had been excluded from full dramatic, hence political, participation. As it turned out, Gomer had been deployed literally and figuratively as a pawn in a power contest not of his own choosing.

The denial of the war in Vietnam in combination with intense domestic discord became part of the psychopathology of everyday life in the United States. It was as if the fictional wars played out in military situation comedies internalized the turmoil of the times and relieved the resultant anxiety through the use of humor. Industrial productivity was supposed to have delivered the goods at home, while the military complex ensured American hegemony internationally. But the liberal vision did not go entirely according to plan. The already high economic cost of maintaining a capital-intensive standing army on a global scale was exacerbated by the allocation of an additional $106 billion between 1966 and 1970 to help pay for the war.[22] The welfare/warfare dualism in American society of the 1960s eventually proved impossible to sustain.

The strains of American society under New Frontier and Great Society liberalism were no laughing matter. What better vehicle than the situation comedy to work through the systemic contradictions of American society revealed to be ever more vulnerable by the hard questions raised by the war and by groups contesting the unequal distribution of social resources. Welfarism and the entitlement revolution, the "continued raising of the level of material desire," eventually pushed the liberal state into first admitting and then trying to satisfy the competing claims of groups newly enfranchised by the internal requirements of liberal democracy itself.[23]

OF EQUINE BONDAGE

The supernatural or fantasy sitcom took its place alongside the military sitcom during the 1960s as one of the conspicuously new subtypes of the genre. Fantasy sitcoms in effect supplanted the ethnic sitcoms of the 1950s, becoming its functional equivalent. The regulatory nature of the situation comedy came to deal less specifically with ethnic Americans and more with their fantasy-induced "body-doubles." The ethnic sitcom was not to reappear on television—but with vital differences—until the 1970s with the programs produced by Norman Lear and Bud Yorkin.

Leaving aside *Topper*, which appeared on television in 1953 after being adapted from the 1937 movie, *Mr. Ed* (October 1, 1961, to September 8, 1965) was one of the first significant fantasy-oriented situation comedies.[24] Although a mere horse, Mr. Ed was in possession of full-fledged human sensibilities. He believed himself to be the equal of any species and resented his treatment as a second-class "citizen" deprived of the rights and privileges of his human counterparts. Mr. Ed's supernatural intelligence was revealed only to his master Wilbur Post (Alan Young), as he rejected the fawning paternalism of other humans who considered him to be nothing more than a serviceable pet. When not with Wilbur, Mr. Ed would play dumb so as to avoid a premature visit to the glue factory.

Figure 3.1
Supernatural Situation Comedies, 1961–1972

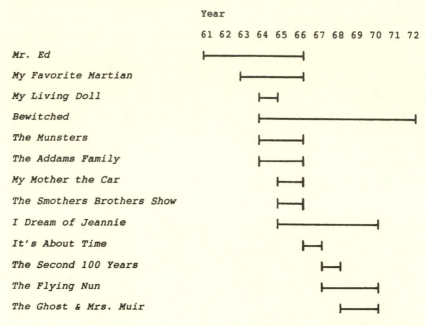

Mr. Ed was a superior human consciousness trapped in an equine body. This transfiguration established him as the disguised object of lingering intolerant attitudes toward newly enfranchised minorities that could no longer be responsibly voiced freely in society, even through humor, without fear of censure. A new national mood of heightened formal civil equality in the years following *Brown v. Board of Education* (1954) attended by increasing acts of civil disobedience on the part of blacks made public declamations of privately held beliefs untenable. Mr. Ed could indulge his human-like tastes and aspire to equality all he wanted. He could peevishly look down his snout at those humans of lesser social attainment or cultural refinement. Mr. Ed after all was a purebred palomino. But when all was said and done, Mr. Ed was still only a horse and would therefore never qualify to stand on equal footing with his biological superiors.

THERE GOES THE NEIGHBORHOOD

Few Americans would have outwardly dismissed the vision of Martin Luther King, Jr., when he spoke of a future time when ''little black boys and little black girls will be able to join hands with little white boys and little white girls as sisters and brothers'' at the March on Washington in the summer of 1963. The speech resonated with echoes of a shared political culture and religious heritage that venerated the principles of justice and equality in the abstract. But within democratic liberal ideology there has existed a curious split between the universal desideratum of justice and the pragmatic compromises involved in attaining it, causing liberalism to be "divided against itself."[25] The formal commitment to the pursuit of liberty, justice, and equality has often run smack dab against the liberal zero-sum concept of power and politics wherein one group's gain meant another group's loss. By this definition of politics, the realization of full equality for all citizens would in practice have meant diminished access to resources by those already enjoying the benefits of complete enfranchisement.

The social legislation of President Lyndon B. Johnson reframed the principal tenets of democratic liberal ideology after a decade of civil rights struggle and often violent protest. The Civil Rights Act (1964), Voting Rights Act (1965), Fair Housing Act (1968), and Federal Jury Reform Act (1968) each granted the claims of minorities against social resources held in common. Justice and equality were assumed to be attainable within the existing democratic pluralist political order.[26] The enlarged pool of competing claimant groups demanding equal access to finite economic resources, however, proved to be particularly distressing to middle Americans, who had only a tenuous hold on economic security.

This "bifurcation of liberalism"—justice versus practicality—was to manifest itself later in the politics of resentment expressed by "white ethnics" and the procedural backlash seen in the "reverse discrimination" U.S. Supreme Court cases of *Bakke* (1978) and *Weber* (1979) in the 1970s. In its earlier, latent stage the bifurcation of liberal ideology reared its head in the form of *The Addams Family* (September 18, 1964, to September 2, 1966) and *The Munsters* (September 24, 1964, to September 1, 1966). Both programs featured a family of monsters plopped down in the midst of middle-class communities.

Prior to the appearance of both programs, the state of California had in 1959 legislated the "Unruh" Civil Rights Act in response to pressures exerted by a coalition of blacks and liberals who sought to end racial discrimination. Four years later, the Rumford Act was passed with the intention of ending patterns of housing discrimination in the state. In Los Angeles County alone, the population had increased eightfold between the years 1940 and 1965, making competition for housing stock in desirable neighborhoods all the more intense. The fear of "black encroachment by the dominant white majority" led to a state initiative that resulted in the 1964 repeal of the Rumford Act by California voters by a margin of better than two to one.[27]

The very presence of the Addams and Munster families stood as a violation of the ordinary neighborhoods in which they resided, much like the "white trash" Beverly hillbillies. In this, these programs were similar to the 1961 film *A Raisin in the Sun*, wherein a black family's move into an all-white neighborhood was cause for alarm. Unlike the characters in *A Raisin in the Sun*, however, neither the Addams family nor the Munsters spent time moralizing about the ill effects of discrimination and intolerance. Both monstrous families went blithely along with their lives as if they were normal and the rest of the world was flawed. The only character in *The Munsters* who was normal in appearance and behavior, Marilyn Munster (Beverly Owen; later, Pat Priest), was viewed as somewhat of a freak by the rest of the family. Such comedic inversion was the source of humor for both programs.

For the economically vulnerable American middle class, the one tangible asset even coming close to resembling wealth in the postwar era has been home ownership. As one of the few means of enjoying financial advantage in middle-class society, such wealth has been aggressively protected and jealously guarded primarily through the maintenance of favorable tax laws. The lowering of property values by the presence of undesirable "block-busting" monsters would be difficult to countenance, even if it meant the contravention of official liberal democratic pieties. In most urban centers across the country the pattern of out-migration known as "white flight" came as a reaction to the lifting of restrictive covenants and informal agreements among home owners and realtors that enforced residential segregation.

The families Munster and Addams notwithstanding, the rise of ghetto rebellion came to the forefront of national awareness beginning with the Harlem riots in the summer of 1964. With the Watts uprising of the following year, urban disturbances and racial violence became increasingly more frequent. Outbreaks of urban unrest had appeared in approximately 75 cities nationwide by 1968. The suburban normalcy of the Mayfield created by Bob Mosher and Joe Connelly in *Leave It to Beaver* became twisted into the necrotic grotesqueries of *The Munsters* written by the same team.[28] Not coincidentally perhaps, the team of Mosher and Connelly had written over 1,500 radio and television scripts for *Amos 'n' Andy*.[29] By 1966 the Addamses and Munsters had moved off the schedule and into syndication where they currently reside in perpetuo in the rerun ghetto.

BEWITCHED

The politics of gender lay dormant for nearly forty years after the passage of the nineteenth amendment (1920) to the Constitution prohibiting the denial or abridgement of voting rights on the basis of sex. In response to criticism about his neglect of women's issues, in 1961 John F. Kennedy formed the Presidential Commission on the Status of Women. The recommendations of the commission resulted in the Equal Pay Act of 1963, which formally banned discriminatory wage structures based upon gender. Title VII of the Civil Rights Act (1964) provided additional legal leverage to end sex discrimination. In 1966, the National Organization for Women (NOW) was formed to advance the economic interests of newly mobilized middle-class, college-bred women.

The year 1963 saw the publication of the liberal feminist manifesto, *The Feminine Mystique*. Author Betty Friedan recounted the forms of domestic (though decidedly middle-class) bondage that held sway during the 1950s domesticity cycle. The image of the "spirited career girl" created by women writers in the late 1930s and early 1940s was replaced by the housewife as the new feminine ideal of the 1950s.[30] Friedan's observations, although never specifically mentioned in her book, came at a time of rapidly deteriorating economic conditions whereby it became "increasingly difficult to achieve or hold on to middle-class standards of living" with a male breadwinner's salary alone.[31] Women were entering the work force not so much out of feminist awareness as out of economic necessity.

The rapid influx of female labor into the work force created social tensions on the same level of magnitude as the earlier interethnic competition precipitated by foreign immigration and the internal migration of American blacks from country to city. In this, the need of capitalism for wage earners came into conflict with the ideology of patriarchy. However, the twin ideologies of patriarchy and liberal democracy were incompatible. In its presence within a liberal democracy, an exploitative patriarchal system was "contradicted by the image of equal opportunity."[32]

The new economic relationship organized now along gender lines was negotiated by a number of notable fantasy situation comedies with women playing leading roles. As in the case of *Mr. Ed, The Addams Family* or *The Munsters*, fantasy was employed in order to identify and grapple with aspects of social conflict that could not be treated in terms of dramatic realism alone. As Tzvetan Todorov observed in his study on the uses of the fantastic in literature, the "fantastic permits us to cross frontiers that are inaccessible so long as we have not recourse to it."[33] Todorov wrote: "We see, finally, how the social and the literary functions coincide: in both cases, we are concerned with a transgression of the law. Whether it is in social life or in narrative, the intervention of the supernatural element always constitutes a break in the system of pre-established rules, and in doing so finds its justification."[34] Fantasy situation comedies, then, allowed for the dramatic working through of social contradictions that could not directly be addressed because of their extreme sensitivity. Although literary realism requires the presence of social contradictions as a structuring device, fantasy allows for such social contradictions to be removed to a less threatening nether world. The fantasy sitcom therefore satisfied both the aesthetic and social requirements of the art form.

The control of transgressions against a normative social order based on male dominance was seen in *Bewitched* (September 17, 1964, to July 1, 1972). The show chronicled the tribulations of the secretly empowered witch Samantha (Elizabeth Montgomery) who was married to a mere mortal, Darrin Stevens (Dick York; later, Dick Sargent).[35] As a condition of their marriage, Samantha promised her husband Darrin that she would behave in a manner befitting a proper suburban housewife by not wielding her magical powers. Samantha's strong-willed mother, Endora (Agnes Moorehead), urged Samantha to use her gender-specific supernatural skills in defiance of Darrin. Endora took every opportunity to thwart Darrin's insistence on male-dominant normality, while Samantha did her best to straddle the gulf between her mother and her husband.

WET DREAM OF JEANNIE

I Dream of Jeannie (September 18, 1965, to September 1, 1970) along with *Bewitched* and *The Flying Nun* (September 7, 1967, to September 18, 1970) were fantasies of female empowerment that was given limited rein within well-defined ideological boundaries. The central female characters in these programs were given magical powers not simply with the intention of having them "do more interesting things."[36] Rather, these tales of female omnipotence were updated versions of the compensatory symbolic dominance enjoyed by the idealized housewife/mother portrayed in the television situation comedies of the 1950s. Given the content of commercial television of the mid–1960s, white male dominance was a core assumption still adhered to by the dominant society, civil rights legislation notwithstanding. On the contested periphery, however, male-centered power was being challenged by the selective use of supernatural social power.

Created by Sidney Sheldon, *I Dream of Jeannie* was a program that fulfilled the sexual fantasies of the American man who grew up with a *Playboy* magazine in hand along with NASA-induced fantasies of deep space exploration. Not only was the hero of the show Major Tony Nelson (Larry Hagman) an honest-to-goodness astronaut, but he lived with a beautiful, scantily clad genie who tended to his every need. The sole mission of Jeannie, played by actress Barbara Eden, was to satisfy the wishes of the man she called "master." "Back into your bottle," Major Nelson would order when Jeannie's presence inconvenienced him.

The politics of feminism and increasingly contested gender power relations in wider society provided the not always subtle subtext for *I Dream of Jeannie*. A representative episode had Jeannie being offered as a "prize" for a male power contest. The episode began with Jeannie grocery shopping at Food City for her master.[37] Having had the good fortune of being the millionth customer passing through the check-out line, Jeannie was annointed "Queen of the Supermarket." Among other prizes, against her will Jeannie was made "Queen of the Coco Beach Rodeo." Interesting to note, Jeannie initially rejected the title not because it was demeaning, but because she wanted to preserve the secrecy, hence status quo of the relationship with her master. As queen, Jeannie was offered as the "prize" to the winner of the rodeo. Major Nelson was thus forced to enter the rodeo as a contestant to preserve his mastery of Jeannie.

After having survived one physical trial after another at the rodeo, Nelson emerged triumphant. His control over Jeannie reestablished, the major then claimed his prize by begrudgingly taking her out on a dinner-date. Major Nelson had blamed Jeannie for having put him through so much torture, even though she had never in the first place consented of her own free will to serve as the rodeo prize. As the prize, Jeannie was made into the passive female object of exchange between competing male wills. Having won the rodeo, Major Nelson succeeded in reasserting his proprietary claim to the exclusive use of Jeannie and her magical powers. The parallels between Jeannie's and her master's contested lordship/bondage relationship and the evolving women's movement seemed too close to be only coincidental.

HOME/WORK

Like other related antinomies in liberal social theory—individual versus society, freedom versus determinism—the divison of home and work was clearly evident in the television situation comedies of the 1960s just as it was in the preceding decade. With few exceptions, such as *The Dick Van Dyke Show* (October 3, 1961, to September 7, 1966), the world of work was kept separate from the home. Most tellingly, there were relatively few programs wherein the values of society, work, and home life commingled as one. Of the notable exceptions, it was usually the case that creative, autonomous, and nonbureaucratic labor was being performed. Professor Russell Lawrence (Don Porter) in *Gidget* September 15, 1965, to September 1, 1966), for instance, taught at a small-town college and Dr. Alex Stone (Carl Betz) in *The Donna Reed Show* (September 24, 1958, to September 3, 1966) maintained a modest private medical practice.

The professional roles of professor or doctor were portrayed in the two programs as allowing for the freer exercise of personal initiative and individual responsibility. This was held in contrast to the common lot of salaried white collar workers who labored within impersonal corporate or state bureaucracies. Professor Lawrence lived and worked in a slow-paced college town where ideas, abstract thought, and commitment mattered. Dr. Stone ran his medical (significantly, pediatrics) practice out of his home office. For both individuals, work was not inimical to life, rather, it was its basis.

One of the few other exceptions to the antimony of work and home in 1960s sitcoms was *The Dick Van Dyke Show*. The focus of the show differed from both *Gidget* and *The Donna Reed Show* in that it dramatized creative group labor, a collectivity that involved professional colleagues, family, and even neighbors Jerry and Millie Helper (Jerry Paris; Ann Morgan Guilbert). The program explored the relationships between Rob Petrie (Dick Van Dyke), his wife Laura (Mary Tyler Moore), and fellow television writers Sally Rogers (Rose Marie), and Buddy Sorrell (Morey Amsterdam). In so doing, the program drew closer together the once mutually exclusive domains of work and home.

RECOMBINANT FAMILIES

The split between home and work can be traced to the development of the capitalist economy in its early stages. Historically, the function of the household as the principal site of economic production in pre-industrial society gave way to its function in the modern liberal state as the center of leisure and consumption. In tandem with the divorce of home and work, the rigors of competitive capitalism forced the bourgeois family to redefine itself "as a place of close, warm, emotive relations."[38] By implication, alienation, inauthenticity, and discontinuity remained the rule in the larger social world of work and politics.

The sheer number of family-oriented situation comedies that have appeared across a span of more than forty years seems to support the notion of the modern family as being a refuge from the harshness of middle-class economic competition, a "haven in a heartless world."[39] During the rare moments when society, politics, and work intrude upon the lives of sitcom families, such occasions are taken as purely personal problems that must be worked through within a delimited sphere of trusted intimates. But for the most part, work—situation comedy shorthand for a constricting, often hostile society—is kept at a far remove.

As a creation of history in process, the 1960s family was not protected from social pressures that forced resolution of its inner contradictions. Variations on the traditionally structured male-dominated nuclear family theme began to appear in more than a few noteworthy situation comedies of the 1960s. There were even hints of the dissolution of the family ideal as constituted by the postwar American social science establishment led by Talcott Parsons.[40] Changes in the social relations of production wrought by corporate capitalism and the professionally managed consumer economy of the postwar period might have meant a "fundamental—if not fatal—alteration in family structure," even as conservative values based on the bourgeois model of the family persisted.[41]

Room for One More (January 27, 1962, to September 22, 1962), *The Brady Bunch* (September 26, 1969, to August 30, 1974), and *My Three Sons* (September 29, 1960, to August 24, 1972) were significant departures from the mom and pop model of the family. *Room for One More* concerned the minor problems of a middle-class couple with two adopted children in addition to their two biological children. Their household served on occasion as a shelter for homeless waifs, giving rise to various and sundry easily solvable situations.

Room for One More lasted less than one year on television. *The Brady Bunch*, however, enjoyed a long run—long enough to qualify it for the lucrative syndication market. *The Brady Bunch* adopted the family situation comedy formula and multiplied it by a factor of two. Instead of the usual nuclear family arrangement, the Brady bunch comprised children of two different families whose parents linked up after the deaths of their respective spouses. The hyperfertility of the postwar baby boom was made possible because of unique economic conditions that made the financial burden of raising children more bearable. But now, if *The Brady Bunch* was an accurate indication, large families such as were glamorized by the Dion quintuplets were to be had only through consolidation and not through natural increase.

Home for *My Three Sons* (September 29, 1960, to August 24, 1972) was an all-male preserve. "Mother" was Bub O'Casey played by William "Fred Mertz" Frawley (later, William Demarest) formerly of *I Love Lucy*. In *My Three Sons* the irascible Frawley was reduced to walking about the house in an apron, cooking, ironing, and performing other domestic chores once restricted to women. Similarly emasculated was Fred MacMurray as widower Steve Douglas, busily raising a household of growing boys. Douglas served in a twin parental capacity until he remarried just before the series ended. As each of the boys grew into manhood, they got married and began families of their own, conferring normalcy to an otherwise untypical "family" sitcom.

The sheer largeness of the clans seen in *Room for One More, The Brady Bunch*, and *My Three Sons* could be understood as at once a salute to the nuclear family and a last hurrah for the generational and demographic aberration known as the baby boom. The positive values of family life were reaffirmed even as its importance as a reproductive unit was being minimized. For in *The Brady Bunch* or *Room for One More* the children were the result of other than natural increase: families in these shows grew to such large proportions through either remarriage or adoption. In *My Three Sons*, reproductive potential was denied by the absence of a wife for widower Steve Douglas during most of the program's twelve-season run. The economics of raising a large family had simply become onerous for most middle-class couples by the mid–1960s.

LOST AND FOUNDLINGS

Even more bizarre than the above deviations from the family sitcom formula was the program *Family Affair* (September 12, 1966, to September 9, 1971). The head of the family was Bill Davis (Brian Keith), a lifelong bachelor quite content in his ways before having been forced to care for his orphaned nieces and nephew. A faithful manservant, Mr. French (Sebastian Cabot), assisted Bill Davis in raising the fraternal twins and the teenager. His ready-made family slightly cramped his freewheeling life as a highly paid professional and confirmed bachelor who enjoyed the company of attractive women. Nonetheless, Bill Davis kindly sacrificed his personal life for the sake of the children. As surrogate parents, Uncle Bill and Mr. French discharged their duties commendably.

Fortunately for Buffy, Jody, and Cissy, fate installed them in affluent surroundings off Fifth Avenue in Manhattan rather than in an orphanage. The precarious status of children raised by potentially uncaring bachelors and their luck in having landed in the best of hands provided a reassuring backdrop for such mawkish episodes as the one where Bill had to search for a doll that was lost by one of the twins.[42] What began in the episode as a touchingly innocent search to recover a lost doll, turned out—inadvertently perhaps—to be a veiled dramatic disquisition on inequality in society.

Bill and his date suspected that the doll might have been accidently thrown out with the trash. In following their hunch, they encountered a street person rummaging through the trash cans outside their apartment. Bill actually apologized to the bum for encroaching upon his exclusive preserve:

STREET PERSON: Help yourself, I got no monopoly.

BILL: Say, um, did you happen to come across a doll? It's about that big, with a blue polka dot dress, it's got kind of a funny looking, sad smile on its.. . .

STREET PERSON: If you want dolls, your best bet is on the Westside. Lotta dolls in that trash.. . .You folks on a scavenger hunt?

BILL'S GIRLFRIEND: No, this is very important.

STREET PERSON: That's life. You'd be surprised the people I meet. Everybody has his approach.

After finding the doll, Bill thanked the man and left him to his pickings. "It's all yours," Bill said. The bum, however, responded with a throwaway line that suddenly injected a critically ironic dimension to their chance social encounter: "Come back anytime," he said. "Competition is the lifeblood of free enterprise."

What transpired in this contingently fleeting exchange between Uncle Bill Davis and the scavenger bared the mechanism of ideological and social domination if but for a short moment. Davis had asked permission to transgress on the trash area implicitly understood by both parties to be the province of the bum. At the same time, the bum unquestioningly conceded the rightness of Bill Davis's superiority, which was coded in the episode in terms of social space— Fifth Avenue apartment above, trash area below. It was this set of class oppositions that propelled the drama to its destination.

The street person had not been coerced, deceived, or manipulated into acceptance of this unequal relationship by either physical force or false consciousness. Rather, the dispossessed man mouthed the half-remembered rhetoric of an obsolete social ideology, laissez-faire capitalism. The street person's comment on the nature of economic competition was simultaneously an affirmation and condemnation of an ideology that "explains" inequality in society. The tension between manifest expression ("free enterprise") and latent content (class society) was the disconcertingly ironic source of humor in this vignette. The bum was therefore both the perpetrator and potential disrupter of an ideological-political construct made vulnerable by its contradictions. The bum was neither a passive agent reproducing the dominant ideology nor fully aware yet of the political implications of his personal dilemma. While the bum was oblivious to the humorous contradiction between his avowal of "free enterprise" and his concomitant powerlessness, the audience no doubt well understood the underlying joke.

COMING TOGETHER

One of the more sensationalized responses to the progressive economic immiseration of the middle-class family was the partial abandonment of the bourgeois " 'till death do us part" nuclear model in favor of serial monogamy. While cultural conservatives such as Daniel Bell criticized the sexual revolution for its hedonism, others welcomed its salutary effects, anticipating perhaps that the sexual revolution would precede social revolution.[43] The sexual revolution had, however, been a long time in coming, at least since more than 100,000 copies of Dr. Alfred C. Kinsey's *Sexual Behavior in the Human Male* sold within the first three months of its publication in 1948. The study documented the historic adaptation of American male sexual behavior to postindustrial society, conferring "a new, scientifically authenticated prestige to these norms."[44]

Television, along with other entertainment media, explored the shifting sands of sexuality in its own rigidly self-conscious manner. The situation comedy in particular toyed with the more sensational aspects of the sexual revolution while remaining firmly on the side of traditional values and attitudes pertaining to family life. Changing sexual mores fit nicely with the generic sitcom interplay of novelty and familiarity. The short-lived program *Hey Landlord* (September 11, 1966, to May 14, 1967) perfectly illustrated the formula.[45]

In "Swingle City, East," landlord Woody Banner (Will Hutchins) tried to transform an unprofitable apartment complex into a money making mecca for young, swinging singles. His friend Chuck Hookstratten (Sandy Baron) had read an article in *Newslife* about "leisure living" in Southern California. As Chuck observed, "They build these apartment buildings out there and they only rent to one kind of people—single guys and single girls." In response to the new social trend, the two renovated the apartment in a way that would attract the targeted clientele. Shortly after the improvements were made, several "girls" moved into the apartment building, as did a few bachelors.

The leisure pursuits of the new arrivals proved to be too disturbing to long-time tenant, Jack Ellenhorn (Michael Constantine), forcing him to move out. He had felt displaced not only by the presence of the new tenants, but by their new ethic as well. "I just don't fit," Jack explained. Jack's departure forced everyone, including the swingles, to reevaluate their revamped lives. Jack's departure was especially hurtful to Woody, who had second thoughts about his innovative business strategy: "I'm right where I've always wanted to be. . .apartments rented, money rolling in. . .and if I'd known it was going to turn out this way, I never would've done it." Fortunately for all involved, some of the singles fell in love, married, and moved away to establish households along more traditional lines. With the new vacancies, Jack felt comfortable about returning and the normal state of affairs was restored.

Like many other situation comedies that have treated novel ideas, social movements, or sensitive topics, the episode flirted briefly with a taboo before settling back to the normative order. What began as an enticing peek at the singles scene proved to be little more than a morality play about the importance of long-term relationships, sexual or otherwise. This episodic dalliance with the notion of sexual freedom served to ultimately repudiate it by having the swingles leaving "Swingle City" to settle down in conventional marriage, an institution antithetical to the unfettered eroticism promised by the sexual revolution of the 1960s.

MARKETING OF THE COUNTERCULTURE

The culture of postwar youth found its expression in a distinct musical form that fused elements of country and western, gospel, and blues.[46] Marketed as "rock 'n' roll," this popular music product celebrated the newfound freedoms made possible by economic prosperity. Performers such as Elvis Presley, Chuck Berry, Little Richard, and Jerry Lee Lewis gave form to the inchoate desires of a semi-autonomous teen culture. Tales of romantic love, sexual danger, and physical sensation slaked the thirst of a historically unique population privileged enough to defer full adulthood. Such teen idols as Pat Boone, Frankie Avalon, and a battery of Bobbys—Bobby Rydell, Bobby Vee, Bobby Vinton—led the retreat into a Never-Never Land where kids never had to grow up.

The situation comedy adopted some of the outward trappings of youth culture by occasionally showcasing its music. In *The Adventures of Ozzie and Harriet*, a segment was sometimes tacked on at the end of the show to present Ricky Nelson performing a tune for a swaying crowd of adoring teens. As a denatured version of the "rockabilly" pioneered by underclass white musicians, Ricky Nelson came to epitomize the culture of American youth for an international audience.[47] *The Donna Reed Show* also boasted two teen idols in Shelly Fabares and Paul Peterson. Both sang on the program to support their hit singles "Johnny Angel" and "My Dad," which were released in 1962. The Douglas boys on *My Three Sons* were also to be seen playing musical instruments on the show from time to time.

The Beatles, like Elvis, were exposed to the mass American audience via television on *The Ed Sullivan Show*. Although cute and as full of charm as other teen idols, the Beatles unwittingly succeeded in reintroducing the American audience to the rich heritage of American music. In the early phase of their career, the Beatles covered many songs written by rock 'n' roll greats including Chuck Berry, Little Richard, Buddy Holly, and Carl Perkins. Similarly, the Rolling Stones paid tribute to black American urban blues artists and in doing so helped revive interest in black music, especially the blues. The "British Invasion" caused many observers of the cultural scene to begin seriously rethinking the meaning and larger significance of rock music.[48]

Critic Lester Bangs attributed the tremendous popularity of rock 'n' roll during this decade in part to the loss of national ideals embodied by the "youth-cult superstar," President John F. Kennedy. In reference to the British Invasion, Bangs observed that "it seems obvious that this elevation of our mood had to come from outside the parameters of America's own musical culture, if only because the folk music that then dominated American pop was so tied to the crushed dreams of the New Frontier."[49]

Susan Sontag in her essay "One Culture and the New Sensibility" described a society that was now "pan-cultural" owing to changed patterns of demographic movement, ease in travel, mobility, "speed of images," and—echoing Walter Benjamin, perhaps—the mass reproduction and distribution of art objects.[50] Sontag inverted the abuse heaped on mass culture by critics regardless of political bent. Rather than reject the transformation brought about by the effects of the culture industry, Sontag enthusiastically embraced the products of the new sensibility.[51] Sontag was not alone in her adulation of the sixties sensibility. Andrew

Kopkind viewed events like the Woodstock Music and Art Fair as evidence of the "reality of a new culture of opposition."[52] Even elite academic critic Richard Poirier came to concede that, indeed, "learning from the Beatles" was possible.[53]

MONKEE BUSINESS

The parameters of acceptability in mass-mediated culture are continually surveyed, reassessed, and redrawn to meet the insatiable demand for new products in a consumer economy. The independent company Sun Records based in Memphis, Tennessee, was an important force regionally with such artists as Carl Perkins, Charlie Rich, Roy Orbison, Johnny Cash, Jerry Lee Lewis and of course Elvis, as part of its stable of talent.[54] But it was not until RCA bought Elvis's contract from Sun Records owner Sam Phillips did the teen phenomenon skyrocket because of the superior marketing capability of the corporate giant.

Elvis had at first been reviled by middle America for thrusting his raw sexuality in the face of postwar youth. The influence of black music and culture was perceived as a threat to white supremacy even as the entertainment industry capitalized on its sheer sales power. By the end of Elvis's career, his place in the pop pantheon was firmly established by his unequaled record sales. Moreover, the bizarre career of Elvis Presley once more demonstrated the seemingly endless capacity of capitalism to "accept potentially subversive influences once they are denatured by becoming commodities."[55]

Vee-Jay, a relatively obscure black-owned Chicago record label, helped introduce to the American public the British working-class lads known as the Beatles. Vee-Jay had specialized in the brand of urban blues geared toward a black audience displaced by the internal migration from the rural South to the industrial North.[56] Corporate power Capitol records later replaced Vee-Jay as the U.S. distributor of the Beatles. By the time of the Beatles's arrival in 1964, rock 'n' roll, formerly "rhythm and blues" or "country and western," proved too great a lure for black and white artists wanting to cash in on the new pop music market created by the baby boom and postwar affluence.

The debasement of the real was fully realized by the creation of *The Monkees*, a carefully researched situation comedy engineered to exploit the antic schoolboy charm of the Beatles as seen in the film *A Hard Day's Night* (1964), directed by Richard Lester.[57] Recording business impresario Don Kirschner served as musical supervisor for *The Monkees* (September 12, 1966, to August 19, 1968) and formed the made-for-television group by bringing together four performers found after a methodical search was conducted. Telegenic qualities were given priority over musical ability since, of the four members, only two Monkees could actually play musical instruments with any degree of proficiency. The enthusiastic reception of *The Monkees* gave credence to the observation that in the age of mass-mediated culture, "teenage idols have been more an artifact of television than of records."[58]

The direct joining of the television situation comedy and the recording industry came to an end and after the four-year run of *The Partridge Family* (September 25, 1970, to August 31, 1974). Other programs such as *A Year at the Top* (August 5, 1972, to September 4, 1977) and *Sugar Time!* (August 13, 1977, to May 29, 1978) were ill-fated attempts at reviving the musical situation comedy format in the 1970s. In their stead, late-night programs such as *Don Kirschner's Rock Concert* (1973 to 1982), *In Concert*, and *The Midnight Special* (February 2, 1973, to May 1, 1981) served as the primary television vehicles for mass-marketed "super groups."

The economics of rock 'n' roll eventually grew to such mammoth proportions that only presold groups could be seen on commercial television. The media conglomerates, ABC, CBS, and NBC, each of which operated recording companies under their respective corporate umbrellas in addition to extensive broadcasting holdings, succeeded in marketing the counterculture.[59] What was once the popular music of marginal people who lyrically told of their quotidian struggles became converted into the leisure time diversion of a highly coveted market segment with large disposable incomes. As a "commoditized dream," rock music became completely absorbed by the system of capitalist production.[60] As in the sitcom, expressions of dissent from ideological orthodoxy were permitted in rock music only so long as they remained purely aesthetic, not political, oppositions.

KENNEDY COMS

The Kennedy-Johnson era represented the apotheosis of the liberal pragmatic tradition in American politics. While democratic liberal ideology admitted to the desirability of reducing economic inequality through the expansion of state-sponsored social welfare measures and progressive taxation used to partially redistribute wealth, it did not confront the basic contradiction between equality and the corporate capitalist form of ownership. Government was seen as an active agency in matters of the political economy that might control inflation, maintain low levels of unemployment, and provide social services not covered by the private sector. But it was equally committed to the preservation of private property even when social resources might have been used for private gain, as in the case of the television industry.

In its underlying assumptions, the Kennedy-Johnson brand of liberalism did not substantially differ from its close counterpart, conservative ideology. It was a difference of degree rather than kind. The notion of "liberal ideology," then, embraced what in popular discourse is referred to both as "liberalism" and "conservatism," for neither liberal nor conservative ideologues would wish to alter the existing structure of power relations. Liberalism and conservatism— then as now—exist as virtually indistinguishable concepts save for the "different relative importance" each respective ideology places on political assumptions held in common.[61]

As might be imagined, elements of reform liberalism turned up in select sitcoms of the mid–1960s. A selection of three situation comedies from the Kennedy-Johnson years reveals many of the ambiguities and unresolved dilemmas of liberal democratic ideology: *Grindl* (September 15, 1963, to September 13, 1964) grappled with juvenile delinquency, *The Smothers Brothers* (September 17, 1965, to September 9, 1966) took up the "dropout problem," and *The Farmer's Daughter* (September 20, 1963, to September 2, 1966) gave a stern warning against the abuses of welfarism.

Grindl starred Imogene Coca, who had risen to prominence on television with Sid Caesar in *Your Show of Shows* (February 25, 1950, to June 5, 1954). In *Grindl*, Coca played the part of a domestic laborer who took various temporary job assignments that placed her in different situations. One such assignment had Grindl in a lower middle-class neighborhood baby-sitting for a couple who had won her services in a raffle.[62] One of the children Grindl was left to care for was a borderline juvenile delinquent named Albert. Grindl tried to rehabilitate Albert and his gang, the Barracudas, by offering them a program that would get the group off the streets and into more productive activity.

Grindl approached her boss Anson Foster (James Millhollin) for start-up capital to develop the Barracuda rehabilitation project, but he proved skeptical. For his money, a more appropriate business enterprise for the gang would be to sell "blackjacks, zip guns, and brass knuckles." Grindl was a persistent social reformer and sympathetically denied that Albert and his gang were "hoodlums." She explained that, "They're just adolescents—too big to be boys and too young to be adult. They just need somebody to give them a feeling of being wanted."

Foster, who represented resistance to the liberal reformist impulse, eventually gave in by contributing a sum of money to be spent on repairing the Barracuda clubhouse. The belief in the redemptive capacity of mankind held by the liberal do-gooder Grindl was thus reconciled with the staunch business and social conservatism of Anson Foster. On a small scale, Grindl's personal campaign was much like the Johnson administration's "War on Poverty." As the "archetypal liberal program," the War on Poverty was described as being a "characteristic blend of benevolence, optimism, innocence and chauvinism."[63] Ultimately, the fiscal drain created by the Vietnam War precluded victory for domestic social welfare programs.[64]

An episode of *The Smothers Brothers Show* tried to draw a correlation between crime and low scholastic achievement.[65] This episode was prefaced by an opening conversation between the two brothers about the "dropout problem." Statistics were cited to convince the viewer of the seriousness of the problem. Into the program proper, Tom (the angel) and Dick (the publishing executive) had overheard plans for a robbery. The robbery was to have been carried out by a group of dropouts who would pose as a musical group in order to gain entry into a posh party. Once at the party, the dropouts could then steal whatever valuables there were.

The brothers intervened by convincing the dropouts that they could make it legitimately as a musical group without having to resort to crime. Tommy even offered to act as their manager. After experiencing difficulty in getting the band booked into local venues on their own merit, Tommy paid some teenagers to scream and shout during one of the group's performances. The manufactured frenzy made possible by payola launched the band on a successful musical career, which in effect spuriously "resolved" the dropout problem. Once Tom and Dick came to realize how much money was being made by the onetime renegades, the two decided to form a group themselves—The Smothers Brothers.

The liberal pragmaticom *The Farmer's Daughter* pitted the virtues held by Katy Holstrum (Inger Stevens), the daughter of an upstanding Norwegian immigrant, against the sordid political realities of Washington, D.C. The program was modeled after the 1947 film of the same title, which starred Loretta Young, Joseph Cotten, and Ethel Barrymore. The original written presentation for the sitcom version of *The Farmer's Daughter* defined the ideological contours of the program by listing the three unwavering beliefs maintained by Katy's father, Lar Holstrum: "his God, his family, and his adopted country."[66] These beliefs were played against the politics and culture of the welfare state as advanced during the Kennedy and Johnson administrations.

Katy Holstrum was a kindhearted soul who combined the pragmatic, traditional values of her father with those of her new home in the nation's capital. It had been Katy's lifelong ambition to work with handicapped children; and she had been offered a position in Washington that would allow her to do just that. But when the job fell through, Katy was forced to look for other employment to help support her family. Luckily, she found a job as a housekeeper for U.S. Congressman Glen Morley, played by William Windom, an actor who bore a close physical resemblance to President John F. Kennedy.

Congressman Glen Morley was described in the show's prospectus as being the scion of a long line of well-established Americans. Morley was portrayed as being independent of mind, but conscious of living in the shadow of his deceased father, a former congressman. Katy often counseled Congressman Morley in matters of realpolitik. She possessed a savvy, down-to-earth sensibility bequeathed her by Lars Holstrum, who saw it as his responsibility to instruct his daughter in the political culture of his adopted country. Katy's commonsense insights on worldly matters helped Congressman Morley navigate the turbulent waters of political life as their relationship grew more intimate.

LIMITED WARFARE ON WELFARE

The original presentation outline for *The Farmer's Daughter* laid bare its author's intention to dramatize conflicting political visions as embodied by the principal characters in the program. In doing so, elements of contemporaneous ideological battles crept into scripts. The issues informing the episode entitled "Jewel Beyond Compare," for example, were from the liberal pragmatic ideology of the Johnson presidency and the politics of the Great Society, a legacy of the Kennedy years.[67] This episode seemed to accept the assumptions and goals of the welfare state even as certain reservations about Great Society reforms were implied. At the same time, the episode tried to reaffirm the primacy of the individual in bourgeois society. "Traditional beliefs about individual responsibility for economic well-being" came into opposition with the expanded role of government in matters of social welfare.[68] Also strongly implied were issues that stemmed from resentment between social classes. Extended scrutiny of this episode is in order.

The Morley household had taken on a male helper by the name of Stevens to lessen some of Katy's work load. Stevens, however, proved to be incapable of performing even the most rudimentary of domestic tasks. Further, he was wont to mock the Morley family's patrician roots. Stevens parodied the family's speech patterns and went so far as to describe them as a "whole crate of eggheads." His outright hostility toward the Morleys was vented through speech that was consciously macaronic: "If I may make so bold, lady, it might be best for you to imbibe it (coffee) right here. It'll rest easier on the old gabonza." The speech marker "old gabonza" identified Stevens as a member of the underclass while the sarcastic use of "imbibe" barely disguised the hostility directed toward his social superiors.[69]

The task of firing Stevens fell to Katy. Confronted by her, Stevens played on her liberal guilt to avoid being let go. Stevens claimed that he was "educationally underprivileged," having been forced to leave school in the fourth grade. Stevens further pressed his advantage by stating, "I have much to learn before I can play my rightful role in today's complex society—right?" By having turned the rhetoric of liberal reformist ideology against itself, Stevens escaped retribution. "It was a happy day when I entered your employ," said the hired hand, "for here I am in contact with cultured, fair-minded people—who don't hold a man's origins against him, however humble they may be."

Stevens' cynical plea—delivered almost as a taunt—struck at the very heart of the Great Society liberalism represented by Congressman Moreley and, to a lesser extent, Katy. Were the congressman to have fired Stevens outright, this would in effect have been a repudiation of his ideological commitment. But Morley found a way out of the dilemma between ideological commitment and practicality: Morely explained to Katy that even if Stevens were fired, unemployment insurance would provide an income safety net for him. "You're sure of that," asked Katy. Glen responded (with a smile), "It's one of my committees."

As it turned out, Stevens had all the while wanted to collect unemployment insurance by having tried to get himself fired. When Katy learned of the ruse, she scolded Stevens by telling him, "Getting fired and collecting unemployment compensation is a privilege that must be earned." Congressman Morley had offered private assistance to help Stevens in getting reestablished. Stevens, however, made it clear that he had no interest in anything other than making use of his unemployment benefits: "Congress created the Social Security system to be *used*. So long as I live—I intend to use it." As Stevens went on his unrepentant way, Congressman Morley shuddered at one of the welfare monsters he had helped legislate into existence.

Oddly enough, there was no mention of welfare unpleasantries in the final scene. The episode simply returned to the original problem of finding another housekeeper to help Katy. Together, Katy and Morley decided against hiring another helper. Said Morley, "I'll settle for the one I've got," meaning Katy. In a switch common to sitcom aesthetics, political imperatives gave way to issues of personal gratification. The larger questions that pertained to the nature of state welfarism were thus diverted by romance. The audience was left with a mild sexual *frisson* and only incidentally an explicitly worded warning against abusing the welfare system. Never mind that welfare programs were "not built for the desperate, but for those who are already capable of helping themselves."[70]

This episode of *The Farmer's Daughter* unfortunately helped perpetuate the myth that welfare cheats like Stevens place a grossly unfair economic burden on society. In truth, the chief beneficiary by far of social welfare programs has been the middle class. Through this not-so-innocent entertainment and its stance on social welfare policies, the audience was given the "false assurance that America is still the free and open society of its cherished image and well-established ideals" by making an exceptionally cynical freeloader the object of scorn.[71] In pre-modern societies, economic relationships based on kinship ties and the principle of reciprocity would have minimized the problem of the "free-loader." But the freeloader in the welfare state has been somewhat more problematic since economic relationships are impersonal, abstract, and market driven. Almost in spite of itself, then, this episode of *The Farmer's Daughter* briefly illumined the shadows cast by inequality in class society. Taken to its full implications in the program, the piecemeal redistribution of wealth in a state-sponsored system of welfarism was seen as perversely inadequate.

CLASS, CASH-AND-CARRY

Author Max Shulman correctly identified college as one of the principal sites of the clash of inconsistent ideals and social ideologies in his novel *The Many Loves of Dobie Gillis*. It was at college, foremost among other social institutions in the postwar era, that the concept of "equality of opportunity" would be tested, for the large number of World War II veterans returning to civilian life had forced the greater democratization of the higher education system. Moreover, the state had institutionalized the concept of compensatory action by granting a disadvantaged group, returning veterans, generous educational benefits through the G.I. Bill. Hence access to higher education, like universal military service, was advanced as the great equalizer in democratic society.

The idea of education as the great equalizer in an unequal society was also put to the test in the television adaptation of *The Many Loves of Dobie Gillis* (September 29, 1959, to September 18, 1963). In the television sitcom version, Dobie Gillis (Dwayne Hickman) progressed from high school student, to peacetime soldier, to professional college student. Dobie's best friend Maynard G. Krebs (Bob Denver) was a beatnik modeled after the characters portrayed by beat writer Jack Kerouac.[72] Although nearly inseparable, Dobie was not tempted by the noncommital bohemianism of Maynard. Dobie tried the best he could to fit in, adjust. Dobie was torn between his class origins and his plans for overcoming the limitations such origins imposed upon him.

The title of the program was somewhat misleading in that rarely was Dobie successful in finding the love he sought. Instead, the program had more to do with the frustrations that arose out of Dobie's blocked access to romantic love because of his humble social origins. Dobie's ongoing plight was due to his desire to amass wealth and attract a beautiful helpmate who would serve as the visible social marker of his achievement. The object of Dobie's desire was the lovely Thalia Menninger (Tuesday Weld). Thalia, however, seemed forever out of Dobie's reach since he lacked the "oodles and oodles" of money she coveted. At a distinct advantage were Milton Armitage (Warren Beatty) and, later, Chatsworth Osborne, Jr. (Stephen Franken), who were both from patrician families. By contrast, Dobie lived with his parents at their mom and pop grocery store. Dobie was humiliated by having to don his clerk's apron at the store after having spent the day attending classes at S. Peter Prior Junior College. His after-school chores were a constant reminder of the vast gulf that stood between Dobie and his well-off classmates.

The plots of select episodes ("I Was a Spy for the F.O.B.," "Lassie Get Lost," "Requiem for an Underweight Heavyweight") were for the most part eminently forgettable. These rambling plots were simply vehicles used to drive home the basic theme of the striver, who by virtue of his low origins, could not quite ascend to the heights of genteel society. While Maynard G. Krebs stood for the dropout who refused to even compete, Zelda Gilroy (Sheila James) presented a more realistic option for a fellow like Dobie, who had so few social expectations. Zelda was plain in appearance, but she was exceptionally smart and pragmatic. She assessed Dobie's native intelligence and his money making potential and found them both deficient. Zelda was nonetheless willing to accept his weaknesses as a tradeoff for her physical unattractiveness and unmarriageability.[73]

A representative episode had Dobie resisting Zelda's entreaties, holding out for the dream girl who is "beautiful, soft, pink, and mine."[74] Zelda was quick to remind Dobie that "To get a girl you need money, to get money you need to work. That lets you out." Zelda tried to make Dobie understand that he could never succeed in a career because of his innate lack of talent and his undistinguished family background. She argued persuasively that the only real choice for Dobie would be to marry her, move to the country, and become self-sufficient by farming. The couple's plans were almost dashed by an attractive co-ed who had shown interest in Dobie, but Zelda successfully rid herself of the competition by having Dobie's grade transcripts and his personality profile sent to the co-ed.

Dobie could never quite bring himself to admit that even romantic love and sexuality were regulated by social class affiliation. Dobie's frustrated amorous ambitions were linked with his lower middle-class status, but he held out in the belief that he had an equal chance at the brass ring. Dobie hoped that his half-hearted attempts at academic achievement meant that he could somehow escape the fate dealt him by the lottery of birth. Only Zelda Gilroy had an objective understanding of Dobie's dilemma. Her sexual unattractiveness marginalized her existence as a marriageable woman/commodity. As such, Zelda exercised her formidable intelligence to circumvent a system of procreative and economic exchange that excluded her from full participation. Unlike Maynard, who had given up all hopes of competing, Zelda seized what little advantage she possessed to gain some small measure of autonomy as expressed by her ambition to operate a farm with Dobie. Dobie remained torn between his unrealistic expectations and the greater probability that he would not be able to escape the sort of life represented by his nice, decent, hardworking, but lower-middle-class, parents.

SHAGGY DOG STORY

The beautiful but vapid love-interests of Dobie Gillis would eventually become the independent career women in the sitcoms of the 1970s, as more professional women made their way past sexist social barriers. But in the sitcoms of the 1960s, for those women who possessed neither exceptional beauty nor super-natural powers, gender equality was still in the early stages of negotiation. Beach bunny Gidget Lawrence (Sally Field) in *Gidget* (September 15, 1965, to September 1, 1966), for example, seemed concerned only with surfing and partying with her friends.[75] However, beyond the trappings of the Southern California surf subculture, *Gidget* betrayed a doubly alienated sensibility that often seeped through all the fun and apparent mindlessness.

For one, the program was the creation of screenwriter Frederick Kohner, whose first novel—*Gidget*—was published in 1957. An immigrant, Kohner was born in central Europe in what is today Czechoslovakia.[76] *Gidget* was the product of Kohner's distanced observations of an American teenage subculture so foreign to him as to evoke the absurdity and humor that arose from the author's multiple dislocation and estrangement from his adopted society. This authorial sensibility made its way into the program through its principal character, Gidget, modeled after Kohner's own teenage daughter. Gidget, while in many ways a typical American teenager, often found herself in predicaments that stemmed from a combination of naïveté and social idealism. Unlike her counterparts, however, Gidget did not hesitate to act on the basis of her heartfelt beliefs.

Second, episodes of *Gidget* were structured through the use of an epistolary dialogue Gidget maintained between her public actions and her private thoughts. The "mindless" beach bunny was in each episode revealed to the audience as an intelligence that could find free expression only through the diary she kept. Gidget religiously recorded the forbidden musings of a young woman coming to terms with an often hostile world. Her father, Professor Lawrence (Don Porter), would try to balance Gidget's idealism with real-world experience, while her older sister Anne (Betty Conner) often gave advice from the perspective of the mature married woman. Anne's husband, John (Peter Deuel), was not shy about applying his half-baked knowledge of psychology to the problems Gidget sometimes encountered.

Professor Lawrence carefully taught his daughter Gidget the facts of the real world. As a college professor who traded in humanistic forms of knowledge, Russell Lawrence fully sympathized with Gidget's passion for abstract ideals, but as a responsible community leader, he also had made his peace with the world as it *is*, not as it *ought* to be. What were often presented in the program as problems of a "generation gap" between Lawrence and his daughter often took on greater meaning as conflicts between opposing social ideologies. To illustrate once more the symbolic resolution of specific social contradictions in the situation comedy, extended examination of a select episode of Gidget might be useful.[77]

Gidget found herself going toe to toe with the establishment when a citizens' group expressed its interest in buying a popular hamburger joint frequented by college students, "The Shaggy Dog." The proprietor of The Shaggy Dog was a gruff but lovable man appropriately named Henry B. Socrates or "Soc." The citizens' group wanted to raze the hamburger hangout and replace it with an art museum. Gidget ran into trouble when she organized a protest against the proposal. Coincidentally, Gidget was confronted by her father, who had been appointed chairman of the citizens' committee. Gidget and Professor Lawrence engaged in a spirited dispute that eventually resulted in a solution acceptable to both parties.

The city had asserted its claim on The Shaggy Dog on the principle of eminent domain. Lawrence had argued that the proposed art museum stood for "progress, beauty" and that it would serve as a "storehouse for history and culture." In opposition, Gidget organized her own committee "for the preservation and protection of private property owned by one private citizen to help him against the militant forces of evil." Russell Lawrence dismissed "these teenage revolutionary tactics" of Gidget's committee as "nonsense." What began as reasoned dialogue between Gidget and the professor escalated into full-blown invective as Socrates was placed on trial:

LAWRENCE: I should have spent more hours teaching you the difference between principle and foolish idealism.

GIDGET: Defending the rights of a man like Soc is foolish idealism? Destroying a man like Soc is your idea of principle?

LAWRENCE: No one is destroying anybody. No one is cheating anybody. Mr. Socrates is being bought out fairly and squarely.

Figure 3.2
Symbolic Resolution of Social Contradictions in *Gidget*

art museum/Shaggy Dog

medical school graduate

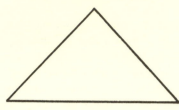

Professor Lawrence	Gidget
citizens' committee	Socrates
eminent domain	private property
States' rights	civil rights
official culture	youth subculture
Picasso	pizza

GIDGET: How can you buy out a man's life? How can you pay him fairly and squarely for a lifetime of hard work? How can you put into dollars and cents what that place means to him? Or to me? Or to all the other kids that go there?

A visit to The Shaggy Dog by Professor Lawrence revealed to him why Gidget and her friends were such staunch supporters of Soc. As Lawrence sat at the counter of the cafe, a well-groomed young man came looking for Soc. The young man had brought a bottle of champagne with him to celebrate with Soc his earning of a medical degree. As it turned out, Soc had convinced the young doctor to stay in college when he had been on the verge of dropping out.

Having finally understood the larger significance of The Shaggy Dog to its college-age customers, Russell Lawrence joined in the toast made to Henry B. Socrates. The amelioration of the conflict between the citizens' committee and the student group was implied by this new level of understanding reached by Professor Lawrence. Also resolved, even more importantly perhaps, was one of the chief contradictions of the liberal state—the conflict between public need (eminent domain) and private property. Friction between official culture and rebellious youth culture was eased in the final scene of the episode.

In the tag scene, Russell Lawrence showed Gidget an artist's rendering of a building that would house both the proposed art museum and The Shaggy Dog in a single facility. The new building would be a combination of "Picasso and pizza," explained Lawrence. The laughable compromise was of course absurdly convenient. But as a sociodramatic model for liberal politics, the compromise summarily neutralized all organized opposition and counterhegemonic ideologies represented by Gidget and her constituency. Issues that had once been vocally contested were drowned out by canned laughter.

CRISIS MANAGEMENT

Throughout the 1960s, many critics continued to express grave doubts about television and its service to the American political economy. Observers over a wide political spectrum commented on the deleterious effects of television on American society. Liberal economist John Kenneth Galbraith noted the effective way in which television was used in the "management of consumer demand," while Paul A. Baran and Paul M. Sweezy noted how the advertising industry waged a "relentless war against savings and in favor of consumption." Anthropologist Jules Henry considered advertising to be "an expression of an irrational economy that has depended for survival on a fantastically high standard of living incorporated into the American mind as a moral imperative."[78] Through television, a specific political economic structure (production, reproduction, exchange, and consumption) and total behavioral superstructure (culture) were being communicated nonstop.

Just as the television and advertising industries have been central to the functioning of the consumer economy, television entertainment programing has been equally important in helping manage the recurrent crises of liberal ideology. As the liberal democratic state sustained challenges to its legitimacy throughout the postwar era, slight accommodative shifts in the dominant ideology have occurred. Such ideological shifts eventually find their way into television entertainment forms such as the situation comedy, but only after having been brought into alignment with mainstream liberal democratic ideology based on a shared belief in the concepts of possessive individualism, private property, pluralism, equality, and procedural justice.[79]

During the 1960s, the cultural and political mobilization of ethnic minorities, students, disaffected upper-class professionals and other similarly disenfranchised groups forced substantial sociopolitical change. Television newscasts were especially compelling in graphically reporting novel conflicts arising from the spread of dissent as seen in the civil rights movement, antiwar protest, new left activism, and countercultural activity in general.[80] The hunger for newsworthy novelties and sense of journalistic mission often combined to produce mixed messages that could be sometimes construed as being critical of the government. Major broadcast news agencies at times even incurred the wrath of fellow establishmentarians, who often accused the media of "liberal" bias.

This was not the case for most television entertainment of the episodic series sort, including the situation comedy. On the contrary, episodic television entertainment through most of the 1960s was noteworthy for its absence of topical, direct references to domestic strife and the war in Vietnam. Still, discussion of politics, religion, and even sexuality was not completely avoidable. *Gilligan's Island* (September 26, 1964, to September 4, 1967), for example, was interpreted by its creator Sherwood Schwartz as being a "socialistic community," while actor Jim Backus described the island as a "benign welfare state."[81]

In that the television situation comedy is a dramatic form ontologically grounded in social discord and conflict, it could not have helped but partially expose the fissures in liberal democratic ideology. Even in their absence, the substantive political issues of the times—civil rights, the growth of the welfare state, American imperialism—were the repressed but persistent subjects of 1960s situation comedies.

Not until the end of the decade with the appearance of *Julia* (September 17, 1968, to May 25, 1971)—a landmark program in that it sympathetically depicted the struggles of a black, female, single parent—did the sitcom begin to reconcile the ideological discontinuities between polity and popular art that had surfaced during the 1960s. By 1968, the "politics of protest" had been modified into the "new politics" of politically committed students, minorities, and members of the underclass who rallied under the banner of the revitalized Democratic party. But by midyear, the era of ideological and political ferment seemed to come to an end with the assassinations of the Rev. Martin Luther King, Jr., and Bobby Kennedy.

In the following decade, the television situation comedy would come to reflect the partial assimilation of counterhegemonic social ideologies that took root during the 1960s. "Social relevance," a catch phrase that gained currency on many a university campus in the push to update curricula, became the watchword for the sitcoms of the 1970s. The pathbreaking sitcoms of Norman Lear and Bud Yorkin were in particular distinguished by their tendency to generate controversy. Despite their daring treatment of certain social taboos, the sitcoms of Lear and Yorkin represented the *consolidation* of, rather than challenge to, the dominant liberal ideology. As already seen, the situation comedy as an aesthetically veiled form of political communication has proven to be a resilient and infinitely adaptable sociodramatic means of achieving and maintaining the structured consensus so vital to the ongoing legitimacy of the liberal democratic state.

NOTES

1. William Appleman Williams, *America in a Changing World: A History of the United States in the Twentieth Century* (New York: Harper & Row, 1978), p. 354.

2. Samuel Bowles, David M. Gordon, and Thomas E. Weisskopf, *Beyond the Waste Land: A Democratic Alternative to Economic Decline* (Garden City, N.Y.: Anchor Press/Doubleday, 1983), pp. 72–73.

3. See Richard A. Blum and Richard D. Lindheim, *Primetime: Network Television Programming* (Boston: Focal Press, 1987), pp. 145–146.

4. J. Fred MacDonald, *Who Shot the Sheriff? The Rise and Fall of the Television Western* pp. 113–114.

5. William L. O'Neill, *Coming Apart: An Informal History of America in the 1960's* (New York: Quadrangle Books, 1971), p. 13.

6. Gary A. Steiner, *The People Look at Television: A Study of Audience Attitudes* (New York: Alfred A. Knopf, 1963).

7. Paul Lazarsfeld, curiously, was associated with the Frankfurt School theorists (Max Horkheimer, Theodor Adorno, Leo Lowenthal, and Herbert Marcuse), all of whom were actively involved in aspects of the mass culture debate. See Martin Jay, *The Dialectical Imagination: A History of the Frankfurt School and the Institute of Social Research 1923–1950* (Boston: Little, Brown & Co., 1973).

8. See Mark R. Levy, "The Lazarsfeld-Stanton Program Analyzer: An Historical Note," *Journal of Communication*, 32 (1982):30–38.

9. Newton N. Minow, *The Private Broadcaster and the Public Interest*, ed. Lawrence Laurent (New York: Atheneum, 1964), p. 57.

10. Steiner, p. 242.

11. Richard Kelly, *The Andy Griffith Show* (Winston-Salem, N.C.: John R. Blair, 1984), p. 17.

12. Robert Metz, *CBS: Reflections in a Bloodshot Eye* (New York: Signet, 1976), p. 224.

13. See Seymour Melman, *The Permanent War Economy: American Capitalism in Decline* (New York: Simon & Schuster, 1974).

14. Andrew Cox, Paul Furlong, and Edward Page, *Power in Capitalist Societies: Theory, Explanation and Cases* (Brighton, England: Wheatsheaf Books, 1985), p. 137.

15. Robert B. Reich, *The Next American Frontier* (New York: Penguin Books, 1984), p. 189.

16. Irving Howe, *Socialism and America* (New York: Harcourt Brace Jovanovich, 1985), p. 135.

17. Conservative apologist Samuel P. Huntington identifies American core political values as being "liberty, equality, individualism, democracy, and the rule of law under a constitution." Samuel P. Huntington, *American Politics: The Promise of Disharmony* (Cambridge: Harvard University Press, Belknap Press, 1981), p. 14.

18. *Hogan's Heroes*. Written by Richard M. Powell, produced by Edward H. Feldman, created by Bernard Fein and Albert S. Ruddy, associate producer Bernard Fein, director Gene Reynolds. Bing Crosby Productions, Inc. Script "Flight of the Valkyrie" bears the date 1960, but the program ran from 1965 to 1971.

19. David Halberstam, *The Powers That Be* (New York: Alfred A. Knopf, 1979), p. 417.

20. *Gomer Pyle, U.S.M.C.*, "Survival of the Fattest." Written by Bob Ross. Script dated May 15, 1964.

21. *Gomer Pyle, U.S.M.C.*, "A Date for the Colonel's Daughter." Written by Bob Ross. Revised script dated August 6, 1964.

22. Joshua Cohen and Joel Rogers. *On Democracy: Toward a Transformation of American Society* (New York: Penguin Books, 1983), p. 108.

23. Michael Walzer, *Radical Principles: Reflections of an Unreconstructed Democrat* (New York: Basic Books, 1980), p. 32.

24. Cleo the talking basset hound in *The People's Choice* (October 6, 1955, to September 25, 1958) only commented on the ongoing action, unlike Mr. Ed who was central to the action.

25. William Connolly, "The Dilemma of Legitimacy," in *Legitimacy and the State*, ed. William Connolly (New York: New York University Press, 1984), p. 233.

26. For a recent account of the tension between radical and liberal politics over issues

of civil rights, see Todd Gitlin, *The Sixties: Years of Hope, Days of Rage* (New York: Bantam Books, 1987), pp. 127–170.

27. Joel Kotkin and Paul Grabowicz, *California, Inc.* (New York: Avon Books, 1982), p. 192.

28. *The Munsters* was developed by Norm Liebman and Ed Haas from a format created by Al Burns and Chris Hayward.

29. Irwyn Applebaum, p. 15.

30. Betty Friedan, *The Feminine Mystique* (New York: Dell, 1963), pp. 47–48. See also Betty Friedan, "Television and the Feminine Mystique," in *TV Guide: The First 25 Years*, ed. Jay S. Harris (New York: New American Library, 1980), pp. 93–98.

31. Marvin Harris, *America Now: The Anthropology of a Changing Culture* (New York: Touchstone, 1981), p. 91.

32. Zillah R. Eisenstein, *The Radical Future of Liberal Feminism* (New York: Longman, 1981), p. 205.

33. Tzvetan Todorov, *The Fantastic: A Structural Approach to a Literary Genre*, trans. Richard Howard (Ithaca, N.Y.: Cornell University Press, 1973), p. 158.

34. Ibid., p. 166.

35. *Bewitched* was created by Sol Saks. Harry Ackerman served as executive producer, a position he also filled with *Gidget*.

36. Gaye Tuchman, Arlene Kaplan Daniels, and James Benet, eds., *Hearth and Home: Images of Women in the Mass Media* (New York: Oxford University Press, 1978), p. 67.

37. This episode of *I Dream of Jeannie* was written by James Henerson, 1966.

38. Mark Poster, *Critical Theory of the Family* (New York: Seabury Press, 1978), p. 171.

39. See Christopher Lasch, *Haven in a Heartless World: The Family Besieged* (New York: Basic Books, 1979).

40. Poster, pp. 79–80.

41. Sidney Willhelm, "Some Reflections upon Work and the Work Ethic in Contemporary America," in *American Minorities and Economic Opportunity*, ed. H. Roy Kaplan (Itasca, Ill.: F. E. Peacock, 1977), pp. 352–353.

42. *Family Affair*, created by Edmund Hartmann. A Don Fedderson Production.

43. For opposing views on sexuality in postwar society, see Daniel Bell, *The Cultural Contradictions of Capitalism*, pp. 72–76 and Theodore Roszak, *The Making of a Counter Culture: Reflections of the Technocratic Society and Its Youthful Opposition* (Garden City, N.Y.: Doubleday, 1969), pp. 14–15.

44. Daniel J. Boorstin, *The Americans: The Democratic Experience* (New York: Vintage Books, 1974), p. 239.

45. *Hey Landlord*, "Swingle City, East." Written by Rick Mittleman. Dated February 1, 1967. Mirisch-Rich TV Production.

46. See Charlie Gillett, *The Sound of the City: The Rise of Rock 'n' Roll* (New York: Dell, 1972); Ed Ward, Geoffrey Stokes, and Ken Tucker, *Rock of Ages: The Rolling Stone History of Rock and Roll* (New York: Rolling Stone Press/Summit Books, 1986).

47. David P. Szatmary, *Rockin' in Time: A Social History of Rock and Roll* (Englewood Cliffs, N.J.: Prentice-Hall, 1987), p. 52.

48. See Morris Dickstein, *Gates of Eden: American Culture in the Sixties* (New York: Basic Books, 1977), pp. 183–210.

49. Lester Bangs, "The British Invasion," in *The Rolling Stone Illustrated History*

of Rock and Roll, ed. Jim Miller (New York: Rolling Stone/Random House, 1976), p. 164.

50. Susan Sontag, *Against Interpretation: And Other Essays* (New York: Dell, 1966), pp. 293–304.

51. See Patrick Brantlinger, *Bread and Circuses: Theories of Mass Culture as Social Decay* (Ithaca, N.Y.: Cornell University Press, 1983). The author surveys the critique of modern mass culture from a variety of political vantage points.

52. Andrew Kopkind, *Rolling Stone*, September 1969:30.

53. Richard Poirier, "Learning From the Beatles," *Partisan Review*, 34 (1967):526–546.

54. Robert Palmer, *Deep Blues* (New York: Penguin Books, 1982), p. 241.

55. Robert Heilbroner, *The Nature and Logic of Capitalism* (New York: W. W. Norton, 1985), p. 138.

56. Mike Rowe, *Chicago Breakdown* (London: Eddison Press, 1973), pp. 153–164.

57. Dallas Smythe, "Buy Something: Five Myths of Consumership," in *In The Marketplace: Consumerism in America*, ed. Editors of *Ramparts* with Frank Browing (San Francisco: Canfield Press, 1972), pp. 167–174.

58. R. Serge Denisoff, *Solid Gold: The Popular Record Industry* (New Brunswick, N.J.: Transaction Books, 1975), p. 429.

59. James Monaco, *Media Culture: Television, Radio, Records, Books, Magazines, Newspapers, Movies* (New York: Dell, 1978), p. 305.

60. Simon Frith, *Sound Effects: Youth, Leisure, and the Politics of Rock 'n' Roll* (New York: Pantheon Books, 1981), p. 272.

61. Ronald Dworkin, *A Matter of Principle* (Cambridge: Harvard University Press, 1985), pp. 187–188.

62. *Grindl*, "There's No Such Thing as a Bad Barracuda." Teleplay by Ed Jurist and Bud Nye, final draft dated December 13, 1963.

63. Godfrey Hodgson, *America in Our Time* (Garden City, N.Y.: Doubleday, 1976), p. 270.

64. Jim F. Heath, *Decade of Disillusionment: The Kennedy-Johnson Years* (Bloomington and London: Indiana University Press, 1975), p. 258.

65. *The Smothers Brothers Show*, "Heaven Help the Drop-out." This episode bears the copyright date of 1966. Written by Gerald Gradner and Dee Caruso, produced by Fred DeCordova, created by Aaron Spelling and Richard Newton, executive producer Aaron Spelling, directed by Richard Kinon.

66. *The Farmer's Daughter*. Presentation by John McGreevey. No date. Screen Gems, Hollywood. U.C.L.A. Theater Arts Archives.

67. *The Farmer's Daughter*, "Jewel Beyond Compare." Written by Stanley H. Silverman. Final draft dated September 15, 1965.

68. Russell E. Smith and Dorothy Zietz, *American Social Welfare Institutions* (New York: John Wiley & Sons, 1970), p. 155.

69. See W. Peter Robinson, "Speech Markers and Social Class," in *Social Markers in Speech*, ed. Klaus R. Scherer and Howard Giles (Cambridge: Cambridge University Press, 1979), p. 213.

70. Michael Harrington, *The Other America: Poverty in the United States* (Baltimore: Penguin Books, 1971), p. 170.

71. Gunnar Myrdal, "Challenge to Affluence—The Emergence of an 'Under-Class,' "

in *Structured Social Inequality*, ed. Celia S. Heller (New York: Macmillan, 1969), pp. 138–143.

72. Rod Amateau. Interview at Burbank Studios. Burbank, Calif. July 17, 1981.

73. Sheila James (Zelda Gilroy), later Sheila Kuehl, gained entrance to Harvard Law School, was elected president of the class of 1978, and currently practices law in the Los Angeles area. As first vice-president of the Women Lawyers Association of Los Angeles, Kuehl maintains an interest in feminist issues. Michael Balter, "Ex-TV Actress Shifts Roles to Become an Activist Attorney," *Los Angeles Times*, June 13, 1985, pt. 5, pp. 1, 34, 35.

74. *The Many Loves of Dobie Gillis*. Copyright date 1960. Produced and directed by Rod Amateau, created by Max Shulman.

75. *Gidget*. Produced by William Sackheim, executive producer Harry Ackerman, created by Harry Ackerman. Pop music packager and purveyor of youth culture Don "The Monkees" Kirschner acted as music consultant.

76. Charles Champlin, "The Novel Origins of 'Gidget,' " *Los Angeles Times*, September 13, 1986, pt. 6, pp. 1, 10.

77. *Gidget*. Produced by William Sackheim, executive producer Harry Ackerman, creator and script consultant Frederick Kohner. Story written by Dorothy Cooper Foote. Directed by Hal Cooper.

78. John Kenneth Galbraith, *The New Industrial State*, 2d ed. (Boston: Houghton Mifflin Co., 1971), p. 209. Paul A. Baran and Paul M. Sweezy, p. 128. Jules Henry, *Culture Against Man* (New York: Vintage Books, 1965), p. 45.

79. See Kenneth M. Dolbeare and Patricia Dolbeare, *American Ideologies: The Competing Political Beliefs of the 1970s*, 3d ed. (Boston: Houghton Mifflin Co., 1976).

80. See Todd Gitlin, *The Whole World Is Watching: Mass Media in the Making and Unmaking of the New Left* (Berkeley: University of California Press, 1980).

81. Joey Green, *The Unofficial Gilligan's Island Handbook: A Castaway's Companion to the Longest-Running Shipwreck in Television History* (New York: Warner Books, 1988), p. 96. Sherwood Schwartz named the S.S. Minnow after Newton Minow, then the head of the FCC.

4

The Liberal Pluralist
Ascendancy

THE SO-SO SOCIETY

The watershed year of 1968 saw the passing of liberal reformist hopes as represented by the "new politics" of Martin Luther King, Jr., Robert F. Kennedy, and Eugene McCarthy. The presidential election year was marked by a wave of political violence and assassinations, widespread urban rebellion, and campus protest against the Vietnam War. Disproving the notion that there are no second acts in American lives, the "new" Richard M. Nixon reemerged from years of self-imposed isolation to win the office of the presidency by a narrow margin. Publicly, Richard Nixon campaigned to bring a tragically divided America back together again. Revelations that arose from the Watergate scandal in 1972, however, later exposed Nixon as a cynical practitioner of pettily vindictive, divisive, and paranoid politics.

With the ascendancy of the "new politics" came a spate of television programs that sought to tap the interest, vitality, and perhaps discretionary income of socially alienated groups, including the counterculture, ethnic minorities women's groups, and young professionals. The market shift toward "social relevance" in television programing was reflected by such programs as *The Mod Squad* (September 24, 1968, to August 23, 1974); *The Flip Wilson Show* (September 17, 1970, to June 27, 1974); *The Bill Cosby Show* (September 14, 1969, to August 31, 1971); *The Young Rebels* (September 20, 1970, to January 3, 1971); *The Young Lawyers* (September 21, 1970, to May 5, 1971); and *Storefront Lawyers* (September 16, 1970, to September 1, 1971). The relatively short lifespan of these programs, however, indicated the audience's retreat from entertainment that dealt with social issues. According to network analysts, the failure of such programs to become popular with the public "was the result of too many dramatic series seeking to be relevant."[1]

The Mod Squad featured an interracial trio (including a woman) of counter-cultural types who, despite their disdain for authority, invariably upheld law and order. *The Flip Wilson Show* was a comedy variety show that featured skits by black comedian Flip Wilson. Self-mocking ethnic stereotypes such as Wilson's character Geraldine abounded on the show, signaling perhaps a partial thaw in racial relations. After *I Spy* (September 15, 1965, to September 2, 1968) ended its run, a funkier, less adventuresome Bill Cosby was found in his self-named situation comedy. Cosby played the part of Chet Kincaid, a caring high school physical education teacher at a predominantly black institution. Bill Cosby had previously been showcased in *I Spy*, the first serious dramatic series to feature a black costar. Dramas that spotlighted politically committed activists including *The Young Rebels, The Young Lawyers*, and *Storefront Lawyers* pushed for incremental change and social reform through the traditional institutions of justice.

All in the Family (January 12, 1971, to September 21, 1983) has often been cited as a breakthrough in situation comedy because of its honest treatment of social antagonisms expressed through the use of unabashed racist and sexist sentiment. However, a program even more significant and far reaching in its implications was *Julia*. It was *Julia* that symbolically represented the reconciliation of the liberal pluralist model of politics with the troubled interethnic power relations of postwar American society. Through *Julia,* the political "drama" of liberal pluralism effected the incomplete reconciliation and consolidation of an American society split along class, regional, gender, religious, ethnic, and generational lines—without resorting to witches, talking horses, ghosts, angels, monsters, or flying nuns.

BLACK ATTACK

By the time *Julia* made it to prime time television, there had already been much public outcry against the pernicious effects of what many black critics identified as the white-controlled mass media. The media, its critics claimed, wielded its immense power to adversely shape public attitudes and perceptions of the *présence noire* in American society. From a black nationalist perspective, the "manipulated image" of blackness had its roots deep in the history of American civilization. The white-dominated media was accused of contributing to the self-alienation of the black individual by first constructing a false identity for him, only to then argue for the rejection of this selfsame image.[2] The only means to escape such domination, went the black nationalist counterargument, would be to pursue the political strategy of separatism. A black separatist state would presumably maintain control of its own social institutions, including media, that would not perpetuate destructive images of blacks.

From a liberal perspective, the observations of Kenneth B. Clark were strikingly similar to those of black power advocates in that he too decried the way in which the mass media tended to "project the values and aspirations, the manners and the style of the larger white-dominated society."[3] Contrary to the separatist stance taken by many black nationalists, however, Clark argued that only by gaining politico-economic power could blacks hope to redress the condition of inequality historically imposed by the dominant white society. Instead of rejecting the culture, politics, and social institutions of the dominant society, Clark sought remedies that would place more minorities in positions of power.

Social research indeed confirmed that the television viewing patterns of the black underclass differed measurably from those of middle-class whites.[4] Among blacks, even the more educated and affluent groups showed a greater "enthusiasm" for television than their white counterparts. Conventional wisdom had always maintained that television viewing tended to decrease among those of higher educational attainment and income.[5] But this was not the case for the black middle class, whose reliance upon television watching "might have at least offered an equal opportunity for vicarious participation in the larger society."[6]

HOT FUN IN THE SUMMERTIME

Beginning with the Harlem riot in the summer of 1964, urban rebellions occurred with increasing frequency. The next major disturbance took place the following summer in Watts. In the summer of 1966, 43 violent incidents were reported, the most explosive of which took place in Chicago and Cleveland. Eight major riots, including an especially brutal outbreak in Detroit, had to be quelled in the summer of 1967. Forty-three people were killed in the Detroit riot. In reaction, that year the National Advisory Commission on Civil Disorders was formed by President Johnson to probe the causes of the widespread riots.

The final report issued by the commission in 1968 made explicit the connection between the media and black underclass rebellion. An entire chapter was devoted to the role played by the news media in the reportage of disturbances. The report was highly critical of news media performance. In an instance of blaming the messenger for the bad news, the commission went so far as to rebuke the media, television particularly, for flaunting white affluence "before the eyes of the Negro poor and the jobless youth."[7]

According to the commission report, simple human envy was cited as the cause—not structured social inequality—for the ghetto rebellions. Similarly, other observers commented on the superficial relationship between television and civil violence. Television, for example, was branded as the "arch-propagandist of the American Dream in all its dangerous obsolescence" by one foreign observer. Television was described as being a "significant agent in showing the nation's under-privileged what they are missing in the way of Scandanavian furniture and holidays in Hawaii."[8] The envy-inducing display of white middle-class affluence on television was supposedly to have "vividly awakened blacks to a new sense of their relative deprivation."[9] Yet another variation on the base human envy theory of urban rebellion stated that holding out the symbols of economic inequality on television before the hungry eyes of the underclass was an open invitation to revolution.[10]

Into this critical juncture in the history of American race relations came Diahann Carroll in *Julia*. The character Carroll portrayed made it seem believable that discrimination and racism were expressions of benighted individuals alone and not attributable to structured social inequality. For those not entirely convinced of the positive results of the equality revolution, *Julia* offered a glimpse into the life of a hardworking, honest, black person who seemed to have "earned" her place in society. And with *Julia* to watch on television, black outsiders to the American dream would presumably have less to be "envious" about.

COLOR TV

The 1968–69 broadcast season was applauded by the press for the programs that finally reintroduced believable blacks to television after a long layoff. Self-congratulatory articles of almost desperate optimism such as "Black Is the Color of TV's Newest Stars," "TV Discovers the Black Man," and "Black Is the Color of Our New TV" heralded a new era in television programing.[11] In the previous year, only 2.3 percent of all commercials had even used minorities as actors. While minorities were represented in approximately one-fourth of all entertainment programs, less than one-fifth appeared in dramatic ("serious") programs. Even so, not quite one-half of those minorities appearing in television drama were used in the capacity of extras only, window dressing for the real focus of attention. Despite this, the fact that fully fourteen blacks were either starring or costarring in prime-time network programs of *any* sort in the new season was cause for celebration on the part of the popular press.

An article that appeared in the January 20, 1968, issue of *TV Guide*, just nine months prior to the debut of *Julia*, addressed the question of television and its relationship to the black audience. "What the Negro Wants from TV," by Art Peters was careful to present the views of only "responsible" black leaders such as civil rights leader Whitney Young of the Urban League and "safe" actors such as Bill Cosby and Diahann Carroll. Peters argued that the outcry from American minorities was coming at a time when the "industry appears to be doing more than ever before in the Negro interest."[12]

The issues and claims pressed by black power groups were not considered to be legitimate by most journalists writing about television and media in the mainstream press. Only the voice of liberal moderation and reform was allowed to be heard. An anonymous television producer was quick to point out that, contrary to much of the criticism, there were "five times as many Negroes appearing on television in feature roles today as there were only a few years ago." The unnamed producer blamed "Black Power groups" for making "this

Figure 4.1
Ethnicoms 1971–1981

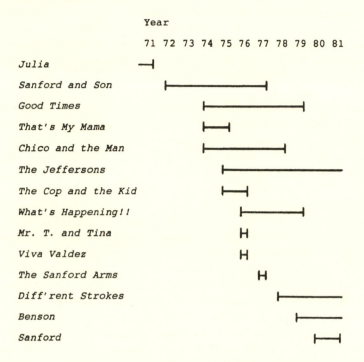

fuss" and indicated that the "responsible Negro leaders" would agree that blacks were making substantive strides in television.[13] The unidentified producer, however, confused numerical presence as being commensurate with roles of substance. Despite their increased visibility, television blacks in the 1967–68 seasons wore "white" clothes and spoke "white" English dialect. Overt references to color or racial topics decreased, particularly in dramatic programs, suggesting that blacks on evening shows "could be interchanged with white actors."[14]

ENTER ETHNICOMS

Once *Julia* entered its third season, the initial enthusiasm over the upgraded role of blacks in television began to cool. The television critic for the *Saturday Review,* Robert Lewis Shayon, assailed both Diahann Carroll and the program for being hypocritical. *Julia,* observed Shayon, ignored the gap that existed between the "national rhetoric of color-blind egalitarianism and the continuing deprivations, economic and psychic, of the larger community of American black citizens."[15] What Shayon perceptively described as a "fluffy piece of warm, plush, middle-class adventurous tokenism in its presentation, on television, of the contemporary black American experience," established the model for later ethnic sitcoms to follow—programs which partially appeased the concerns of ethnic special interest groups while not alienating the larger white audience.

The common denominator for such ethnic sitcoms, as discovered by *Julia*, proved once more to be the resilient, ever-adaptable set of assumptions that compose American liberal democratic ideology. While the television situation comedy has been cloaked by liberal ideology since its inception, beginning with *Julia* it was recut and custom tailored to fit the sizeable demands of politically mobilized claimant groups.

After more than a decade of neglect, *Julia* harkened the return to situation comedies that featured ethnic performers. Not since *Amos 'n' Andy* (1951–53) had a black person starred in a television situation comedy. There was one historically significant difference in emphasis, however, between the ethnicoms of the 1950s and *Julia*. In *Julia*, the traditional desideratum of assimilation and acculturation according to the dominant white Anglo-Saxon Protestant model was relaxed ever so slightly. Instead, self-respect and ethnic pride was allowed a little more room in which to assert itself. This in part represented a concession to more militant black organizations that refused to be judged on the basis of mainstream values and instead offered the alternative of "black pride."

Although the character of Julia Baker might conceivably have been played by a white actress, the program nonetheless implied that Julia possessed a distinctive black self-consciousness. Unlike some of her more stridently vocal black brethren, Julia rarely called attention to her ethnic identity. Beyond her quiet sense of ethnic pride, Julia was seen as being like any other black, female, single parent trying to survive in a sometimes less than sympathetic world. The program implied that Julia Baker lived in a society that did not systematically discriminate against her or anyone else in a similarly disadvantaged position. Rather, well-intentioned individuals sometimes merely "misunderstood" what it meant to be a single black woman raising a child. Of course it helped that Julia was beautiful, did not lack for male attention, and was financially secure as a nursing professional.

EQUAL OPPORTUNITY DEPLOYER

An early episode of *Julia*, "Julia's Man," explored the program's tripartite premise of a single black woman trying to succeed in the world of work.[16] All within the bounds of one episode, Julia faced and then overcame job discrimination, sexism, single parenthood, and even loneliness. After a long, presumably self-imposed absence from the work force, Julia found herself applying for a nursing position at Astrospace Industries. It was simply assumed that Julia would never stoop so low as to accept welfare assistance from such Great Society program as Aid to Families with Dependent Children (AFDC).

Julia's goal of self-sufficiency, however, was threatened by the residual racism of the personnel manager of Astrospace Industries, Mr. Colton. During an employment interview, Mr. Colton had stated that Julia's training, background, and references were in perfect order. Colton also averred that he had not considered the possibility that Julia's credentials were those of a black person. Colton's observation pointed out a persistent contradiction in liberal democratic society, that of the official ideology of status through individual achievement versus that of ascription on the basis of color caste. Knowing that he could not possible disqualify Julia on the basis of credentials or ethnicity alone, Colton patronized her through sexism:

MR. COLTON: You ought to be on television. . .a beautiful girl like you.

JULIA: I'm not a girl, I'm twenty-six years old. . .a qualified registered nurse.

Colton's reluctance in hiring Julia was explained when a black maintenance worker told her that, prior to his present position, he "was a draftsman back in Milwaukee." The maintenance man warned Julia of the "normal person," mundane prejudice of Mr. Colton.

To reinforce the notion that not all white people, only select individuals, are prejudiced against blacks, a subplot established the color-blind relationship between Julia and her neighbor Marie Waggedorn (Betty Beaird). It was through their sons, Corey (Marc Copage) and Earl J. Waggedorn (Michael Link), that their friendship was forged. Corey and Earl formed an innocent, color-blind friendship free of prejudice. The world viewed through the eyes of the two boys was simple, direct, and uncomplicated:

EARL: Your mother's colored.

COREY: So am I colored too.

EARL: Oh boy!

With that exchange, the boys tumbled gleefully over the sofa and the issue of color was effectively dismissed. The childish, romanticized mutual understanding between Corey and Earl J. Waggedorn, it was implied, negated the learned racist and sexist behavior of adult society as embodied by Mr. Colton. While children might indeed identify more with character than with ethnicity in television portrayals, as one study has determined, the fact of institutional racism remained intact and unaddressed in this episode.[17]

After a brief flirtation with a television repairman (hence "Julia's Man") whom Corey had hoped would marry his mother, Julia received a telegram informing her that she had been hired for the nursing position with Astrospace Industries. Not certain whether her new boss Dr. Chegley (Lloyd Nolan) knew of her ethnicity, Julia called the doctor to confirm the job offer:

JULIA: Has Mr. Colton told you?

DR. CHEGLEY: Told me what?

JULIA: I'm colored.

DR. CHEGLEY: What color are you?

JULIA: I'm a Negro.

DR. CHEGLY: Have you always been Negro or are you just trying to be fashionable?

With this deadpan exchange, Julia was reassured that racial prejudice, at least in this instance, had been overcome. It helped that the black maintenance man and former draftsman had complained to Dr. Chegly about Mr. Colton's obvious prejudice. As a remedy, the liberal humanism of the crusty Dr. Chegly painlessly excised the racism of Mr. Colton. In doing so, this tidy sociodrama transposed the systemic, institutional dimension of racism into the isolated action of a lone misguided individual.

In keeping with the piecemeal approach to change that has typified the sitcom, Julia Baker was still described as being "colored" or "Negro" rather than as "black" or "Afro-American." Blackness as self-identity even as late as 1968 had "militant" connotations and was therefore unacceptable to the mass audience. In addition, *Julia* was also strangely silent on the issue of sexism. Dr. Chegley accepted her as a "Negro," but the issue of gender segregation in the nursing field, with its high concentration of women working in the profession, went unmentioned.

For the black underclass, Julia Baker did serve as a model minority member. Julia would not permit herself to become part of the droves of free riders entering the welfare rolls of the Great Society during the peak years of 1965 to 1970. Her sense of pride and self-reliance would not allow such a descent into individual helplessness. Not until well into the episode was it revealed that Julia's husband had died in combat as a helicopter pilot in Vietnam—no unearned, premature sympathy here. This withholding of information injected pathos into the program without sentimentalizing the death of Julia's patriot husband. *Julia* taught an important lesson to members of the black underclass about overcoming adversity through personal adjustment, about not being too demanding of the political system.

AFFIRMATIVE REACTION

The rediscovery of middle America by the news media in the late 1960s coincided with the September 1968 debut of *Julia*. A sitcom concerning the mundane problems of an apolitical, mild mannered, nonaggressive "good Negro" who betrayed no sign of hostility or resentment posed no threat to a viewing audience grown weary of contentious groups aggressively demanding their fair share of the entitlement revolution. The character Julia Baker was far from typical of black single heads of households, however. The U.S. Bureau of the Census reported that 30 percent of black families were headed by women in 1970. Of this percentage, over half lived in poverty.[18] Instead, Julia was shown comfortably ensconced in a nicely furnished apartment much like that of any respectable middle-class white person like her neighbor, Marie Waggedorn.

The "bold" move by NBC to air *Julia* during the 1968–69 season was in part due to the urging of Paul Klein, director of the NBC audience research department at the time. One argument advanced in favor of the *Julia* experiment concerned the consistently strong ratings earned by *The Red Skelton Show* on rival CBS during the same time slot. Klein argued that since any program in that particular time slot was probably doomed to failure anyway, it would be wise (in light of criticism that television was a "lily-white medium") to take the moral high ground by offering *Julia* as something new and relevant in an otherwise bland and boring 1968 schedule of programs.[19] Business acumen and political expediency dovetailed in the case of *Julia*, and thus was the ethnic situation comedy revived.

Against all expectations of *Julia* ending as a noble failure, the program became popular with the audience. The series ended its first season occupying the seventh position, even beating the once invulnerable *Red Skelton Show* in the ratings. The novelty wore off soon thereafter, however. *Julia* never cracked the top twenty-five programs after its first season. But by then *Julia* had made its impact. Perennial ratings underdog ABC introduced two new shows the following season to capitize on the latest programing trend—ethnic chic.

GOOD GIRLS/BAD GIRLS

ABC followed CBS's example by offering *The Courtship of Eddie's Father* (September 17, 1969, to June 14, 1972) and *Room 222* (September 17, 1969, to January 11, 1974). Both programs were similar in that they often worked at solving problems that arose between people of dissimilar social backgrounds. The programs lightly alluded to the milder forms of discriminatory treatment suffered by certain groups in society. But like *Julia*, neither of the two programs probed the deeper reasons for the differential treatment of minorities within a social system that has maintained a commitment to equality, at least on a formal level.

In *The Courtship of Eddie's Father*, questions of race, ethnicity, or gender were subsumed by the overarching male parental authority of widower Tom Corbett (Bill Bixby). Corbett held didactic power over his young son Eddie (Brandon Cruz) and his Japanese servant, Mrs. Livingstone (Miyoshi Umeki). Each episode of the show was prefaced with a private dialogue between father and son. The show was capped at its conclusion with an epilogue that was usually lighthearted and humorous despite its serious underlying social message. These precious moments were meant to be instructive to the young boy, who was just beginning to learn about life from his father.

The always touchy theme of "interracial" romance was delicately treated in one episode of the program.[20] The prologue led with Eddie having taught (erroneously) his father how to distinguish the "good girls" from the "bad girls." The bad girls always had "squinty eyes," explained Eddie. Tom was confused by Eddie's line of reasoning until he realized that his son had come to his warped observation through the reading of comic books. The vignette foreshadowed what turned out in the episode proper to be an object lesson in the dangers of prejudging individuals on the basis of stereotypes.

As in the episode "Julia's Man," the blind evaluation of an individual on objective criteria brought the persistent problems of discrimination to the fore once again. Tom had spoken on the telephone with Betty, the mother of Eddie's friend Max. During the course of their telephone conversation, Tom learned that Betty was a fashion model and that they shared similar taste in wine. After having invited Betty for dinner, household servant Mrs. Livingstone counseled caution, invoking a folk expression of her native Japan: "A smart eagle hides his claws." Mrs. Livingstone presciently asked whether Tom's unrestrained amorous intentions toward Betty was advisable.

Mrs. Livingstone's caution proved justified once Betty arrived for dinner. She was black! After the initial shock wore off, Tom and Betty enjoyed each other's company the rest of the evening, which presumably did not include much more than dinner and dessert. The lesson, as it was adumbrated in the prologue, was driven home: Judging people categorically is wrong. People should be judged on an individual basis and not as a member of an ethnic group, class, or profession.

Lest the lesson in cross-cultural understanding be taken too far, to the point of miscegenation, a cautionary tale was inserted in the epilogue. Eddie asked his father a seemingly innocent question: "Do grasshoppers marry grasshoppers? Well what happens if a grasshopper marries a bird?" Tom Corbett answered, "You get a very jumpy bird." Translated into adult terms, the parable of the grasshopper and the bird implied that, while friendship and understanding between persons of different ethnic groups is acceptable, the mixing of "races" was quite another matter.[21]

AMERICAN SHIBBOLETHS

It was Mrs. Livingston, the Japanese servant for the Corbett household, who supplied the eccentric title of the program, *The Courtship of Eddie's Father*. She referred to her boss Tom Corbett periphrastically as "Mr. Eddie's Father"; not "Mr. Corbett," "Tom," or even "master." Mrs. Livingston's linguistic inadequacies connoted "Oriental" servitude, a condition she worked hard to overcome by attending English language school. Mrs. Livingston, for example, had trouble understanding the distinction between the words "people" and "pupil." She reasoned in the flawless logic of the alien, that one term necessarily implied the other. Such grammatically flawed but poetically correct utterances were the shibboleths that kept Mrs. Livingston from passing into the larger American society.

How Mrs. Livingston ever got her decidely Anglo-Saxon last name was not made clear in the program. Most likely she was a Japanese war bride once married to an American G.I. whose patronymic was Livingston. The life of actress Miyoshi Umeki, married to comedian Red Buttons, did not at all resemble the many subservient roles she played throughout her acting career. Umeki had first gained professional recognition as a jazz singer. She later went on to win an Academy Award for her supporting role in *Sayonara* (1957). Her first major exposure on television came in 1955 as a regular on the variety show *Arthur Godfrey and His Friends*.

Given the high level of professional success she enjoyed, it seemed particularly ironic that Umeki was cast as a docile servant. But given the general drift of late 1960s civil rights activism and increased network sensitivity to charges of media exploitation of blacks, the choice of an Asian performer such as Umeki to act as a servile side-kick made sense. The Asian-American actor, such as Jack Soo in *Valentine's Day* (September 18, 1964, to September 10, 1965), was according to social stereotypes a "safe," "model minority" that could be used, with a minimum of controversy, to mediate the social tensions that existed between the white-dominated institutions and black activist organizations. Use of an Asian-American character actor could connote subservience and subordination without directly offending other minorities held equally at a disadvantage.

By the late 1960s to early 1970s, mainstream social science literature had conferred "model minority" status to Asian Americans. In contrast to other ethnic groups, so the argument implied, Asian Americans were a shining example of how quiet patience in the face of injustice, hard work, and self-help allowed a formerly disadvantaged group to take its rightful place within a democratic pluralist society.[22] Having been given the unofficial seal of approval, the use of Asian Americans in subordinate roles—Peter Tong (Sammee Tong) in *Bachelor Father*—generated less controversy than using black actors to fulfill the same function.

It was not until the appearance of *Barney Miller* (January 23, 1975, to September 9, 1982) that an Asian-American character was given equal status as a three-dimensional human being. Jack Soo played Detective Nick Yemana, a world-weary police officer who worked in a melting pot of a bureau that included a black, a Jew, a Pole, a German, and a Puerto Rican. The program showed men from diverse backgrounds united against the sordidness of police work. Beyond the wisecracks and twisted observations on street life, *Barney Miller* was guilty of glossing over at least two hidden falsehoods when it came to Nick Yemana and Jack Soo. For one, "Yemana" was a fabricated "Japanese" name. No such Japanese surname exists. Second, "Jack Soo" was born Goro Suzuki. Suzuki changed his name to a more acceptable Chinese-sounding name in order to get work as a comedian during a period of residual anti-Japanese sentiment in California after World War II.[23]

BORED BLACK JUNGLE

Perhaps because it was part serious drama, part sitcom, *Room 222* (September 17, 1969, to January 11, 1974) drew a refreshingly candid portrait of an inner-city public school and the complex functions such an institution serves in the larger society. Regular cast members portrayed believable characters who each represented one specific sociopolitical point of view. Slightly on the left was the liberal reformer Alice Johnson (Karen Valentine), an enthusiastic, middle-class white woman fresh out of one of the better colleges and armed with the latest, most progressive theories of learning. Somewhat naive about the practical realities of the teaching profession, Alice Johnson was a dedicated professional full of good (if sometimes misguided) intentions.

At the opposite end of the political spectrum stood the principal of Walt Whitman (poet of the democratic spirit) High School, Mr. Seymour Kaufman (Michael Constantine). Kaufman represented the second-generation realization of the American Dream. He had fully internalized the standard lessons of American society and assumed the responsibility of transmitting this legacy to the younger generation. It disturbed Mr. Kaufman greatly that not a few of the students at Whitman High seemed unconvinced that a solid education was the ticket to entering middle-class society. He could not fully understand the apathy of those students who in his mind squandered the opportunity to make something of themselves through self-discipline and learning. As a believer in the myth of socioeconomic advancement through formal training and education alone, Mr. Kaufman disregarded the high opportunity cost of education for nonwhites living in inner-city ghettos.[24]

Completing the ensemble were Pete Dixon (Lloyd Haynes) and Liz McIntyre (Denise Nicholas), a history teacher and counselor, respectively. Both Pete and Liz had pivotal roles as black middle-class teaching professionals. They functioned as visible signs of attainment to both aspiring blacks of the underclass and the dominant white society, who could point to them as singular examples of the liberal pluralist ideal in operation.[25] Pete and Liz also carried on a half-secret love affair to which they could retreat whenever conditions at school became overheated. As a complementary pair, Pete and Liz occupied the middle ground between Mr. Kaufman and Alice Johnson.

Although having outgrown the naive optimism of Alice, they still demonstrated willingness to work for modest changes in school and society. In contrast to Mr. Kaufman, Pete and Liz had not yet settled into the hardheaded realism of experienced, battle-weary educators. Yet Kaufman himself seemed at times torn between a youthful past commitment to progressive politics and his official role as high school principal. In this, Mr. Kaufman's dilemma presaged the social and intellectual movement known as neoconservatism, a movement that gained momentum in the mid–1970s and culminated with the election of President Ronald Reagan in 1980.

BENEATH THE UNDERCLASS

The limitations of public education in society and its emancipatory potential for the individual were dramatically treated in "Man, If You're So

Smart . . . ''[26] The episode dramatized the new political realism that developed from the collapse of the new left, the rediscovery of middle America, and, most importantly, the decline of the American economy. The golden age of Keynesian state capitalism since the end of World War I showed serious strains by the time Richard Nixon was elected president in 1968. Several downward turns in the American economy forced rethinking of social welfare programs that were installed during the expansive years of the Great Society. Throughout the 1970s, increased levels of inflation, high rates of unemployment, stagnant industrial production, capital flight, and the energy crisis dictated a reordering of political economic priorities.[27] *Room 222* dramatized this growing ambivalence and even disatisfaction with ''liberal'' Great Society experiments in reducing inequality in society.

Unlike the liberal pragmatic pieties of the Kennedy-Johnson years that found expression in such sitcoms as *Grindl* or *The Smothers Brothers Show*, *Room 222* challenged many of the operating assumptions of Great Society liberalism, a favorite target of Richard Nixon during his 1968 presidential campaign and subsequent terms in office. The story concerned a problem student on probation who gained the trust of the correctional and educational establishment only to crush its misplaced faith in him. Mr. Kaufman and his teaching staff had gone to great lengths to ensure the student's success. The student, Henry Drucker, was described in the script notes as having ''about him an air of casual insolence'' and had spent time in reform school before reentering the mainstream.

Neophyte teacher Alice Johnson had believed that she had achieved a breakthrough with Henry when she learned of his interest in birds. Street-wise Henry knew how to gain sympathy and evoke liberal guilt as he played on Alice's unrealistic hopes for his rehabilitation. Her faith in Henry was shattered when, as she handed him a book on birds, a gun fell to the floor. Not wanting to betray the trust that had developed between the juvenile parolee and herself, Alice decided to turn the matter over to Mr. Kaufman. A search of Henry Drucker's pockets and locker turned up no weapon, which caused the staff some doubt as to the propriety of their search. They agreed, however, that the possibility that Henry had a gun on campus outweighed his right to privacy.

After the confrontation, Henry slipped unnoticed into Alice's classroom as she prepared to leave for the day. Alice expressed her regret at having reported Henry, but he would have none of it. Henry pulled out the pistol and menaced Alice with thinly veiled threats of retaliatory violence. Black male sexual violence against defenseless white womanhood was strongly suggested by the encounter: ''You almost blew it for me, Miss Johnson. But you wouldn't do that again, would you?. . .The way I figure it, you owe me something.'' Fortunately for Alice, Pete came to her rescue and managed to subdue Henry with assistance from the parole officer who had come to check up on his ward.

The closing act was devoted to a reexamination of Great Society premises and values. Pete told of his feelings of guilt over having not been able to rehabilitate Henry Drucker according to their expectations. Principal Seymour Kaufman, the seasoned professional, helped put the incident into perspective for all concerned:

KAUFMAN: Pete, don't let Henry Drucker hang around your neck like an albatross.

PETE: What's that supposed to mean?

KAUFMAN: Just that we've had other kids from reform school here at Whitman. We were able to help them, and they turned out fine. But some kids it's just too late for.

PETE: Maybe you're right

KAUFMAN: We're educators, Pete, not miracle workers.

The view voiced by Mr. Kaufman rang true in its implication that schools were not always able to deal with deep-seated problems stemming from the social structure. Society exists prior to the secondary institutions of socialization such as schools. The schools were therefore able to accommodate only those individuals who were already within reasonable reach of goals established by educational institutions for the greater good of society. The rest, like Henry Drucker, were presumably to be written off as losses.[28]

Mr. Kaufman's observations on public education in American society frequently bordered on pessimism. Because of its realism and willingness to admit wider social problems into the drama, *Room 222* went beyond the run-of-the-mill classroom sitcoms that featured kids living happily through an adolescent Never-Never Land as in the later *Welcome Back, Kotter* (September 9, 1975, to August 10, 1979). In this, *Room 222* showed slight skepticism at the mythology of upward social mobility achieved through educational attainment. As the data bore out, while enrollment parity between white and black high school students had been realized by 1965, there remained a grossly divergent gap between whites and blacks of this age group so far as unemployment and labor force participation were concerned.[29]

True to form, *Room 222* never went so far as to question the existing structural arrangement that kept minority enrollments high but minority labor force participation low. The Henry Druckers of the world were portrayed as being more the exception than the rule. More representative of black aspirations as viewed through the sitcom was Whitman High student Jason Allen, played by an actor by the name of Heshimu. Originally planned for a onetime appearance on the show, the "sullen Negro boy" Jason received strong reactions from a preview audience of about 400 people. His unexpectedly high ASI (Audience Survey, Inc.) rating ensured Jason a continuing role on *Room 222*.[30] Although Jason wore a *dashiki* and an Afro as an expression of black pride, he also held to careerist middle-class norms that place high value on training and education as means of achieving success in the world. Jason Allen was allowed his display of ethnic identity so long as he otherwise conformed to the democratic pluralist ethos of Whitman High's namesake.

BLACK PROBATIONARY IMAGES

Like Henry Drucker, images of black Americans on the networks went through a probationary period during the late 1960s through early 1970s. Their appearance, conduct, and thoughts as represented on commercial television were scrupulously controlled by those involved in the overall production process. Cedric C. Clark (1969) went so far as to suggest that minorities were made to pass through three stages of representation in the media before legitimacy was conferred upon them by the dominant society. The three stages were nonrecognition, ridicule, and regulation.[31] As of 1969, Clark observed that blacks were in the third or "regulation" stage of mass media portrayal. Clark noted the peculiar irony of blacks being cast in establishment or law and order roles far out of proportion to their actual numbers in the total population. Just as the 1950s housewife was the beneficiary of compensatory symbolic dominance on television, so too were blacks falsely elevated in much entertainment programing.

Even as blacks were gaining greater visibility on network television of the late 1960s through early 1970s, their symbolic empowerment was selectively channeled. The middle-class surroundings of Julia Baker, for example, were very much at variance with the actual living conditions of many blacks whose "humble" dwellings were "recognized only in television newscasts and documentaries and certain public television programs."[32] From other quarters, it was argued that the manner in which blacks were being portrayed on television had improved. In the condescending words of a research team, blacks on television were "treated very well" and shown as being "industrious, competent, and law abiding."[33] In sum, the paternalistic solicitude toward blacks and their numerical overrepresentation on television entertainment was employed as a form of compensation for their relative powerlessness in class society.

Therapies of personal adjustment masked paternalism as a form of social control in a 1977 episode of *The Bob Newhart Show* (September 16, 1972, to August 26, 1978).[34] The episode had psychotherapist Dr. Bob Hartley (Newhart) leading a small group of prison inmates in a series of rehabilitation sessions designed to prepare them for a life of freedom on the outside. Alone among the prisoners, a black man named Tatum resisted treatment. Contrasted with Tatum was a self-described "Harvard man" by the name of Coppleson, who by his comments ("I am not a crook") was in prison presumably because of a Watergate-type crime. Unlike Tatum, Coppleson was filled with the therapeutic self-regard of the white upper strata of society as he read from a thick manuscript that detailed his prison experiences.

Ultimately, Tatum was brought into the therapeutic fold and forced to accept the societal constraints negotiated by Dr. Hartley. Tatum confessed that the burden of living as a free man turned out to be too much for him to handle, after the parolee turned up at the Hartley household to rob them. Dr. Hartley, however, recognized the "robbery" as a cry for help. Bob offered to help Tatum in his return to freedom if Tatum agreed to lead, like a Judas goat, his fellow immates back into therapy. Strongly suggested by the episode was that only by submitting to the white middle-class therapeutic model of adjustment offered by the likes of a Dr. Hartley could Tatum hope to free himself of self-imposed probationary shackles.

BLACK BANDWAGON

After *Julia,* there was no dearth of situation comedies that featured black performers. *Julia* succeeded in bridging the gap between commercially marketable entertainment values and the political push for increased minority visibility on television. By relegating nonwhite ethnics to the situation comedy ghetto, the classic democratic liberal contradiction between concentrated politico-economic power and popular representation was once more, on a symbolic plane at least, apparently overcome. The increased number of ethnic-oriented situation comedies that appeared in the 1970s provided a nearly ideal dramatic solution to an otherwise persistent and vexatious problem of the liberal democratic system of governance—how the disenfranchised come to believe and accept "that those with power have the right to rule."[35] In sum, the age-old political question of legitimacy had been forestalled once more.

As a transitional program, *Julia* tread lightly in the area of American intergroup tensions. Moreover, the show diminished the contradictions inherent in divisions along social class lines by foregrounding ethnic pluralism. Julia Baker was portrayed as a typical middle-class individual save for her skin color. In that the content of the television situation comedy since the 1950s has been synonymous with the world of the middle class, *Julia* ran true to form. The conflation of ethnicity and social class in *Julia* was in keeping with the cultural pluralist conception of power, which tolerated ethnic self-identity while leaving the fact of class domination untouched.

Sanford and Son (January 14, 1972, to September 2, 1977) appeared the season after *All in the Family* (January 12, 1971, to September 21, 1983) made its network debut. Led by *Sanford and Son,* black Americans moved out of the regulatory ghetto of mass media portrayal and into the integrated television neighborhood of liberal pluralist respectability. Granted, Fred Sanford (Redd Foxx) and his son Lamont (Demond Wilson) did live in a junk yard in the midst of a black ghetto. But in keeping with the relativistic drift of the cultural pluralist model of society, the Sanfords's squalid surroundings and black subcultural style was accorded the same degree of respect and acceptance as any other household.

Whereas Julia gave no evidence of her blackness through her appearance (no Afro), lifestyle (employed professional), or language (media English), both Fred and Lamont were readily identifiable as members of the black underclass. Fred, Lamont, and their assorted friends had little truck with the outside white world save for collecting its castoff goods for resale. Whenever white authority asserted its presence in the junk-strewn Sanford domain, Fred was particularly resentful.

Like Archie Bunker, no ethnic groups—whites included—were safe from the slings and arrows of the embittered Fred Sanford.

Fred's reverse racism was viewed as funny, even acceptable. By the time *Sanford and Son* appeared, the 1960s quest for political power, which to a large degree took the form of ethnic mobilization, had already been transmuted into the cultural pluralism of the 1970s. That the burlesqued reverse racism of a Fred Sanford could hold such appeal for its audience confirmed that the equalitarian political goals of the 1960s had been thrown over for the cultural politics of liberal pluralism. Once more, the issue of class politics was shunted into the rhetoric of the 1970s version of liberal democratic ideology.

By the 1970s, the dearly held belief that America was becoming a middle-class society was severely challenged by the continuing decline of the political economy. Theories of class convergence popular in the immediate postwar period were challenged by the many debilitating shocks dealt to the American economy in the 1970s. Spiraling inflation, sluggish economic growth, intensified foreign industrial competition, and the precipitous rise in the cost of imported oil had a severe destabilizing impact on the political economy. The great middle-class society promised by the economic bounty of the 1950s became less plausible as American class relations in the 1970s began to exhibit "characteristics of the more highly stratified European model."[36]

After lying dormant for many years, the politics of class reawakened with the appearance of *All in the Family* during the final season of *Julia*. The sanctity of the home as an apolitical refuge from the outside world was thrown over, as Norman Lear "portrayed the family as a political arena—as *the* political arena."[37] The much aggrieved working-class hero Archie Bunker (Carroll O'Connor) was solidly locked into the blue collar stratum of the class system. Advanced middle age also precluded upward mobility for Archie. The best Archie could hope for was just to be left alone, insulated from the irritants of the outside world. Rather than point to the larger source of his frustrations, Archie targeted ethnic and normative minorities for blame. Archie was simply incapable of comprehending the brave new world wrought by the equality revolution. Sadly, those closest to him—wife Edith (Jean Stapleton), daughter Gloria (Sally Struthers), and son-in-law Mike Stivic (Rob Reiner)—suffered the most from Archie's generalized resentment. Beyond his bluster and anger, however, Archie Bunker was toughest on himself. Archie evoked audience sympathy because he bore the all-too-familiar burden of having to live with his individual failure in the face of insurmountable objective circumstance.

Norman Lear, equipped with both an artistic acumen born of vast writing experience and an objective understanding of the larger social transformations taking place, adopted the sociodrama of the more rigid British class system and applied it to a uniquely American setting. Unlike Great Britain, issues of social class and power in American society have been more typically transcoded into issues of ethnicity, gender, or profession. Out of his intuitive grasp of an emerging system of exacerbated class relations in the 1970s, Lear adapted *All in the*

Family from the British program *Till Death Do Us Part*. Lear's prescience spurred him to duplicate his original success by producing *Sanford and Son*. *Sanford and Son* (January 14, 1972, to September 2, 1977) was an adaptation of *Steptoe and Son,* also a British situation comedy.

For the better part of the 1970s, Norman Lear's and Bud Yorkin's Tandem Productions appeared to have solved the dilemmas of class-based politics through more ideologically neutral explorations of intergroup tensions in general and ethnicity in particular. This time, however, the new vision of American society presented on television was colored by over two decades of political struggle, struggle that had forced adjustments in the dominant liberal democratic ideology. While the unbridled optimism of *Mama* or *The Goldbergs* had disappeared along with the loss of political innocence, the 1970s ethnicoms retained the liberal world view undergirding capitalist relations of production and society. The basic assumptions of capitalist society—competitive individualism, materialism, the sanctity of private property, profit taking, and the primacy of the market—remained consistent throughout.[38]

BAD GOOD TIMES

The ideological subtexts of situation comedies produced by Tandem Productions were largely in line with the political beliefs held by Norman Lear. Producer Lear, for example, developed the black ethnicom *Good Times* (February 1, 1974, to August 1, 1979) with an express "sense of social consciousness and a degree of serious purpose rare in television situation comedy."[39] In keeping with his personal and professional commitment. Lear stressed the need to "incorporate the 'issues of the day' into the half-hour comedy slot" in his 1978 address to the Edinburgh International Television Festival.[40] In an art form that has scrupulously avoided controversy and overtly political messages, Lear sitcoms were noted for references and observations on American economic and foreign policy that were often critical in tone.

In addition to his outspoken advocacy of certain political issues, Lear has been credited with the realistic and honest treatment of such subjects as death, prejudice, abortion, marital infidelity, the black family, and homosexuality. Because of his politics, Lear had once been the target of Moral Majority leader the Reverend Jerry Falwell. Falwell denounced programs produced by Lear as being "anti-family," "anti-moral," and "anti-Christian." In response, Norman Lear founded the People for the American Way in September 1984 to help stave off the assault on American culture and politics by the religious right.[41]

As a spin-off from *Maude* (September 12, 1972, to April 29, 1978), the concept for *Good Times* was attributed to two black writers, Eric Monty and Mike Evans. Despite the initial involvement of Monty and Evans, most of the scripts for *Good Times* were written by white writers. Lear had at the beginning sought to involve black writers in the creation of *Good Times,* but when no new scripts written by blacks were deemed acceptable, there were questions raised as to whether sincere efforts on the part of Lear were indeed being made in recruiting black writing talent.

In the attempt to directly involve minority writers in a competitive, highly specialized, and exclusive industry, Lear was confronted with an affirmative action issue that as of early 1974 had not been fully institutionalized. In the 1970s the question of how to correct historic imbalances in given occupations without compromising quality and discriminating against more qualified applicants was one of the salient dilemmas of the liberal pluralist ascendancy. In the legal arena at least, the dilemma was partially resolved by the U.S. Supreme Court ruling *Bakke v. University of California* (1978)[42]

In explaining his dilemma as a producer, Lear stated that there were few black writers with the necessary "long list of credits in television" that established a track record in a high-stakes business.[43] In sum, while Norman Lear was willing to give aspiring black writers an equal opportunity in competition with seasoned professionals who have been in the writing profession for twenty years or more, he did not go so far as to break the vicious circle by granting black writers equality of condition, not even on a trial basis. In the competitive, costly business of producing television programs where there is little chance of seeing a return on investment unless a given show can be sold into syndication, betting on untested talent was considered to be too much of a risk.[44]

BLACK REDEMPTION

Good Times took as its subject the quotidian concerns of a black family living in the South Side of Chicago struggling to make its way out of near poverty. The undisputed head of the household, James Evans (John Amos), provided security and stability for his wife Florida (Esther Rolle) and their three children James, Jr., or "J. J.," (Jimmie Walker), Michael (Ralph Carter), and Thelma (BernNadette Stanis). Although hardworking and industrious, James often suffered long layoffs from work. He was one of the "working poor" who straddled the official poverty line from month to month. James was seen as being devoted to his family, someone who would not dream of deserting them just so they could qualify for welfare subsidies. Unlike her husband, Florida was able to keep herself out of the ranks of the underemployed for she had steady work as a domestic laborer.

The standard list of individual rationalizations for the existence of poverty—shiftlessness, immorality, lack of ability, unrestrained spending habits—only by the broadest implications applied to the Evans family.[45] Although each family member was engaged in some form of productive activity, there were certain aspects of their class-specific behavior that somehow stood outside the pale. The supposed obsession of blacks with games of chance, their dependance on luck, and predisposition toward superstitious beliefs were explored as themes in an episode of *Good Times* written by Jon Dunley and Kurt Taylor.[46]

J. J. Evans had been painting a portrait of a well-known neighborhood hustler when his precocious younger brother Michael arrived home bearing plans for Black History Week. Michael wore a fatigue army jacket, which signified his budding militancy. The jacket was also emblazoned with the black, green, and red Afro-American nationalist flag that flew during the 1960s in revolutionary opposition to the Stars and Stripes. Although a talented painter, J. J. was apolitical and seemed resigned to his fate as a suffering artist. His spirited brother Michael suggested that J. J. paint a subject other than "Sweet Daddy Williams," someone more "relevant" to Black History Week. In J. J.'s mind, however, there was no one better than Sweet Daddy Williams to represent black aspirations: "Relevant? Are you jiving? Sweet Daddy Williams owns three apartment houses, two Cadillacs, and a Lincoln. . .ain't never worked a day in his life, and never been to jail. He's the same dude who got shot five times and ran seven miles to the hospital. Now if that ain't Black History then I don't know what is." Michael succeeded in having J. J. enter a painting entitled "Black Jesus" into an art show sponsored by the "Pan-African Council." "Black Jesus," as it turned out, was modeled after a street character better known as Ned the Wino.

Michael, with all the enthusiasm of youth, espoused the objectives of black cultural nationalism. He argued passionately before his kin that, as a black family, a portrait depicting a *black* Jesus would be more appropriate to have in their home than that of a white man. Florida had been angered by the seeming blasphemy of J. J.'s "Black Jesus." Michael calmed his mother's anger with the support of black cultural nationalist readings of the Bible that described the Lost Tribe of Israel as being black. J. J. was quick to agree. "I bet they were," said J. J. "If ever a people were lost, we're it." Florida allowed the portrait to hang in her home after Michael read a passage from the Book of Revelations (1:14) that described the historical Christ as being black in physical appearance.

In a parallel development, James Evans learned that he was being audited by the Internal Revenue Service for irregularities in his income tax return. The unfairness of the audit was put into perspective by a neighbor, Willona Woods (Ja'net DuBois), who observed that the president of the United States paid only $700 in taxes on an income of $200,000 that year. When James returned from the IRS audit having been cleared not only of suspected improprieties but with a refund as well, all eyes turned to the portrait of "Black Jesus" as the cause of the "miracle."

As the voice of reason and bearer of dominant middle-class values, Florida stated firmly that "Jesus has nothing to do with luck." Before Florida's statement had time to sink in, a numbers runner arrived at their apartment to inform James that his combination had hit. The assembly of the faithful again gazed reverently at "Black Jesus." Florida held fast to her denial of luck playing any part of her family's sudden good fortune. Further, she was angered by James having broken his promise not to gamble any more. "This isn't gambling," James assured his wife. "With this cat blowing on the dice, ain't no chance of me crapping out."

The uncanny run of good luck continued as Willona brought news that a rich fellow who owned a chain of gas stations had asked her out on a date. Young

Michael was similarly blessed with luck after reporting that he was given five dollars to say nothing about an automobile accident that he did not even witness. At that, Florida took down the portrait of "Black Jesus," having seen the baleful influence it had on her household. In desperation, James wrested the portrait away from her. James pleaded that he needed all the luck he could get, having had very little social advantage with only a sixth grade education. Florida remained adamant that the solid foundation of her family would not be undermined by a false reliance on luck. By her actions, Florida reaffirmed the middle-class values of deferred gratification and self-achievement against the implied values of the black underclass, which prized immediate gain realized through a combination of luck and hustle.

James was eventually won over to the cause of individual achievement when he selflessly gave up his good luck piece for J. J. to exhibit at the art show. James had been reluctant to surrender the painting, since it probably meant an end to his lucky streak. James's decision had been hastened by J. J.'s doubts about whether he had the necessary formal training and talent to succeed as an artist. James told J. J. not to "run down his thing" and encouraged him to pursue his art. By James's act of sacrifice, the false god of luck was rejected in favor of J. J.'s quest for individual distinction and achievement.

By the conclusion of the episode, Michael's black nationalist identity had been duly acknowledged, J. J.'s cynicism and despair had been held in abeyance, and James's honest aspirations for himself and his family were set right. Black matriarch Florida Evans emerged triumphant over the intractable forces that threatened to disrupt the poor but honest life she provided her family. Although strongly alluded to at the beginning of the episode, the structural reasons for black unemployment and underemployment were left at the threshold of understanding as the Evans family beat a loving retreat into their privatized homelife.

GOOD ENGLISH

As in all liberal sociodrama, in *Good Times* conflicts were articulated within and contained by the ideological parameters defined by the commercial system (sponsors, producers, networks, audiences) responsible for their creation. In spite of these contraints, *Good Times* was unique among other black ethnic situation comedies because of its stronger emphasis on "forbidden" problems of black underclass life such as racism and unemployment. Each principal character in the program, with the exception of Florida, was a source of possible trouble for the larger system to which they tried to adapt. James was sometimes tempted by gambling and a life of enforced indolence, J. J. often slipped into self-denigrating despair, and Thelma seemed a prime candidate for unwed motherhood. In short, these characters were living examples of the failings of liberal democratic ideology. As in other sitcoms, it was the family that helped lessen the pain of the larger social world. Ironically, it was also the family that forestalled an objective understanding of their bondage.

One of the more intriguing of all principal characters in the black ethnicoms of the 1970s was Michael Evans in *Good Times*. As a dedicated black nationalist, young Michael envisaged sweeping changes for the betterment of the black underclass. Still, Michael conceived his family's objective condition of subordination in exclusively *cultural* rather than *political* terms. Perhaps because of his relative youth, Michael was allowed to put forth unusually harsh critical comments on the dominant society without suffering reprisals, ridicule, or censure. For example, an episode produced in 1974 had Michael refusing to take an intelligence test because it was biased, or in the words of Michael, a "white, racist test." "It doesn't tell you how intelligent you are," said Michael, "but how white you are." Had Michael been an adult black, such a statement would have been considered inflammatory. Because childhood enjoys protected status, in Michael's case such truths were allowed to pass. The strategy of having black children utter adult truths was later put to use in such shows as *Diff'rent Strokes* and *Webster* in the latter part of the 1970s and early 1980s once the ideological climate changed.

Michael's critical observations, however compelling, were blunted by his age and relative inexperience. His anger, though probably justified, could have been too easily dismissed as simple youthful idealism, an example of every child's discovery of unfairness in the real world. The true locus of power in the Evans family resided in the person of Florida Evans. Florida's role as the ultimate "regulator" of black family behavior was reflected by her use of language. Like the other central female characters on such black ethnicoms as *Sanford and Son* and *The Jeffersons*, Florida Evans spoke in a dialect more akin to standard English while the comic characters spoke a sanitized version of black English. Just as the black matriarch was portrayed in the television situation comedy as the "keeper of the standard language," by implication she also acted as the bearer of the dominant liberal ideology.[47]

MOVE ON UP

The Great Society's War on Poverty officially began with the passage of the Economic Opportunity Act of 1964, out of which was formed the Office of Economic Opportunity (OEO). Numerous OEO programs serving diverse constituent groups were created with the intention of correcting the more obvious signs of inequality in American society. The massive infusion of federal dollars into monumental social welfare programs domestically while simultaneously financing an undeclared war plunged the American economy into a sustained crisis. The OEO was budgeted for a total of $2.8 billion between 1965 and 1973, which was roughly equivalent to the cost of waging war in Vietnam for one month.[48]

Whether the Great Society experiment in social reform as interpreted by social scientists ultimately proved to be a means of regulating the poor, a symptom of capitalism in its twilight, or a futile exercise in "maximum feasible misunderstanding'' the Economic Opportunity Act reflected the willingness of the state to minimize the worst effects of corporate capitalism.[49] The ameliorative but often conflicting goals of Great Society social welfare programs were incorporated into the sitcom *The Jeffersons* (January 18, 1975, to July 23, 1985). One of the more salient themes explored in the program was the contradiction between equality of opportunity and equality of condition. The aesthetic and political problem established for *The Jeffersons* was one of how social inequalities historically suffered by newly enfranchised minority peoples could be corrected without at the same time violating the rights of the majority.

George Jefferson (Sherman Hemsley), the relatively successful independent entrepreneur in *The Jeffersons*, was depicted as a direct beneficiary of Great Society social legislation and private industry efforts to assist minorities in breaking out of the "cycle of poverty." George Jefferson was both scrappy and ambitious. Jefferson was somewhat defensive of his personal shortcomings as any parvenu might be, but he was clearly proud of his achievements as a businessman, almost to the point of arrogance. Although he benefitted from Great Society "set-asides" for minorities, the show made it obvious that it was hard work and dedication that were largely responsible for the success George Jefferson enjoyed.

George Jefferson shared the struggles of the past with his family one day as they sat on the living room sofa.[50] Together they reminisced about their difficult advance toward economic well-being. A flashback transported the episode to the fateful day in 1968 when George first applied for the loan that would enable him to start his own business. This signal event in the Jefferson's lives happened to coincide with the height of racial violence that occurred in the aftermath of the assassination of Martin Luther King, Jr.

George had hoped that he could finance his start-up business through a "Minority Lending Program" designed to help minorities pull themselves up by their own bootstraps. The scope and method of the "Minority Lending Program" closely resembled that of the Urban Coalition headed by John Gardner. The Urban Coalition was established as a way to "facilitate money into the ghetto, clean up the corporate image of the Chase Manhattan Bank," and placate black activists.[51] George claimed that in order to qualify for a business loan, "All's you have to do is be colored, ambitious, and have a great personality." George was tired of working for someone else and having little to show for his efforts. In this, the expectant capitalist George Jefferson shared the same unabated entrepreneurial drive as such sitcom progenitors as Chester Riley or Ralph Kramden. Even though small business actually works at a disadvantage in comparison to the corporate sector, the dream of being his own boss fueled George Jefferson's ambition.

A Mr. William Drew from the Mercantile National Bank visited the Jefferson home to discuss the terms of the business loan. After being welcomed into the Jefferson apartment, Mr. Drew looked curiously about as if he were in an alien world. The loan officer saw that the apartment was neat and orderly, contrary to his expectations. As a not quite willing participant in the equality revolution, Mr. Drew was obviously uncomfortable with the Jeffersons. He took every opportunity to self-consciously point out similarities between the dominant white society and the Jeffersons, more to reassure himself of their normalcy than anything else. George was angered by the invidious comparisons drawn by Mr. Drew and was offended by Drew's unthinking condescension. When, for example, George mentioned that he had only one son, the banker was genuinely surprised. He had simply assumed that most "colored people have large families."

The tension built even more when George's son Lionel (Mike Evans) returned home covered with bruises he received while attending a demonstration. He had been clubbed by a policeman. Lionel explained that he and the "brothers" were beaten when they were out demonstrating against dismal conditions in the black community. Mr. Drew was surprised to learn of Lionel's involvement with his "brothers," especially since George had claimed to have only one son.

Lionel took an immediate dislike to Mr. Drew. He correctly assumed that the car parked outside with the "America: Love It or Leave It" bumper sticker belonged to Mr. Drew. Mr. Drew said that there was no place for protest or dissent in America. If only people were more willing to work, he averred, and less inclined to complain, America would be a better place for everyone. Having seen a portrait of the Reverend Martin Lurther King, Jr., hanging in the living room, Drew went so far as to imply that the civil rights leader was a communist. Although livid with anger, George put up with the humiliation because he badly wanted the loan to be approved. As he left, Mr. Drew paid George a backhanded compliment by saying, "You know, Jefferson, I wish all Negroes were like you."

George took Louise and Lionel down to the future site of "Handy Dandy Cleaners" in the heart of the black ghetto. Lionel was skeptical of his father's prospects for surviving in what he believed to be a fatally flawed economic and social system. George insisted that he would succeed against all odds and Louise sided with her husband. She felt that the violent political protest of Lionel and his fellow community activists was counterproductive. As for George, he espoused the nonviolent gradualism of Martin Luther King, Jr., and rejected Lionel's model of social change that sometimes employed violence and confrontation with authority. As the three of them spoke, a brick came flying through the storefront window. Someone ran by yelling that Martin Luther King, Jr., had just been murdered. George picked up a chair and hurled it through the window in rage and shouted, "Bastards!"

Safely at home, the Jeffersons watched the rioting unfold on a television set that worked only intermittently. George and Louise were both demoralized by the violent turn of events. George went so far as to state that the country was going nowhere but downhill. In mourning, Louise called to inform her employer that she would not report for work that day. But Louise's boss Mrs. Warren was having guests that night and insisted that she come to work. Incensed by Mrs. Warren's insensitivity, George called her up and told her to find a new maid. Lionel's response to the crisis was to go out and find a new television to steal. He reasoned that stealing was no crime at all in comparison to the murder of their spiritual and political leader.

Since the black community was in an uproar over the assassination, Mr. Drew skulked back to the Jefferson household with a coat drawn over his face. The loan officer advised George that he would be better off locating the proposed cleaning business in a "respectable neighborhood," meaning a white neighborhood. Said Drew, "My bank can't lend you the money to open a store in an area where people behave like animals." At this last unbearable insult, George threw Drew out of the apartment. George's wounded pride dashed all hope of obtaining the business loan.

The recent turn of events had George begin to side with the radicalism of Lionel. George even stated that the only way to get anything in this society was to take it by force. Louise, acting once more as the mouthpiece of liberal democracy, restated her belief in the system. She said that social change would not come out of violence. Lionel sharply rejected his mother's reaffirmation by pointing to the irony of their leader having been assassinated while preaching the nonviolent tactics of Gandhi. Lionel remained steadfast in his position that nothing had ever changed in American society for the better and that nothing ever would.

Alarmed, George did not want his son Lionel to abandon all hope for progressive social change. George quickly retreated from his temporary radicalism and sided with his wife Louise. George tried to convince Lionel that their lives *had* changed for the better, albeit not so fast as they would have liked. George reaffirmed his belief that anyone regardless of social background could achieve anything so long as the desire to succeed was there. Said Louise, "Your father's right. We *shall* overcome!" The program ended with a moving voice-over excerpt of the "I Have A Dream" speech delivered by the Reverend Martin Luther King, Jr., at the March on Washington on August 28, 1963. The Jefferson family, Lionel included, drew close to one another in the closing tableau.

Moderation and gradual reform, both prominent features of the dominant liberal ideology, were planted firmly back in place by the end of the episode. The use of the flashback technique covering a span of over ten years added historical weight and legitimacy to the liberal reformist approach to correcting social inequality. The obvious message was that positive change would come about eventually, but only by sticking patiently to the rules and procedures of the dominant liberal democratic paradigm. Moreover, the distance traveled by the Jeffersons up the mobility ladder during that ten-year span of time falsely implied similar improvement in the economic lives of blacks and other nonwhite minorities. This was a strategy that carried over into the ethnicoms of the 1980s.

A HOUSE DIVIDED

It was perhaps only appropriate that this episode of *The Jeffersons* concluded with a reference to the march on Washington. Like the march on Washington,

The Jeffersons as liberal sociodrama brought together three incompatible schools of thought concerning social change and strategies for realizing political goals: (1) revolutionary nationalism (Lionel), (2) religio-conservatism (Louise), and (3) liberal reformism (George). This entire ideological spectrum was represented by members of the Jefferson household.

The character who bore the underlying message or moral was of course Louise, who fulfilled a function similar to that of Florida Evans in *Good Times*. Louise, like many other black women in television entertainment, relied on "explanations of feelings and actions in the attempt to increase understanding in others, resolve strife, or reassure others."[52] In sum, black women held out hope for interpersonal adjustment in lieu of political solutions to social contradictions. Competing models of power relations and social change were, through this strategy, pushed into the background by the therapeutics of personalistic psychology.

The three-part interplay of competing ideologies had its objective correlative in the black civil rights movement. Events surrounding the March on Washington brought into relief the ideological divisions among the various recognized civil rights organizations. Traditionally conservative civil rights groups, like the NAACP or the Southern Christian Leadership Conference (SCLC) led by the Reverend King, contended most notably with the Student Non-Violent Coordinating Committee (SNCC). Disenchantment with the gradualist strategy of the SCLC led to the radicalization of the once closely aligned Student Non-Violent Coordinating Committee. Taking a separatist position altogether was Malcolm X, who referred to the March—the signal event of the civil rights movement—as the "farce on Washington."

Like so many other memorable figures in American popular culture, the character of George Jefferson was but a new twist in the myth of the self-made man.[53] In the person of George Jefferson, the updated liberal pluralist version of the myth now gave minority people club membership so long as the proper dues were paid. *The Jeffersons* showed that the dues for "Movin' On Up," as the program's gospel theme song expressed it, were heavy indeed. While the Jefferson family might not have been representative of the average black American family, *The Jeffersons* dramatized better than most other programs the heavy emotional and economic toll exacted by a competitive society wherein opportunities are largely determined by social class. For George Jefferson and so many others like him, regardless of ethnicity, the myth of the self-made man retained its special urgency and palpability simply because the social vision of a realistically achievable alternative was not part of popular discourse.

"YOU'VE COME A LONG WAY, *BABY*?"

The television career of Mary Tyler Moore marked the changing social aspirations and roles of the American woman during the past three decades. Moore debuted as Sam, the unseen receptionist on *Richard Diamond, Private Detective* (July 1, 1957, to September 6, 1960). (Only her legs appeared on camera.) From disembodied, sultry siren, Mary Tyler Moore then became helpmate to Rob Petrie on *The Dick Van Dyke Show* (October 3, 1961, to September 7, 1966). Her function as housekeeper and nurturing parent was later replaced by that of the youngish single career woman trying to make her way in the big city in *The Mary Tyler Moore Show* (September 19, 1970, to September 3, 1977).

There is little doubt that the liberal feminist agenda of the middle to late 1960s helped set the ideological stage for *The Mary Tyler Moore Show*. Developing alongside the civil rights movement, the women's movement joined other "minorities" as yet another claimant group clamoring for a piece of the pluralist pie.[54] Along with the liberal feminist rejection of the double standard, the strongly implied sexual freedom of Mary Richards was a legacy of the counterculture. She was not engaged, had no steady boyfriend, was never married, and further, "Mary Richards didn't even seem to care."[55] But even as "*MTM*" seemed to have assimilated some of the lessons of the 1960s, the national mood was beginning to swing toward cultural and political conservatism, which coalesced under the banner of the "new right."

As a counterpoise to the perceived toppling of traditional American beliefs concerning family, church, patriotism, and morality, the new right sought to restore balance to a society it believed to have gone out of kilter. The conservative resurgence of the 1970s took vastly different forms, ranging from experientially based evangelical Christianity to the intellectual movement known as neoconservatism. Numerous single issue organizations also cropped up in response to a civilization gone awry: The Supreme Court decision in *Roe v. Wade* (1973), which partially excluded state and federal government intervention in reproductive matters, spawned the "right-to-life" movement. With the passage of the the Equal Rights Amendment by Congress in 1972, assorted conservative groups mounted efforts against its ratification by the states, demonstrating their substantial political clout.[56]

SURROGATE FAMILY

The acceptance of *The Mary Tyler Moore Show* by the general television audience and critics alike was due to the ability of its creators to mediate two countervailing tendencies in the culture and politics of the American 1970s— the careerism of the liberal feminist agenda versus the persistence of the family culture ideal in mainstream American society. Mary Richards' quest for personal autonomy through the single-minded pursuit of a career and her search for self-fulfillment beyond lifetime monogamy and childbearing was part of the progressive legacy of the 1960s equality revolution. The danger, however, in this quest lay in the possible destruction of the last remaining bastion of community that has resisted the total commodification of life, the family.

The network of friends, neighbors, and co-workers seemed to be a surrogate family of sorts for Mary Richards. Like a family formed of blood bonds, they sheltered each other from the shortness, brutishness, and nastiness of the Hobbesian vision of social life. In this way, *"MTM"* blended the progressive gains of the previous decade with the traditional "ideology of the familial." The emotional closeness of the principal characters in the program salvaged the "family-as-community" ideal, but only at the cost of reinforcing the "conservatism associated with gender and family hierarchy."[57] The *Mary Tyler Moore Show* therefore succeeded in balancing two contradictory imperatives—career versus family—that continued to serve as a highly serviceable premise for many sitcoms of the 1980s.

MAKING IT

The premiere episode of *The Mary Tyler Moore Show* limned the thematic and ideological contours of the entire series. As in most sitcoms, the inaugural episode sets into motion the premises and problems that drive the program. This episode for example took up a surprisingly wide range of contemporary issues including male/female social roles, female subordination in the workplace, and sexual harrassment. In each case, the problems at hand were ultimately depoliticized by foregrounding the therapeutic role played by Richards's "family" in mediating social contradictions. Despite this general tendency of the liberal sociodrama, it can be observed that *The Mary Tyler Moore Show* managed to introduce elements of counterhegemonic thought, that is, social thought that systematically or informally proposes alternatives to dominant social and political ideologies.[58] In the final analysis, even in *The Mary Tyler Moore Show,* counterhegemonic thought concerning sexuality, work, authority, and leisure was for the most part contained and controlled by presocial "explanations" rooted in personalistic psychology.

In the first installment of *The Mary Tyler Moore Show,* Mary Richards was seen beginning a new life in Minneapolis after having ended a two-year relationship she had mistakenly assumed would lead to marriage.[59] Mary had supported her boyfriend for two years during his medical internship. As he was about to enter a residency program, Mary's boyfriend balked at the idea of their getting married. In a departure from the familiar female role of faithful and constant companion, Mary did not wait for his final decision. Instead, she moved to Minneapolis to establish her own career. With the help of a close friend, Phyllis Lindstrom, (Cloris Leachman) and a lovingly intrusive neighbor, Rhoda Morgenstern (Valerie Harper), Mary Richards sought to establish a career independent of a male partner.

Mary's professional ambitions were modest. She first applied for a secretarial position in the newsroom of a failing television station. The newsroom was staffed by a domineering manager (Lou Grant), a newswriter who kept above the fray (Murray Slaughter), and an egoistic anchor man (Ted Baxter). The key personnel at the station came to form Mary's workplace "family." At a job interview with the gruff station manager Lou Grant (Ed Asner), Mary was informed that the secretarial job had been filled. Instead, Grant offered Mary a position as associate producer of the news program. At first elated by her good fortune, Mary began to wonder why the producer's job paid ten dollars *less* than the secretarial job. The unspoken implication was that the ten-dollar differential between the window dressing secretarial job and the position of substance as associate producer represented the price of "making it" in a male-dominanted profession.

Mary's fear of a sexual shakedown surfaced when Lou Grant appeared unannounced one evening at her apartment. Knowing that Lou's wife was out of town, Mary assumed that he was there to collect the "favor" owed him. Before she could express her indignation, however, Mary's former boyfriend Bill arrived. Bill explained that the purpose of his visit was to propose marriage, but only if Mary would agree once more to postpone their marriage to some unspecified time in the future. This time Mary informed her former beau that the relationship was over for good. What with her new career and circle of faithful friends, Mary no longer had to rely on any one man for financial or emotional support.

In the person of Mary Richards, two contradictory aspects of liberal thought were held in momentary equipoise. The quest for individual autonomy, previously restricted to men, was now extended to Mary Richards and others like her reaping the gains of the feminist critique. Yet the equally compelling communal values represented by the family were kept intact by Mary, her friends, and co-workers as they resolved mundane problems and minor crises. In *The Mary Tyler Moore Show*, the radical individualism summarized in the credo, "I have the capacity to choose my life, my world and finally my own self," was temporarily reconciled with the objective demands imposed by family and society.[60] In that there is no final resting place for the historically grounded battle of conflicting ideas, "*MTM*" slowly sank in the ratings as the political climate changed to one of reactionary happy days.

RETROGRADE DAYS

Throughout the better part of the 1970s and into the early 1980s, situation comedy program production was dominated by the firms MTM, Tandem or T.A.T., and Miller-Milkis. While MTM and Tandem/T.A.T. consciously pushed out previously established ideological boundaries, Miller-Milkis pursued a counterstrategy, that of ideological retrenchment. Miller-Milkis exploited the nation's fascination with the retro cultural styles of the American 1950s and in doing so scored a big hit with *Happy Days* (January 15, 1974, to July 12, 1984). As in so many products of mass-mediated culture that attempt to deal with the past, history was reduced to visual style and song cues. The "premature nostalgia" of the baby boom generation as reflected by retro sitcoms denied the unpleasant realities of the un-"silent" 1950s, but instead directed attention to only the most superficial aspects of the era.[61]

A spin-off from *Happy Days, Laverne & Shirley* (January 27, 1976, to May

10, 1983) was set in the late 1950s to early 1960s. Producer Garry Marshall congratulated himself for having correctly perceived blue collar reactionary sentiment demonstrated by the success of *Laverne & Shirley*. The program hovered near the top of the ratings in its very first season. According to Marshall, *Laverne & Shirley* came at the "perfect time in history" because for the first time working-class life was portrayed in all its humanity, opposing depictions of middle- and upper-class women in "literature and movies saying that women have rights."[62] As might be inferred by its popularity, *Laverne & Shirley* articulated working-class America's opposition to a liberal feminist agenda that had no social, economic, or cultural relevance to their lives.

After twenty years at the top as a military-industrial power, America showed distressing signs of vulnerability both domestically and internationally. Within the context of deepening economic crises and embarrassing impotence in foreign affairs, the collective mid–1970s yearning for the happy days of the golden decade, the 1950s, made absolute sense. The Arab oil embargo in 1973 during the Yom Kippur war was but a glimpse of the gas shortages to come, dramatically demonstrating the U.S. dependence on the resources of foreign powers. The American automobile and steel industries took a drubbing by German and Japanese manufacturers who succeeded in outcompeting their former conquerors. The United States was proven unable to protect its citizens living abroad as Iranian revolutionaries led by the Ayatollah Khomeini overran the American embassy and held American citizens hostage for over a year.

In retro shows like *Happy Days*, Americans were once more able to revel in a highly romanticized remembrance of their glory years. Such programs also served as ideal vehicles to revive the regressive dominant ideologies of the past by transporting them to an earlier point in time. By such means could beliefs discredited by the liberation movements of the 1960s be sneaked in through the back door. In the pilot script of *Happy Days*, for example, the cult of virginity was nostalgically revived to titillate the viewer without fear of accusations over sexism.[63] The virgin/whore Madonna complex, wherein certain "bad" women are pursued as objects of sexual conquest while others are saved for marriage, was explored and partially reaffirmed. It was as if the movement known loosely as women's liberation or feminism had never taken place, its historic presence having been effaced by nostalgia.[64]

MILITARY-INDUSTRIAL MADONNA COMPLEX

The setting for the pilot script of *Happy Days* was noted as "Anywhere, U.S.A." In actual practice it was Milwaukee where the drama of extended adolescence unfolded. The central character, Richie Cunningham (Ron Howard), was a wholesome young man who lived at home with his family. Richie aspired to be a journalist but felt somewhat at a disadvantage by not having experienced life at its fullest. Dreams of worldly adventure and excitement made Richie's lack of sexual experience all the more troubling to him. The prospect of being initiated into the mysteries of sex came when his friend Potsie (Anson Williams) arranged for Richie to meet a young woman who was reputed to "go all the way."

Richie visited Mary Lou Milligan at her baby-sitting job looking, as described in the script notes, "as nervous as a kid awaiting his first visit to the brothel." Having screwed up his courage for the seduction attempt, Richie promptly got his hand entangled in Mary Lou's brassiere. Upset, Mary Lou repelled Richie's advances and scolded him for such effrontery. Richie tried to defend himself by explaining that the word was out among the guys that Mary Lou welcomed all manner of sexual advances and that she had even come to expect as much on dates.

Mary Lou defended her virtue by recounting an incident of sexual harassment where a male gym teacher "tried to grab my bra." The gym teacher had told Mary Lou that "built" girls get "talked about" and, by implication, that they were more likely to be victims of sexual harassment as well. The stories that circulated about her promiscuity, said Mary Lou, did not bother her since there was nothing she could do to silence the rumors anyway. In keeping with the social conventions of the 1950s, Mary Lou Milligan accepted sexual harassment with resignation. Interestingly, Richie apologized to Mary Lou not for his unsolicited sexual advances but for his having believed the false tales of her promiscuity.

Having situated *Happy Days* in the "innocent" 1950s, the producers of a contemporary 1970s program were able to convey, without challenge, condescending and even openly antagonistic attitudes toward women and other social subordinates. The 1950s setting of *Happy Days* offered refuge for obsolete social thought. The shield of the nostalgic past allowed such eternal verities as there being "two kinds of girls—those you marry and those who go all the way"— to be uttered without a trace of self-consciousness. There was, however, an element of opposition and antagonism in the character of Arthur Fonzarelli (Henry Winkler), better known as "Fonzie" or simply "The Fonz." The role of the Fonz was at first meant to support that of Richie Cunningham. Fonzie was a "greaser" type who complemented Richie's squeeky clean image. The Fonz's outsider status, however, was revised after the viewing public took him to heart. Once Fonzie moved in with the Cunninghams, it was only a matter of time before he came to represent the wholesome goodness originally intended for Richie Cunningham.

BLOOD BROTHERS

At its best, the use of past history as a distancing device in drama enables contemporary social realities to be placed into sharp relief. The film *American Graffiti* (1973), which *Happy Days* resembled, demonstrated the aesthetic effectiveness and truth of understanding the present through the lived experience of the past. At its worst, the historical revisionism of programs like *Happy Days* and *Laverne & Shirley* helped to perpetuate regressive social ideologies. Sexism, ethnic stereotypes, and social inequality—all of which were challenged by the activist climate of the 1960s—were kept intact by the surface style of 1950s culture. The television situation comedy, however, is not inherently incapable of articulating the lived connection between past and present history. The enormously successful program *M*A*S*H* (September 17, 1972, to September 19, 1983) showed how historical distance and irony could be employed to comment on the society that waged war in Vietnam.

The singular role of race and racism in American society was examined directly in a *M*A*S*H* episode written in 1973 by Larry Gelbart and Laurence Marks.[65] The story centered on a career soldier by the name of Condon, who was to receive a blood transfusion. Condon informed surgeon Hawkeye Pierce (Alan Alda) that he was concerned about the possibility of receiving blood from a black donor. Condon said to an incredulous Hawkeye that he "wouldn't want any of that darkie stuff." Hawkeye and his colleague Trapper John (Wayne Rogers) played a prank on Condon by swabbing his face, as he slept, with iodine to darken his skin.

A black nurse was brought in on the gag. She teased the now "black" Condon about his trying to "pass" for white. "They got you down as 'white,' " said the nurse, Ginger. "Good work, baby." A short while later, Trapper stopped by Condon's bed to extend the prank a bit more by offering his patient a meal of fried chicken and watermelon. The serious moral message of the episode was stated in a bedside conversation:

CONDON: (desperately) What're you guys doing to me? D'you give me the right color blood or not?

TRAPPER: All blood is the same.

HAWKEYE: Ever hear of Dr. Charles Drew, soldier?

CONDON: Who's that?

HAWKEYE: Dr. Charles Drew is the man who invented the process for separating blood so it could be stored.

TRAPPER: Plasma.

HAWKEYE: Dr. Drew died last April in a car accident.

TRAPPER: He bled to death because the hospital wouldn't take him in.

HAWKEYE: It was for whites only.

As in the above example, the use of irony in *M*A*S*H* often had a critical edge to it that was sometimes lost amid the chaos of the battlefield setting. The dialogue moved quickly from topic to topic. It was urgent, hurried, lucidly manic, and as incisive as operating room procedure. This had the effect of hiding or at least disguising politically offensive jokes among ordinary banter and less sensitive gags.

Throwaway pieces of information were also inserted into the text to provide oblique commentary on the American presence in Southeast Asia. A news broad-cast that Dwight D. Eisenhower and running mate Richard M. Nixon had just been nominated for office at the Republican National Convention not only sup-plied a heightened sense of contemporaneity to the episode, but had the effect of establishing the historical and political continuity between the Eisenhower (1953–61) and Nixon (1969–74) administrations in the conduct of the Cold War.

While *M*A*S*H* did take a few game pokes the American war machine, by the time the show appeared in 1972 public opinion was already mobilized against continued U.S. involvement in Vietnam. As early as 1968, Richard Nixon's presidential campaign promise of achieving "peace with honor" found a recep-tive audience among the electorate. By the year 1968, the major television networks and national news publications had with greater frequency begun to depict the Vietnam war effort in a negative light.[66] The 1972 reelection campaign of President Nixon further capitalized on the desire of the American public to end the Vietnam debacle. By September of 1972, about the time of *M*A*S*H's* debut on television, Nixon had reduced the number of American combat troops in Vietnam from a high of 543,000 to 39,000.[67] *M*A*S*H*, rather than mobilizing antiwar opposition, merely reflected the prevailing national mood against the U.S. presence in Vietnam.

SNOW IN THE PICTURE

The social and cultural revolution of the 1960s placed issues of equality and personal autonomy high on the social agenda. Overt forms of discrimination were given legal and legislative remedy; equality of opportunity as an ideal of social justice gained institutional legitimacy, and the federal government ex-panded its role by creating social welfare programs that eased the more serious symptoms of a political economy in permanent crisis.[68] Television situation comedy of the 1970s—albeit fitfully and incompletely—assimilated the mo-mentous sociocultural changes that took place in the previous decade, all within the framework of the liberal pluralist paradigm of power in society.

The ethnic situation comedy, redolent of liberal democratic rhetoric, extended a spurious equality to all peoples. Through the symbolic embourgeoisement of ethnic peoples, especially blacks, the television sitcom achieved symbolically what had not yet been fully achieved politically. The proliferation of ethnic situation comedies of the 1970s, like the liberal reforms wrought by the expanded corpus of civil rights law during the 1960s, offered a "credible measure of tangible progress without in any way disturbing the basic class structure."[69] In the linked relationship of both the symbolic and the political, the structural contradictions that placed the 1970s ethnicoms in such stark contrast to the sitcoms that preceded them went unmentioned. The unprecedented accommo-dative strategies of both civil rights legislation and ethnicoms breathed new life into a seriously ailing liberal state gasping for a revived legitimacy that could promise, under vastly changed circumstances, to restore it to health once more.

NOTES

1. J. Fred MacDonald, *Blacks and White TV: Afro-Americans in Television Since 1948* (Chicago: Nelson-Hall, 1983), p. 156.

2. E. U. Essien-Udon, *Black Nationalism: A Search for an Identity in America* (New York: Dell, 1964), p. 140.

3. Kenneth B. Clark, *Dark Ghetto: Dilemmas of Social Power* (New York: Harper & Row, 1967), p. 12.

4. For quantative data pertaining to the viewing patterns of blacks and the urban poor, see Bradley S. Greenberg and Brenda Dervin, *Use of the Mass Media by the Urban Poor: Findings of Three Research Projects, with an Annotated Bibliography* (New York: Praeger, 1970), pp. 12, 116.

5. Leo Bogart, "Negro and White Media Exposure: New Evidence," *Journalism Quarterly* 44 (1972): 15–21.

6. Robert T. Bower, *Television and the Public* (New York: Holt, Rinehart and Winston, 1973), p. 181.

7. U.S. National Advisory Commission on Civil Disorders, *Report of the National Advisory Commission on Civil Disorders* (Washington, D.C.: U.S. Government Printing Office, 1968), p. 92.

8. Max Hastings, *The Fire This Time: America's Year of Crisis* (New York: Taplinger, 1969), pp. 145–146.

9. Harvard Sitkoff, "The Preconditions for Racial Change," in *A History of Our Times: Readings on Postwar America,* ed. William H. Chafe and Harvard Sitkoff (New York: Oxford University Press, 1983), p. 123.

10. Roger Daniels and Harry H. L. Kitano, *American Racism: Exploration of the Nature of Prejudice* (Englewood Cliffs, N.J.: Prentice-Hall, 1970), p. 119.

11. Joseph R. Dominick and Bradley S. Greenberg, "Three Seasons of Blacks on Television," *Journal of Advertising Research* 10 (1970): 21–27.

12. Art Peters, "What the Negro Wants from TV," *TV Guide: The First 25 Years,* ed. Jay S. Harris (New York: New American Library, 1980), p. 141.

13. Ibid., p. 141.

14. "For the 1967 and 1968 seasons, data showed that most (Negro actors) wore 'white' clothes and used 'white' language. References to race or racial topics actually decreased during prime time from 1967 to the current season. These data suggest that Negro actors, especially in nighttime drama, are in roles that could be interchanged with white actors." Dominick and Greenberg, p. 27.

15. Robert Lewis Shayon, "Changes," *Saturday Review* 53 (April 1970): 46.

16. "Julia's Man," written and directed by Hal Kanter, created and produced by Hal Kanter, associate producer Bernard Wiesen, n.d.

17. In the case of children, identification with character overrides the ethnic factor in television portrayals. See Bradley S. Greenberg, "Children's Reaction to TV Blacks, *Journalism Quarterly* 49 (1972): 5–14.

18. H. Roy Kaplan, ed., p. 17.

19. Les Brown, *Television: The Business Behind the Box* (New York: Harcourt Brace Jovanovich, 1971), p. 79.

20. *The Courtship of Eddie's Father,* written by James Komack. Director Ralph Senensky. Copyright 1969, MGM Television. Based on a novel by Mark Toby. A film version was directed by Vincente Minnelli (1963). In the film, Mrs. Livingston is white.

21. On the spurious use of the concept of "race" as an explanatory concept, see Ashley Montagu, *Man's Most Dangerous Myth: The Fallacy of Race,* 5th ed. (New York: Oxford University Press, 1974).

22. The "model minority" thesis is found in William Petersen, *Japanese Americans: Oppression and Success* (New York: Random House, 1971). For an an updated version of this interpretation including other "model" minorities, see Thomas Sowell, *Ethnic America: A History* (New York: Basic Books, 1981), pp. 133–179.

23. The persistence of anti-Asian sentiment in television is seen, ironically enough, in the overrepresentation of Asian-American females as both newscasters and as exotic objects of desire in commercials. Their male counterparts do not enjoy the same degree of media exposure.

24. Bennett Harrison, *Education, Training, and the Urban Ghetto* (Baltimore: Johns Hopkins University Press, 1972), p. 68.

25. The concept for *Room 222* is attributed to writer Allan Burns, who has extensive credits on many other situation comedies. The consistency of liberal ideological purport is in part due to the circulation of cultural workmen, such as Burns, within the industry.

26. "Man, If You're So Smart.. . ." Written by Martin Donovan, produced by Jon Kubichan, executive producer Wm. P. D'Angelo. Final script dated December 1, 1972. Twentieth Century-Fox Television.

27. Joseph Bensman and Arthur J. Vidich, *American Society: The Welfare State and Beyond*, rev. ed. (South Hadley, Massachusetts: Bergin & Garvey, 1987), pp. 313–322.

28. See Edward C. Banfield, *The Unheavenly City Revisited* (Boston: Little, Brown & Co., 1974), pp. 148–178.

29. Charles Murray, *Losing Ground: American Social Policy 1950–1980* (New York: Basic Books, 1984), pp. 73, 98.

30. Martin Mayer, *About Television* (New York: Harper & Row, 1972), p. 86.

31. Cedric C. Clark, "Television and Social Controls: Some Observations on the Portrayals of Ethnic Minorities," *Television Quarterly* 8 (1969): 18–22.

32. Churchill Roberts, "The Portrayal of Blacks on Network Television," *Journal of Broadcasting* 15 (1970–1971): 50.

33. James L. Hinton et al., "Tokenism and Improving Imagery of Blacks in TV Drama and Comedy: 1975," *Journal of Broadcasting* 18 (1974): 431.

34. Directed by Michael Zinberg, produced by Glen Charles and Les Charles, story editor Mark C. Tinker, executive producer Michael Zinberg. Production #7056, 1977.

35. Jonathan H. Turner and David Musick, *American Dilemmas: A Sociological Interpretation of Enduring Social Issues* (New York: Columbia University Press, 1985), p. 54.

36. Paul Blumberg, *Inequality in an Age of Decline* (New York: Oxford University Press, 1980), p. 211.

37. Richard P. Adler, ed. *All in the Family: A Critical Appraisal* (New York: Praeger, 1979), p. xxxix.

38. Kenneth M. Dolbeare and Patricia Dolbeare (1976), pp. 24–25.

39. Norman L. Friedman, "Responses of Blacks and Other Minorities to Television Shows of the 1970s about Their Groups," *Journal of Popular Film and Television* 7 (1978): 97.

40. Mick Eaton, "Television Situation Comedy," in *Popular Television and Film,* ed. Tony Bennett et al. (London: British Film Institute, 1981), p. 42.

41. John Dart, "Norman Lear Leads a Battle Against Politicking by the Religious Right," *Los Angeles Times,* October 27, 1984, pt. II, p. 20.

42. While denying a redress of historical inequalities through the use of racial quotas, the *Bakke* decision upheld the principle that race, among other factors, should be considered in the admissions procedures of federally assisted institutions. See Philip Green, *The Pursuit of Inequality* (New York: Pantheon Books, 1981), pp. 168–169.

43. Norman Lear, "Dialogue on Film," *American Film: Journal of the Film and Television Arts* 2 (June 1977): 33–48.

44. For a discussion of production costs and their relationship to syndication practices, see Martin H. Seiden, *Who Controls the Mass Media? Popular Myths and Economic Realities* (New York: Basic Books, 1974), pp. 168–171. More recently, see Michael Botein and David M. Rice, eds. *Network Television and the Public Interest: A Preliminary Inquiry* (Lexington, Mass.: D. C. Heath & Co., 1980).

45. Joe R. Feagin, *Subordinating the Poor* (Englewood Cliffs, N.J.: Prentice-Hall, 1975), p. 97.

46. *Good Times* episode written by Jon Dunley and Kurt Taylor, produced by Allan Manings, developed by Norman Lear, created by Eric Monty and Mike Evans.

47. Marlene G. Fine, Carolyn Anderson, and Gary Eckles, "Black English on Black Situation Comedies," *Journal of Communication,* 29 (1979): 27.

48. William Appleman Williams, p. 442.

49. For differing interpretations of the rationale and efficacy of Great Society social welfare programs, see Frances Fox Piven and Richard A. Cloward, *Regulating the Poor: The Functions of Public Welfare* (New York: Vintage Books, 1971); Michael Harrington, *The Twilight of Capitalism* (New York: Touchstone, 1976); Daniel P. Moynihan, *Maximum Feasible Misunderstanding: Community Action in the War on Poverty* (New York: Free Press, 1969).

50. *The Jeffersons.* Executive producers, Jay Moriarty and Mike Milligan, developed by Norman Lear, directed by Bob Lally.

51. Peter Schrag, *The Decline of the WASP* (New York: Simon & Schuster, 1971), pp. 131–132.

52. Patricia C. Donagher et al., "Race, Sex and Social Example: An Analysis of Character Portrayals on Inter-racial Television Entertainment," *Psychological Reports* 37 (1975): 1032.

53. See Irvin G. Wyllie, *The Self-Made Man in America: The Myth of Rags to Riches* (New York: Free Press, 1966).

54. See Sara Evans, *Personal Politics: The Roots of Women's Liberation in the Civil Rights Movement of the New Left* (New York: Vintage Books, 1980).

55. Nora Ephron, "A Fond Farewell to the Finest, Funniest Show on Television," *Esquire* 87 (February 1977): 74.

56. Burton Yale Pines, *Back to Basics: The Traditionalist Movement That Is Sweeping Grass-Roots America* (New York: William Morrow & Co., 1982), pp. 130–154.

57. Serafina Bathrick, *"The Mary Tyler Moore Show:* Women at Home at Work," in *MTM 'Quality Television,'* ed. Jane Feuer, Paul Kerr, and Tise Vahimagi (London: BFI Publishing, 1984), p. 100.

58. The notions of hegemony and counterhegemony are of course derived from Gramsci. For an incisive explication of an updating of this fruitful concept, see Carl Boggs, *Social Movements and Political Power: Emerging Forms of Radicalism in the West* (Philadelphia: Temple University Press, 1986), pp. 242–247.

59. *The Mary Tyler Moore Show.* Premiere, September 19, 1970. Written by James L. Brooks and Allan Burns, directed by Jay Sandrich.

60. Peter L. Berger, "Western Individuality: Liberation and Loneliness," *Partisan Review*, 52 (1985): 326.

61. Landon Y. Jones, *Great Expectations: America and the Baby Boom Generation* (New York: Coward, McCann & Geoghegan, 1980), p. 246.

62. Marc Eliot, *Televisions: One Season in American Television* (New York: St. Martin's Press, 1983), p. 100.

63. *The Happy Days*, revised pilot script dated October 15, 1973. Created and written by Garry Marshall. A Miller-Milkis Production.

64. The script notes for *Happy Days* are invaluable in uncovering the ideological biases of its creators. In one such note, Richie's mother Marion (Marion Ross) was described as having a mentality that predated "woman's [*sic*] lib."

65. "Dear Dad. . .Three." Revised final script dated September 24, 1973. Written by Larry Gelbart and Laurence Marks. Twentieth Century-Fox Television.

66. Peter Braestrup, *Big Story: How the American Press and Television Reported and Interpreted the Crisis of Tet in Vietnam and Washington* (Garden City, N.Y.: Anchor Books, 1978), pp. 464–507.

67. William E. Leuchtenburg, *A Troubled Feast: American Society Since 1945* (Boston: Little, Brown & Co., 1973), p. 230.

68. See Marshall Kaplan and Peggy L. Cuciti, eds. *The Great Society and Its Legacy: Twenty Years of U.S. Social Policy* (Durham: Duke University Press, 1986), pp. 216–217.

69. Alan D. Freeman, "Antidiscrimination Law: A Critical Review," in *The Politics of Law: A Progressive Critique*, ed. David Kairys (New York: Pantheon Books, 1982), p. 110.

5
Neoconservative Death Valley Days

CONTRADICTORY SITUATIONS

Barely articulated principles of exchange, reciprocity, and larger questions of social justice help to compose the content of the television situation comedy. What is presumed to be right, fair, and just in a liberal democratic society is negotiated and brought to partial resolution within each 30-minute moral, ethical, hence political, contest. The special attraction of the television situation comedy for its large and demographically diverse audience are the inventive ways in which old and new questions of equity are framed and then decided upon, all within a highly formulaic format. As a site for the symbolic "negotiation and exchange between classes and social groups," the television situation comedy thus conceived cannot help but reveal the paradoxes and contradictions of the larger society.[1] Conflict inheres in the sitcom because infinite equity decisions constitute the material processes of social life itself.

What follows is a necessarily abbreviated survey of selected television situation comedies from the point in time when the sitcom first began to address, perhaps obliquely, questions of equity posed by the neoconservative political and cultural agenda set during the late 1970s. The present discussion extends to the second-term presidency of Ronald Reagan, which succeeded fairly well in placing government at the service of corporate oligopolies and wealthy individuals. Of special interest here are those groups—women, children, the elderly, minorities—who most acutely suffered from the contradiction between the logic of capitalism, which posits profit maximization as its summum bonum, and the humanist principles that lie at the core of liberal democracy.[2] Also given extended discussion are the twin questions of recent immigration and the internationalization of production, both of which have brought to the fore a new set of contradictions to be symbolically, if not politically, mediated.

The term "neoconservatism," while admittedly nebulous, is nonetheless based on certain tenets that distinguish it from other ideologies on the liberal/conservative continuum. At the risk of glossing over the more subtle distinctions and variants of neoconservative thought, it can be safely stated that the neoconservative critique assumes a crisis of authority in government and social institutions, crises in culture and values, and sheer governmental "overload."[3] The situation comedy, if it is true to its defining aesthetic characteristics of contemporaneity and realism, partially reveals the ongoing "legitimation crises" sustained by the structures of power in advanced capitalist society.[4]

FROM ME TO MEAN DECADE

By the latter part of the 1970s, an axial assumption of postwar American liberal democratic ideology—that American capitalism had found the secret of sustained economic growth—was severely shaken. Given, however, the dynamism of the American economy between the years 1945 and 1970, this heady optimism seemed justified. Average family income, for example, more than doubled during these years of plenty. Closely related to the assumption of ever-expanding economic growth was the notion that deep-seated social contradictions of advanced capitalism would be minimized if not eliminated due to the increased size of the economic pie.[5]

With the slowing of national economic growth accompanied by high rates of inflation and unemployment, television situation comedies had to grapple with the dilemma of lowered expectations and economic retrenchment while preserving the accustomed high level of consumption that fueled postwar American economic growth. Programs as diverse as *One Day at a Time* (December 16, 1975, to September 2, 1984), *Alice* (August 31, 1976, to January 16, 1985), *Angie* (February 8, 1979, to October 2, 1980), *Taxi* (September 12, 1978, to July 27, 1983), *Three's Company* (March 15, 1977, to September 18, 1984), and even *Diff'rent Strokes* (November 3, 1978, to August 30, 1986) conveyed to varying degrees the widespread sense of falling expectations but without an observable drop-off in material comfort. Instead, as material expectations fell, the salience of "socially relevant" themes in the television situation comedy as seen in the 1970s gave way to the micropolitics of intimacy.

The symbolic resolution of dilemmas inherent in interpersonal relations have long been the signal strength of the television situation comedy. As such, the sitcom has been well-suited to the dramatic elaboration of the contemporary American "emphasis on the details involved within the management of interpersonal relations."[6] If macroeconomic events were beyond all comprehension and personal control, then at least a certain measure of solace, security, and autonomy might be found at the level of interpersonal relations revolving around domestic life. In the situation comedy, sociopolitical contradictions become transcoded into personal problems.

Both *One Day at a Time* and *Alice* concerned the lives of female single parents raising children during tough economic times. *Taxi* featured a ragtag and bobtail group of outcasts including an aspiring actor, a burnt-out acid head from the 1960s, a would-be boxer, a foreign-born mechanic of undetermined nationality, and part-time art dealer. In both *Angie* and *Diff'rent Strokes,* the central characters were fantastically rescued from less than affluent circumstances by their social betters. Angie Benson, nee Falco (Donna Pescow), had incredible luck in latching onto a handsome physician, from a prominent Philadelphia blueblood family, no less.

In *Diff'rent Strokes,* Arnold (Gary Coleman) and Willis Jackson (Todd Bridges) were two black brothers (i.e. blood relations) plucked off the streets of Harlem to live in the posh apartment of a middle-aged white millionaire, Philip Drummond (Conrad Bain). In an act of noblesse oblige, Drummond took in the orphaned sons of his deceased housekeeper, proving perhaps that the rich are not without feelings, even toward members of the black underclass. As a newly constituted family, together they confronted issues of discrimination, racism, class conflict, and other, more mundane problems of late childhood and early adolescence.

In one episode, a friend of their stepsister Kimberly (Dana Plato) proved to be a budding racist and was taught a lesson for her intolerance. In another episode, Willis threatened to sue his school for "reverse discrimination" when a white student with less talent was picked for the basketball team over Willis in order to achieve racial balance. Willis's girlfriend pointed out, however, that the "brothers" were equally guilty of discrimination when they froze out the white guys in pick-up games on the playground. Willis reconsidered his intention to press the issue once he decided that discrimination was strictly a personal matter, practiced only by people with "closed minds." In this incident as in most situation comedy, structured social inequality took on the guise of individual failing and frailty alone.

Three's Company flirted with incest taboos by bringing two attractive young women and an aspiring male chef together in a single household. This "family" of unrelated adults of mixed gender was formed out of economic necessity, since none of them could alone afford the fashionable apartment they kept. Jack Tripper (John Ritter) had to pretend he was gay so as not to rouse the suspicion of their prying landlords and disapproving parents. The show's premise made for a humorous clash of contradictory values pertaining to the family as at once a reproductive and economic institution. *Three's Company* in its way seemed almost a swan song of sorts for the classic American nuclear family, the likes of which were celebrated in such vintage programs as *Leave It to Beaver* or *The Donna Reed Show*. Beyond the high "jiggle" quotient of *Three's Company* (which drew the ire of not a few opinion leaders both religious and secular), the show gave teasingly belated recognition to the widespread practice of cohabitation, a family form at odds with the traditional model of domestic organization.

The loss of confidence in America as postwar world economic leader was even seen in *The Facts of Life* (August 24, 1979, to present). Although the program was set at the exclusive Eastland School, a girl's prep school, even these students were not unaware of larger macroeconomic trends. In a telling peripheral conversation with their housemother Mrs. Garrett (Charlotte Rae), these bright scions of the corporate and managerial elite expressed the growing sentiment that American economic dominance could no longer be simply assumed:

MOLLY: Mrs. Garrett, I don't think we should buy a Yamaguchi stereo. If we don't start buying *American* products, our economy is going into the toilet.

MRS. GARRETT: Delicately put, Molly.

TOOTIE: Molly, Yamaguchi *is* an American company.

NATALIE: Yeah, they gave it a Japanese name so people would have more confidence in the quality.[7]

Implicit in the foregoing dialogue was a perceptive critique of the sorry state of American business moving into the 1980s and a surprisingly sophisticated understanding of the rapid internationalization of the economy.

Like *Three's Company,* the surrogate family in *The Facts of Life* was formed out of economic necessity, albeit that of the upper class. The girls' forced separation from their families and the creation of their tightly knit unit offered them a slightly eccentric view of society that was both critical and imbued with the spirit of skepticism, two potentially subversive components of comedy. Even so, the legitimacy of the girls' social class advantage was sometimes seen as problematic. In a December 1986 episode, Blair Warner's (Lisa Whelchel) father was accused of stock market fraud, this coming on the heels of the Wall Street insider-trading scandals.

TUBE OF SCARCITY

The television industry has functioned as one of the central legitimating institutions in the politics of postwar plentitude. Television and the allied advertising industry were indispensable to the stoking of ceaseless consumer demand, which industry gladly satisfied with a parade of the latest, new and improved consumer items. The complementary relationship between television and advertising is clear: Television accounted for only 3 percent of advertising volume in 1950, totaling $171 million. But by the year 1984, this figure rose to over $15 billion as the percentage of television advertising came to constitute 22 percent of total advertising expenditures.[8]

So long as the economic system provided for the material needs of most

Americans, the legitimacy of the liberal democratic consumerist social order would remain relatively intact.[9] If American industry could only deliver what the tube of plenty promised, then a high degree of political consensus could be maintained. Deteriorating economic conditions throughout the 1970s, however, spurred a rethinking of the ideological premises that undergird postwar American society. Although better protected than the poor or blue collar workers, even the middle class was not immune from the most bedeviling array of economic ills to befall America since the Great Depression. The dilemma of rising middle-class expectations in the midst of economic malaise led to a conservative reaction calling for "more modest expectations and a return to traditional values."[10]

The downsizing of the American Dream during the 1970s was articulated by the new rhetoric of "scarcity," which in essence advanced a "moral argument for the decline of real wages and the deterioration of the quality of everyday life."[11] The politics of scarcity tended to blame the individual for wastefulness, excessive wants, and a general lack of self-restraint. Unmentioned went the structural and institutional causes of economic malaise, including the existence of corporate oligopolies, public subsidy of private profit taking, a massive defense and aerospace budget, and international noncompetitiveness due to the ill-advised protection of domestic markets.

Neither the caretaker presidency of Gerald Ford nor the moralistic drift of the Carter administration could shake America out of its economic doldrums. By the time Ronald Reagan was elected in 1980 to the most important role of his public career, the rate of inflation stood at 12 percent, the prime rate soared to 15½ percent, and real wages declined by 3 percent over a span of only twelve months.[12] In 1980, the unemployment rate exceeded 7 percent, rising steadily over the next three recessionary years to a postwar high of almost 11 percent. In 1981, the federal deficit reached $1 trillion for the first time, causing conservative ideologues to call for massive cuts in social spending to balance the budget. The "balanced-budget ideology" helped justify reducing the tax liability of corporations and higher income households thereby shifting the burden of a weak economy to the poor and the working class by cutting back income-maintenance programs.[13]

For those voters who supported him in the presidential election of 1980, Ronald Reagan held promise for the revitalization of America that went beyond politics, ranging into the realm of myth. The appeal of the Reagan promise lay in its ambitions to restore America to its former economic and military glory. While President Reagan invoked timeworn but effective verities about the minimal state, excessive government interference, and a no-nonsense foreign policy, his protective helpmate Nancy drew attention to problems of the family and the local community that could be solved ("Just Say No") without tapping into public funds.

Politically, the "Reagan Revolution" had a direct social impact through its substantial reduction of corporate and personal income taxes, cutbacks in social welfare spending, and increase in defense spending as part of the largest military buildup since the Vietnam War era.[14] Even adjusted for inflation, from 1982 to 1984 those earning less than $10,000 per year suffered a 22 percent increase in tax liability, while those earning over $200,000 saw their liability decrease an average of 15 percent.[15] The Reagan administration presided over the increased "privatization" of public services, the depression of the wage structure due to the de-unionization of the work force, and the erosion of hard-won individual rights and legal protections.[16]

THIS IS LIVING?

It was perhaps fitting that on the eve of Ronald Reagan's election to the presidency the disadvantaged condition of the female American worker found expression in the sardonically titled *It's a Living* (October 30, 1980 to present). Despite increased media attention given the handful of white middle-class women who managed to defy all odds by making it to the top of the corporate hierarchy, the fact remained that women "hold the dubious distintion of having made the least progress in the labor market."[17] The waitresses seen in *It's a Living* certainly bore out this observation. Not only were they held down by sex role stereotypes, but they were oppressed by the rule of law as well. When a male "waitress" sued the restaurant for sex discrimination after a woman is hired for an advertised position, the all-female crew was shown to be victimized by the very social legislation designed to protect it.[18]

Jan Hoffmeyer (Barrie Youngfellow) expressed the collective anger of the waitresses over the inequity of the system: ". . .for years men have been exploiting women. Making us take menial, low paying jobs.. . .Now they're making us *share* them." Jan Hoffmeyer was an intelligent woman who by her own description "almost graduated from law school." Her professional ambitions and training gave Jan an objective understanding of her subordination not only in the workplace but in larger society as well. It was usually Jan who acted as the catalyst for the changes that took place in the workplace, which benefited the waitresses as a group. It was usually Jan who resisted the arbitrary dictates of hostess and manager Nancy Beebe (Marian Mercer), and it was Jan who delivered the most cutting verbal swipes at the sexually predatory lounge singer Sonny Mann (Paul Kreppel).

At bottom, the waitresses in *It's a Living* were "wanna-bes." Although they worked in a classy restaurant located in a high-rise hotel in downtown Los Angeles, each of them had career aspirations that out of necessity had been placed on hold. There was great poignancy in the realization that chances were, unlike for Mary Richards, these contemporary women were not "gonna make it after all." Substantive reasons—such as the persistence of an inherently unequal dual labor market despite Title VII of the Civil Rights Act—for their inability to achieve individual career goals were not explored to any extent. Rather, they were shown to be held back by a laundry list of gender-specific personal failings, including excessive concern with romance and sexual gratification, a preoccupation with "relationships," falling prey to the lures of consumerism, and being controlled by personal obsessions or bad personal habits.

The futility and despair of the struggling waitresses in *It's a Living* as they ministered to the needs of wealthy customers were made somewhat more tolerable by the bonds of closeness they formed out of their common labor. The individual search for self-fulfillment and personal intimacy among the waitresses kept them in bondage, yet it gave the collectivity strength enough to resist complete dehumanization at the hands of the institution and its management. Not until the appearance of such Monday evening "lady's night" programs as *Kate & Allie, My Sister Sam, Valerie,* and *Designing Women,* were the traditionally female virtues of intimacy and nurturirng more fully reconciled with the pursuit of careers, professional life, and personal autonomy beyond the family.

FASCINATING SISTERHOOD

Although the equality revolution of the 1960s set women free as economic actors in the grand marketplace of life, it also had negative consequences for the American family, chief among them being the "feminization of poverty."[19] Despite the growing economic distress of female-headed households over the past fifteen years, this fact of contemporary life had only partly made its way into situation comedies that revolved around domestic life. Aspects of *Mama's Family* only hinted at the problem of economic inequality based on gender, while in *Kate & Allie* a female-headed family was seen as one of the trade-offs in the quest for selfhood. In *My Sister Sam, Valerie,* and *Designing Women,* the absence of spousal support in the household seemed to have actually benefited the careers of the central female characters in each of these shows, but not without twinges of guilt or remorse.

Thelma Harper (Vicki Lawrence) in *Mama's Family* was the feisty resigning matriarch of a midwestern family living in a small community, Raytown.[20] Her helpless son Vint (Ken Barry) was often caught in the periodic strife that broke out between his mother Thelma and his wife Naomi (Dorothy Lyman), who held an outside job as a cashier at Food Circus. Completing the household was Thelma's grandson Bubba (Allan Kayser). Bubba was only slightly less competent than his uncle Vint, having even spent time in juvenile hall. Although Vint earned a modest but steady income as a locksmith, it was Mama Harper who made the important decisions for the family, usually after having done battle with Naomi.

Kate McArdle (Susan Saint James) and Allie Lowell (Jane Curtin) were 1960s parents of 1980s teenagers who lived *en famille* in a Greenwich Village apartment.[21] Beyond the stock intergenerational misunderstandings between parents and children, *Kate & Allie* was a highly original portrait of a radically restructured family unit that would have been unthinkable until recently. Unlike many female-headed families, however, Kate and Allie seemed fairly able to provide for their children without experiencing undue hardship. Their former husbands, absent from the home because of divorce, were mentioned often enough to imply continued financial support of this composite family.

Kate & Allie also dramatized the uneasy truce between the progressive politics and culture of the 1960s and the difficult social and economic realities that characterized the conservative reaction of the 1980s. While Kate and Allie found themselves having difficulty in adapting to a changed social landscape, the personal values of the two were often also in opposition. The patrician, security-minded Allie, for example, had been married to a physician in residency, while the free-spirited Kate married and subsequently divorced a struggling actor. The intragenerational clash of values between Kate and Allie was given expression in a flashback when, as expectant mothers in the 1960s, Kate and Allie discussed prospective names for their children. For Allie, the baby was to be named Brooks if a boy. If a girl, her name was to be Tiffany. By contrast, Kate selected the names Che or Angela for her child:

ALLIE: Che? What kind of name is Che?''

KATE: Che Guevara; Angela Davis.

ALLIE: You're naming your children after communists?

KATE: You're naming your children after stores.

By the time the mean 1980s arrived, Kate and Allie both had to adapt to changed objective circumstances. Although the promise of complete financial security eluded Allie and the dream of unbounded personal freedom dimmed for Kate, they each managed to gain a small measure of both by benefit of their blended family unit that had no permanent adult male presence. By its fourth season on television, both Kate and Allie continued to suffer mild setbacks in matters of the heart. But they had at least achieved a modest level of autonomy through the catering service they operated out of their crowded but happy home.

COTTAGE INDUSTRY

While the declining economy forced the movement of more women into the labor force, their unpaid domestic responsibilities, which included the rearing of children, did not decline proportionately.[22] The twin pull of career and domestic work often led to the so-called superwoman syndrome and even forced many female fast-track corporate professionals out of the running entirely. One of the ways in which the situation comedy tried to mediate the contradiction between the economic necessity of having two income earners per household and the persistence of female noncompensated household production (estimated at 44 percent of the GNP) was to portray women engaged at fulfilling careers in the home.[23]

The conflation of home and work place in television situation comedy programs made for the illusion of women capable of earning independent incomes without ever having to leave the home. This allowed women, symbolically at least, to retain the more gratifying aspects of parental and domestic activity while escaping the rigors of corporate life. The cottage industry image also stirred memories of the romance of precapitalist forms of productive autonomy. In this idealized vision of organic society, the self-sufficient professional portrayed on television was most often engaged in a "clean" occupation that was not harmful and perhaps even beneficial to society.

One such mother/professional was Valerie Hogan in the eponymous *Valerie*. "I was a good mother. I repressed my own competitive drive in favor of your emotional development," said Valerie (Valerie Harper) to her two teenage sons over a hotly contested game of Trivial Pursuit.[24] Unlike TV moms of times past, Valerie projected a strong sense of self that included, but was not necessarily restricted to, tending to the needs of her family. Her career as a free-lance designer allowed Valerie to spend a good deal of time at home, while her husband (a pilot) was usually gone. This clever premise allowed the program to play with problems of the single-parent household without risking the financial stability that comes with a second paycheck.

Having lived through the rights revolution of the 1960s, Valerie as a parent was now faced with having to mediate intergenerational clashes of values. While she tried hard to raise her son David as a sensitive, caring individual, Valerie was disturbed that his preferences in girlfriends did not reflect her own values. As Valerie's friend Barbara expressed it, "You may have tried to raise a Phil Donahue, but you ended up with a David Lee Roth."

David, however, surprised his mother and reaffirmed her values by dating a young woman, not particularly attractive, who showed an interest in the music of the sixties and was of an intellectual bent. In this episode, the positive legacy of 1960s feminism (and its critique of sexism in society) scored a victory over the resurgence of the traditional, ideologically conservative concept of femininity and womanhood at a time when "female competition for two scarce resources—men and jobs—is especially fierce."[25]

Like *Kate and Allie* and Valerie Hogan, (and the Sugarbaker sisters in *Designing Women*), Samantha Russell (Pam Dawber) in *My Sister Sam* also owned and operated a successful cottage industry out of her loft located in the city of San Francisco. With the help of friends, co-workers, and her high-school age sister Patti (Rebecca Schaeffer), Sam's commercial photography studio operated as a thriving business. But as the sole proprietor of Russell Studios, Sam had neither time enough nor opportunity to sustain a romance which would, presumably, complete her otherwise fulfilling life.

Strongly implied by the program was the notion that Sam's professional advancement was achieved only through the sacrifice of interpersonal intimacy. That is, Sam's lack of a permanent male companion was the trade-off for her success. Her emotional vulnerability was demonstrated in an episode in which Sam was plunged into bitterness and despair after her boyfriend called an end to their two-year, dual time zone romance. After a whirlwind romance, Sam's boyfriend had wound up proposing to a woman he had known for only a week. Expressing her anger in the rhetoric more akin to a salesperson than that of a lover, Sam said, "I was the one who softened him up. I was the one who laid all the groundwork. And then some babe named Melody comes along and cashes in."

By this scenario, the politics of the equality revolution became secondary to, perhaps even the cause of, the emotional/monetary loss suffered by Samantha. If Sam had not been overly ambitious in pursuing her career, it was implied, then maybe her personal life would have been much happier. Thus the thrust of 1960s feminism—a social movement based on the premise of radical equality between men and women—was contained by the threat of being cut off from the real human need for intimacy and love.

In yet another episode, Jack Kincaid's (David Naughton) residual political activism was derided as an act of selfishness when Sam was made to perform his domestic chores while Jack followed his conscience locked in a jail cell.[26] After Sam rejected her supporting role in Jack's fight against land developers who wanted to raze a local ballpark, Jack conceded "I guess one guy can't make a difference any more." The show ended with Jack and Sam self-mockingly mouthing two well-known slogans of the 1960s: "Power to the People" and "Make Love Not War." With the shouting of the latter slogan, Jack withdrew his challenge to the power structure and decided he would rather make love and grabbed Sam. As in the other episode, the constraints of personal intimacy precluded sustained engagement with the broader society.

THEY'RE SO CUTE WHEN THEY'RE YOUNG

Attesting to the "success" of the conservative agenda, the Center on Budget and Policy Priorities reported in late 1986 that government reductions in 1979 of antipoverty programs resulted in a 30 percent rise in poverty among families with children.[27] Dismal economic conditions, the rising divorce rate, and persistent gender inequality dramatically increased the number of single-parent families, pushing approximately 13 million or "20 percent of all children" below the official poverty line.[28] The child poverty rate hit blacks and Hispanics especially hard. Almost half of all black children, 46.5 percent, and 39 percent of Hispanic chidren were classified as poor.[29]

While the situation comedies of the 1980s did not directly depict the squalid lives led by impoverished children, neither could programs wholly avoid portraying contingent social reality without risking severing their dialogical ties to the audience. Instead, the fact of child poverty was indirectly addressed by means of two strategies: (1) the absence of a second parent was "explained" by his or her loss through illness, injury, accidental death, or other unavoidable circumstances (*Gimme A Break, Who's the Boss?, Full House, Valerie's Family, Out of This World, My Two Dads*); (2) the idealization and romanticization of the family (*Silver Spoons, The Cosby Show, Family Ties, Growing Pains*). Also noteworthy for the sheer audacity of its paternalism were *Diff'rent Strokes* and *Webster*. Both shows were based on the implausible premise of parentless black children being rescued and raised by well-to-do white families.

At the other end of the age spectrum, the plight of older men and women facing poverty was, for the most part, finessed in programs such as *Me & Mrs. C, The Golden Girls, You Can't Take It with You, The Cavanaughs,* and *One Big Family*. Despite U.S. Census Bureau data that counted 8.7 percent of all men and 15 percent of all women 65 years old and over living below the official poverty level as of 1984, evidence of this growing trend was not directly reflected in recent sitcoms.[30] Instead, elderly persons in American society were usually depicted as having secure financial resources and rich emotional lives.

The campaign to reinstate the family as the primary provider of health care and welfare benefits to individuals was an important agenda item in the conservative reaction.[31] This change in public policy dictated the reduction of state-subsidized social services and income support programs that had grown as part of the "new politics" of the Great Society during the 1960s. The financial burden once assumed by the state now reverted to the family, placing tremendous pressure on an already besieged institution.

With the rise of the religious right and its move to revive the traditional family, *Love, Sidney* (October 28, 1981, to August 29, 1983) could not have appeared at a worse time. In the pilot for the series, *Sidney Shorr*, the main character played by Tony Randall, it was implied, was homosexual. The situation comedy version, however, was devoid of its sexual dynamic. Appeasement of both the gay lobby and the religious right by NBC turned an interesting premise into little more than a clever plot device that enabled Sidney Shorr to maintain a platonic relationship with an unmarried pregnant young actress, Laurie Morgan (Swoosie Kurtz)[32]

In keeping with the return to "conservative verities" in the 1980s, the neighborhood, the church, the family, and other "mediating groups" were increasingly called upon to cope with personal crises whose resolution had been to a large degree ceded to the welfare state in the postwar era.[33] The fall 1987 debut of *Mama's Boy* provided an opportunity to examine how one aspect of the conservative agenda translated into interpersonal conflict in want of symbolic resolution. In the inaugural episode of *Mama's Boy,* a successful columnist for a major metropolitan newspaper, Jake McCaskey (Bruce Weitz), was forced to take in his mother (Nancy Walker) after the death of her husband left her without any means of support.[34] Having to house his elderly but combative mother posed quite a problem for Jake, who was used to the independent, carefree life of a bachelor without family responsibilities.

Embarrassed by his mother's presence, Jake lied about living alone in a magazine interview given after he was nominated for a bachelor-of-the-year award. Jake was racked by guilt after his mother learned of his disavowal, especially since he had recently written a column about the injustices suffered by the aged in society. At the bachelor-of-the-year banquet, Jake confessed his sin of omission as he accepted the award. In his acceptance speech, Jake suggested that the definition of a "real man" in the age of scarcity be revised: "Well, it may be time for me—maybe for a lot of us—to redefine what a real man is.. . .A man can't turn his back on his family and remain a real man.. . .I live with my mother. And if that makes me a mama's boy, then it's a label I'll wear proudly, like the Medal of Honor."

In effect, the liberal democratic realist sociodrama *Mama's Boy* attempted to bridge the false division interposed between the private and public realms, a dichotomy inherent in liberal democratic thought.[35] In keeping with the neoconservative reinstatement of the family as principal caretaker and provider of services to the aged, *Mama's Boy* imperfectly reconciled the contradiction between the state as conservator of corporate profit (in the guise of reducing the federal deficit through cuts in social spending) and the private realm of the family, an institution whose well-being was less actively being ensured through government intervention than in times past.

EQUAL BUT SEPARATE

Not since *All in the Family* had a situation comedy so handily outstripped its competitors as *The Cosby Show*. *The Cosby Show* not only routinely captured half of the viewing audience, but it gained much critical acclaim as evidenced by its fifteen Emmy nominations and three Emmys awarded in September of 1986.[36] Bill Cosby had originally conceived of a show with less grandiose pretensions. Cosby was to have played the part of a janitor and his wife was to have been a construction worker.

Instead, Marcy Carsey and Tom Werner, two former NBC television executives who went into independent production, transformed Bill Cosby into Dr. Cliff Huxtable, a likeable upper-middle-class obstetrician and father of five children.[37] Completing the family was Clair Huxtable, played by Phylicia Ayers-Allen (later Phylicia Rashad). Her profession as an attorney pushed the combined household income of the Huxtables into a bracket much higher than that of most American families, black or white.

The Cosby Show, whose scripts were reviewed by Harvard professor of psychiatry Dr. Alvin Poussaint, was intended by Bill Cosby to educate and inform as well as to entertain. Program consultant Poussaint stated that "TV shapes the perception of Black kids who watch these shows." He was also aware of the potential of television to shape the "perception of White children who might think that all Black children are comedians who conform to racial stereotypes."[38] Not only did the program idealize the lived experience if not "perception" of most black American families, the *Cosby Show* pointed up the widening rift between contending social classes within the black community. The show dramatized, inadvertently perhaps, what William Julius Wilson described as the "declining significance of race" as a barrier to privilege and power in contemporary American society. Rather, Wilson observed that a "deepening economic schism seems to be developing in the black community, with the black poor falling further and further behind middle- and upper-income blacks."[39]

While *The Cosby Show* might possibly have been an accurate portrayal of those black professionals who had broken through ethnic and class barriers, it was pure fantasy for the many more members of the black underclass who could only dream of the material comfort and security enjoyed by the Huxtables and their brood. In *Designing Women,* the black ex-con who played man Friday to the beauteous Southern belles, the Sugarbaker sisters, mocked *The Cosby Show* by telling a dinner guest, "I like to watch the Cos because he's a wonderful role model for blacks. My goal is to finish high school, get my degree in medicine, and completely stop using the word "be" as a verb."[40]

Other black-oriented situation comedies including *Amen, 227, The Redd Foxx Show, What's Happening Now!!, Bustin' Loose, Frank's Place* (a hybrid of drama and comedy called "dramady"), and the short-lived but excellent *Better Days* were, like *The Cosby Show,* middle-class in value orientation. Unlike *The Cosby Show,* however, these shows depicted aspects of black American culture that were sometimes at variance with WASP standards of expressive behavior and perhaps even embarrassing to the newly arrived black middle class.[41] For one, the above shows admitted street culture—spatially and experientially—into the lives of their respective central characters.

In *The Cosby Show,* most of the drama unfolded within the confines of the home, while other black sitcoms celebrated the richness of urban street life. The opening credits of *Amen* rolled over an unfolding minidrama that had a scene with Deacon Ernest Frye (Sherman Hemsley) actually skipping double Dutch rope with children playing outside his church. In *227,* Pearl (Helen Martin) remarked on the comings and goings of visitors to her Washington, D.C., apartment and often dispensed unsolicited advice to neighbors while leaning from her window sill. The stoop in *227* was just as important as the bourgeois drawing room of *The Cosby Show* as a site where significant social exchange occurred.

Second, the expressive use of language in black sitcoms, such as that voiced in *Amen,* was a living reminder of the oppositional political power wielded by such diverse charismatic religio-political leaders as Martin Luther King, Jr., Malcolm X, and Jesse Jackson, each of whom has relied upon vividly rendered speech acts as tools for social transformation. (Even Cliff and Clair Huxtable would sometimes modulate into "black" dialect when they wanted to "get real" in making certain high context, instructive points to their children.) In accordance with the long tradition of the black church as an oppositional social institution, *Amen* featured an episode wherein the Reverend Ruben Gregory (Clifton Davis) voluntarily went to jail for offering his church as a sanctuary to those Deacon Frye referred to as "illegal aliens."[42]

While in jail on behalf of those he preferred to term "political fugitives," the Reverend Gregory brought salvation to a hardened criminal through the sheer force of his oratory. By the end of the episode, however, the politically charged question of "illegal aliens" was obscured by the fact of one particular individual's personal salvation. Even in *Amen*, the potential for the political mobilization of a dissident social group centered around the church was held in check by reasserting the priority of the individual and his personal salvation over the needs of the community at large.

Among recent ethnic situation comedies, *Better Days* embodied all that *The Cosby Show* denied either by omission or default. The rhythms and sounds of working class Brooklyn streets and playgrounds helped compose the self-consciously rendered textures of *Better Days*, which made a brief appearance on ABC.[43] Similar in spirit, although uniquely different in style, to the classic 1970s Tandem Productions ethnic sitcoms of Norman Lear and Bud Yorkin, *Better Days* dared to tackle major social problems and issues most other programs had long abandoned.

Better Days extended the perimeters set by 1970s ethnicoms by going beyond the easy jokes and laughter that had often been employed to take the edge off serious underlying issues. Reggie Theus of the Sacramento Kings once appeared on the program as "Double D," a basketball hero returning to Braxton High School to award a scholarship he had established. Two students were shown spontaneously breaking into rap artist Kurtis Blow's ("blow," that is, cocaine) "Basketball," which foreshadowed Double D's cocaine overdose at the school. There were no quick, easy answers offered in *Better Days*. Instead, the humor had an aggressive, embittered cast to it. "When did Double D know he had a problem?" asked a student and talented basketball player who had idolized the pro athlete, "When he tried to snort the free throw line." Heavy stuff indeed for prime time network fare.

THE INVISIBLE HAND

In the 1980s, with the exception of most sporting events and a few news and information programs, consistent black and minority presence on network television was largely restricted to the situation comedy. By their high visibility on contemporary ethnicoms, it was falsely implied that minorities had become fully integrated into the polity, the economy, and the dominant culture as well. But the symbolic presence, perhaps even overrepresentation, of blacks and minorities on sitcoms shifted attention from the relative absence of political and economic equality they in fact enjoyed in relation to their white American counterparts.

Blacks on the television sitcoms of the 1980s had conferred upon them a form of compensatory symbolic dominance not seen since the heyday of 1950s domestic situation comedies that paired strong and decisive housewives with bumbling fathers. This form of aesthetic inversion could also be observed in recent sitcoms based on slightly veiled themes of class, ethnic, or gender antagonism such as *Mr. Belvedere, Who's the Boss, Charles in Charge, She's the Sheriff, He's the Mayor, I Married Dora, Me & Mrs. C, Marblehead Manor,* or *Trial and Error*. In each program, the causes of class, ethnic, or gender subordination were strongly implied but finally repressed. Sitcom aesthetics, like the liberal democratic political culture that informs it, conforms to the harmonious model of the self-regulating, equilibrium-seeking system that ultimately brings into balance the play of conflicting demands as if guided by an invisible hand.

He's the Mayor, for example, was based on the premise of an ambitious young black man (Kevin Hooks), who won a hotly contested mayoral race in an upset victory, coming to grips with actually managing a city.[44] Unlike similar real-life scenarios that have been played out in major urban areas across the United States over the past ten years, the "race question" never once was broached in the program. That the mayor's staff, friends, advisors, and even the police chief were white was seen as being of little consequence, an incidental matter that paled in comparison to the larger problem that faced them all. Instead, each member of the mayor's team was faced equally with the problem of finding a way to "solve the deficit."

The overarching problem of a fiscal crisis that faced the mayor and his constituents, like life during wartime, reduced the level of social strife and dissidence that might have ordinarily fragmented or polarized the group. Further, the program strongly suggested the inability of government to generate enough revenue for its ongoing operation. Most disturbing of all was the implication that government lacked the wherewithal to redistribute equitably the social wealth in an era of economic hard times. In a final nod to the prevailing neoconservative agenda, the program cast blacks and other historically disadvantaged minorities among the total pool of economic supplicants without regard to indurate structures of inequality.

The hidden irony of the show was that the mayor was voted into political office at a time when white flight, corporate disinvestment, suburbanization, and the shift from heavy industry to the service economy had left heavily populated (almost 25 percent of total population), black core urban areas with severely eroded tax bases. By gaining political power, according to Michael Harrington, black mayors elected to office in such cities as Newark, Philadelphia, Washington, D.C., Gary, Atlanta, Detroit, and Chicago had "won the right to allocate poverty, not wealth."[45]

He's the Mayor suggested that having at last overcome the barrier of blocked political participation, blacks could now take their place among other fully vested groups that competed according to the liberal pluralist model of power relations. At one swipe, the ignominious history of social discrimination and economic exclusion was done away with by renegotiating the terms of the struggle for black economic equality: Compensatory social action and redress of historical injustices gave way to the pluralist model whereby "special interests" contended with one another in a free and open marketplace only to balance eventually their respective claims on the social wealth.

To a certain extent, the liberal accommodationist strategy of institutionalizing the notion of "equal opportunity" through legislation and antidiscrimination law since the mid–1970s served to confer legitimacy on an inequalitarian society by making the "problem of racial discrimination go away by announcing that it has been solved."[46] By extension, the legitimation of current, insidious forms of racial discrimination found its expressive correlative in recent ethnicoms that similarly assumed that persistent social contradictions already had been overcome. Together, the political system and its expressive superstructure helped to maintain the system of stigma and exclusion attached to minorities via the ideology of equal opportunity, a "strategy for keeping a plural society unequally plural."[47]

ALIEN STATES

Adding to the general socioeconomic crises of the 1980s was the continued wave of immigration, the likes of which had not been experienced since the first two decades of the century. From 1975 to present, approximately six million legal immigrants entered the United States. Add to this number the estimated 500,000 to 1 million immigrants per year who illegally entered the country. The massive influx of immigrant labor during a time of high unemployment and lowered productivity caused much resentment among American workers and a boon for many employers. It was popularly perceived—despite studies that provided evidence to the contrary—that undocumented aliens took jobs away from American citizens, depressed wages, and placed additional weight on an already overburdened welfare system.[48] The Immigration Reform and Control Act of 1986 was designed in part to deflect criticism directed against official government policy. The act did little, however, to eliminate the advantage of having at hand a ready supply of workers who were motivated, compliant, relatively cheap, and easily exploited.

Immigration was crucial to the development of industrial capitalism in America. Earlier waves of immigrant peoples, while strongly resisted by nativist organizations and other groups that felt directly threatened, were responsible for the economic dynamism and growth of American society. Varied languages and customs notwithstanding, a guiding assumption among social philosophers of the day was that the diverse immigrant groups would by and by come to "constitute a single people."[49]

Without denying the subjective differences between the current immigration flow and that of an earlier era, a similar ensemble of questions and contradictions that informed liberal pluralist political culture and society remained to be resolved. How, for example, did the principles of liberal democracy based upon equality, freedom, and nonexclusive membership square with the existence of a frankly exploitative unequal economic system? In the television situation comedies of the past as well as those of the present, the disjunction between democratic values and economic practice was imperfectly mended by moralistic appeals to patriotism, tolerance, and understanding.

NEEDED BUT NOT WANTED

As in the case of American ethnic minorities, the new immigrants were a protected species on television sitcoms. Despite a *New York Times/CBS News Poll* in June 1986 that reported that 49 percent of adult Americans were in favor of reducing the number of immigrants admitted to the United States, immigrants depicted in sitcoms were only good-naturedly mocked, rarely humiliated, never discriminated against or in any way abused. More troubling, 44 percent to 34 percent held the opinion that the new immigrants "cause more problems than make contributions."[50] That recent immigrants were treated with such solicitude in current sitcoms suggested deeper motives at play. Close readings of recent episodes of *The Facts of Life* and *The Golden Girls* illustrated the wide gap between spurious solicitude and the far less charitable opinions that were in fact held by a large percentage of Americans.

Jo Polniazek (Nancy McKeon) in *The Facts of Life* had been tutoring a foreign student, Enrico Quinteras, in English.[51] She learned that Enrico's father had fallen ill, forcing Enrico to earn money by taking a job, a violation of the terms of his student visa. Jo planned to help Enrico gain U.S. citizenship by marrying him. She believed (mistakenly) that by marrying Enrico he would be able to obtain a green card. Immigration and Naturalization Service (INS) agent Arnold Jensen paid a visit to Enrico and Jo just prior to their "marriage." He warned them that they were required to live together two years before Enrico would be eligible to apply for citizenship. The confrontation initiated an impromptu discussion between Jensen and Beverly Ann (Cloris Leachman) that trivialized the contemporary debate over the historically shifting definition of citizenship:

BEVERLY ANN: What about the Pilgrims?

ARNOLD JENSEN: What about them?

BEVERLY ANN: When the Pilgrims came to this country they didn't have any green cards. All they had were big dreams about freedom and big buckles on their hats.

The episode fulfilled a twin ideological and aesthetic objective: Its barely disguised public service message warned against the abuse of laws governing immigration while it sustained the liberal pluralist purport of most sitcom dramas. "This country was built by people who came from somewhere else. In a way, we're all immigrants," said Beverly Ann. This noble sentiment, however, gave way to the rule of law when Enrico was arrested by Jensen.

A similar scenario was played out in a 1986 episode of *The Golden Girls*, wherein Dorothy (Bea Arthur) tutored a young Latino student, Mario Sanchez.[52] With Dorothy's help, Mario won first prize in an essay contest. The essay described Mario's fresh impressions of America, formed in a movie theater like many of the immigrants who preceded him. Wrote Mario: "The very first night he was in America, his uncle took him to a movie. He felt more excited than he ever had in his whole life watching that movie. Because of the feeling he got sitting in that theater with all those other people, laughing together, getting scared together, he felt like those people were his friends. To him, that feeling was the feeling of living in America. In America, you always felt like you were among friends." Friendship or not, Mario's essay earned him the attention of the INS, which promptly picked him up. After Mario's deportation hearing, Dorothy vowed that she would pursue all legal avenues to get him back into the country. "This is your home," said Dorothy. "This is where you belong. You're what this country is all about."

Enrico Quinteras, Mario Sanchez, and others like them occupied an ambiguous role in contemporary American society. From a purely economic standpoint, immigrants—"illegal" or otherwise—helped prop up sagging profits and depress wages in labor intensive small businesses. At the same time, immigrants posed a threat because of the potential politico-economic power they might gain according to the commonly understood rules of liberal democracy. In terms of sheer numbers, immigration accounted for almost 20 percent of current U.S. population growth, compared with about 11 percent during the late 1950s. Moreover, not only had the growth rate of the native population been in decline, but the relative youth of the immigrant population meant an even greater increase in the number of problematic people in the near future.

These select episodes of *The Facts of Life* and *The Golden Girls* at once identified and masked the contradiction between the economic necessity and social expendability of "illegal aliens" that underlay the immigration problem. Both programs raised fundamental questions about the nature of community, citizenship, and polity only to retreat into the apologetics of patriotism, tolerance, and understanding. In deciding such questions, both programs placed an inordinate degree of faith in the legal system for formal relief and redress of grievances. This emphasis was consistent with liberal democratic norms that, in response to ingrained problems, favor evolutionary adaptation and piecemeal reform over structural change. By personalizing a larger social problem, these episodes induced pathos enough to sustain viewer interest. But this selective concern for the individual immigrant, however well-intentioned and generous, effectively overlooked the larger importance of the international (unequal) divirsion of labor within a historically specific "world economic system."[53]

DISPLACED POLITICS

Perfect Strangers, *What a Country!*, and *I Married Dora* were three recent sitcoms that treated problems of contemporary immigration from the point of view of the immigrant. To varying degrees, each of these programs skirted the politics of immigration and instead focused on the individual's adjustment to alien environments. The glorification and idealized romance of the Americanization process was in full evidence, although exhausted political symbolism, myths, and worn patriotic pieties were sometimes mocked. With the partial exception of *I Married Dora*, these programs extended the myth of the "open door'' by assuming the immigrant presence in contemporary America to be an accepted and unproblematic aspect of political life for the majority of citizens, which clearly was not the case.

The new world of the immigrant Balki Bartokomous (Bronson Pinchot) in *Perfect Strangers* was often confusing and harsh. Having left behind life as a shepherd on the Mediterranean island of ''Mypos,'' Balki lived and worked with his similarly striving American cousin, Larry Appleton (Mark Linn-Baker). With the help of Larry, who had also pulled up roots to make a go of it in Chicago, Balki encountered and passed routine tests of his fitness to become a full-fledged American. In one instance, Balki tried to obtain a driver's license, which he referred to as his passport to the ''American dream.''[54] After a series of disasters, including an accident in Larry's beloved Mustang, Balki was on the verge of abandoning all hope of ever being licensed. Larry joined Balki in a chorus of ''America the Beautiful'' as he encouraged his foreign-born relation. ''Hanging in there is part of what the American spirit is all about,'' said Larry.

What a Country! linked the new immigration to earlier waves of immigration. The opening title sequence featured sepia still photographs that portrayed immigrants of earlier decades, including one of Albert Einstein presumably taking the Oath of Citizenship. The idea was conveyed in the photo montage that the new crop of immigrants would likewise contribute to the vitality and growth of American society.[55] In the program, a citizenship class provided the pretext for bringing together a mixed bag of immigrants who learned that there was much more to context-rich American life than legal residency alone. As such, *What a Country!* abounded with wordplay, malapropisms, puns, and diastrous misreadings of the social text.

Students in the citizenship class included an African expatriate who ''lost'' his country to revolutionaries, an Asian woman, a Hispanic, an older man from Eastern Europe (Hungary), a Latina, a Russian, and an East Indian. The mix of national types drew upon the familiar pluralist conception of society with the implication that the students studying for American citizenship would eventually form a culturally diverse but ideologically uniform social order.

Unlike *Perfect Strangers* or *What a Country!*, *I Married Dora* took as its central character not an immigrant, but a displaced person.[56] Set in the Hollywood Hills, the premier episode established how Dora Calderon (Elizabeth Peña) became installed as housekeeper for architect Peter Farrell (Daniel Hugh Kelly) and his children after his wife's airline flight was diverted to Syria by ''three swarthy men.'' Prior to her sudden disappearance, Janet Farrell had been a hopelessly spoiled and insecure Southern California housewife who lived in anguish because she did not ''know who she is.''

Dora's new life went well until her legal residency status was called into question by the authorities. Dora had hoped to benefit from the Reagan administration's immigrant amnesty program put into effect in May 1987. The amnesty program was designed to deflect public criticism over the lack of federal governmental action in controlling illegal immigration into the United States. Unfortunately for Dora, she could not positively prove five years continuous residency in the United States as required by the amnesty program.

After a bit of coaxing, Dora Calderon told Peter Farrell how her sister Cecilia, living in an unspecified Central American country (probably El Salvador), had been killed by what she directly referred to as a "death squad." Dora's sister was one of the *"desaparecidos."* Cecilia Calderon had been accused of subversion by having innocently provided food to opposition guerrillas. Less innocent was Dora who hinted at her political involvement while a university student. Farrell expressed his concern for Dora's safety:

PETER: They weren't after you were they?

DORA: No. Not until I got a *little* political in my sophomore year.

PETER: Couldn't you just have gone out for cheerleading?

No mere "economic migrant," housekeeper Dora Calderon as it turned out had studied for two years in preparation for a career as an orthopedic surgeon. It was established, therefore, that repressive political conditions—not simple economic need—forced Dora to seek sanctuary in the United States. As a premise for a sitcom, the trials of a political refugee from a totalitarian state made the program stand out from other shows.

I Married Dora was an exceptional program given that its premise was so solidly grounded in urgently debated issues of contemporary domestic and international relations. But as might be expected, this program did not go much beyond the conventional wisdom regarding the United States presence in Central America. For one, the program expressed a clear preference for a certain *kind* of immigrant—political refugees—instead of merely economic refugees. The flight of political refugees to the United States testified to the moral superiority of the American system over totalitarian regimes, while the influx of economic refugees forced the issue of America's crucial role in perpetuating third world underdevelopment.

At a time of revived anticommunist sentiment reminiscent of the Cold War era, the immigration issue became a key weapon in the rhetorical arsenal deployed in the global campaign against Soviet influence. Prior to his conciliatory summit meeting with Soviet Premier Mikhail Gorbachev in May 1988, President Ronald Reagan had gone so far as to call the Soviet Union an "evil empire." The passage of the Refugee Act of 1980 formalized preferential treatment for those immigrants requesting asylum provided they "claimed persecution at the hands of Communist governments."[57] Ironically, many of those denied entry into the United States as "economic refugees" were political refugees fleeing totalitarian regimes supported by the American government. *I Married Dora* as an aesthetically veiled polemic, managed to have it both ways by taking the moral high ground while sustaining ideological justifications for unequal domestic and international power relations.

LET'S "GUNG HO" ("WORK TOGETHER")

The international character of labor and production in the present was made more obvious by the new immigration. Similarly linked to the transformation of the global economy and perhaps even more problematic was the economic ascendancy of East Asian countries led by Japan. A vanquished nation once mocked for its cheap imitations of Yankee products, Japanese exports to the United States grew twenty-three times in value between 1963 and 1980. As a world-class economic region, East Asia had replaced Europe as "America's chief supplier of manufactured goods" by the mid–1970s.[58]

Panic induced by the threat of "Japan, Inc." set off a minor explosion in popular literature that tried to explain the Japanese economic miracle. Management gurus, many with academic affiliations, dispensed advice to receptive corporate audiences eager to understand the secret to increased profitability.[59] While special attention was paid to the supposedly superior cultural values that made for better business in the context of Japanese society, American business management "innovations" in accounting, tax avoidance, litigation, and corporate acquisitions that spawned unproductive "paper entrepreneurialism" largely escaped identification as key factors in the U.S. economic decline.[60]

The superficial but intense fascination of Americans with Japanese management practices and cultural life in general held a curious ambivalence. While grudging admiration was extended to the first nonwhite people to successfully compete with American industry on an equal footing, long-time assumptions of Anglo-Saxon superiority were at the same time called into question. The popular literature and official thought of late nineteenth-century America, for example, were filled with dubious explanations for the cultural and racial superiority of Anglo-Saxon peoples over those of the East. Not coincidently, such literature helped justify the economic domination of the United States over Asian countries.[61]

Given the legacy of racism in American society, the so-called Japanese challenge likewise carried overtones that found expression in various popular arts. According to two contemporary observers, the decline of American economic and military might beginning in the 1970s had "implicit racial dimensions." Michael Omi and Howard Winant observed how "Popular ideology often makes use of racial themes as a framework by which to comprehend major problems, be they declining US dominance in the world, dislocations in the workforce, or the fiscal crisis of the state."[62] It was in this highly volatile context that the television situation comedy *Gung Ho* made its debut.

Gung Ho appeared on television late in 1986 after the original movie version starring Michael Keaton proved to be a big box-office success. The film earned over $25 million in the four weeks after it opened in March of 1986. ABC committed to running six episodes of *Gung Ho* without so much as a pilot, primarily on the strength of the track record of the program's executive producers, Ron Howard, Babaloo Mandel, Lowell Ganz, Tony Ganz, and Deborah Blum.[63]

Despite the fact that "gung ho" was a Chinese—not Japanese—expression that gained wide currency as the result of the imperial American military presence in Asia, the program ostensibly dramatized the problems associated with the imposition of Japanese management techniques on American workers.

In *Gung Ho,* it was the job of "employee liaison" Hunt Stevenson (Scott Bakula) to mediate the clash of cultures between the upper management of Assan Motors and its production line workers.[64] Stevenson had been instrumental in bringing Assan Motors to Hadleyville, a company town dependent on a moribund automobile manufacturing plant before Assan took over and revived the facility. Hunt worked closely with Kazuhiro Takahashi (Gedde Watanabe), the plant manager in charge of operations. The most obvious source of cross-cultural conflict was found in the person of the rigidly authoritarian Saito (Sab Shimono), Takahashi's second-in-command.

Hunt's first professional challenge arose when the production workers refused to adopt the practice of task rotation employed by Japanese automobile manufacturers. Strangely enough, the workers actually voiced a preference for specialized job assignments as if boredom, routinization, and alienation played no part in the advanced form of Taylorism that organized the production process at their factory.[65] Rather than direct their anger at the abstracted relations of production that were the deeper source of their discontent, the workers's rebellion took the form of racial and cultural antagonisms.

Predictably, shop floor friction disappeared once cross-cultural inconsistencies were exposed for their laughably arbitrary and contingent nature. The stern disciplinarian Saito continued with his amusingly funny conniption fits, but Takahashi attained a deeper level of understanding and compassion for his American employees as Hunt worked at bringing the antagonistic groups together in mutual harmony. All was made right after the ringleader of the intractable workers led them in a communal swim in the river along with their new bosses.

CHINAMAN'S CHANCE

Industrial competition, cultural superiority, nationalism, class, and race were some of the more obvious themes that formed the subtext for *Gung Ho.* In the end, however, the program played down these sensitive themes and arrived at a not entirely convincing state of group harmony. Absent were the very real politico-economic, nationalistic, and racial antagonisms that informed the Japanese industrial presence in the United States. Although only fourth behind Britain, West Germany, and the Netherlands as foreign holders of U.S. assets, the pouring of $14.7 billion into U.S. investments during 1987 by Japan spurred backlash at the federal, state, and local levels.[66]

The somewhat condescending title of the program itself, *Gung Ho,* was a linguistic barbarism used to symbolically apprehend (but managed to confuse) two unique and distinctive Asian civilizations, those of China and Japan. The reduction of all Asian societies and peoples to one simplistic cliché by the writers and producers of *Gung Ho* was not without racist overtones. Decidedly more than harmless stereotype or race awareness, this long-standing feature of mainstream American social knowledge has had devastating consequences in the past.

The most notable historic example was the incarceration of American citizens of Japanese ancestry in concentration camps during World War II, when racial membership overrode constitutional rights guaranteed by American citizenship. More recently, in June 1982, a Chinese-American engineer, Vincent Chin, died at the hands of Michael Nitz and his stepfather, Ronald Ebens, a foreman at Chrysler Motors. Nitz and Ebens beat Chin to death with a baseball bat after they saw him give a large tip to a white dancer at a topless bar, where Chin was celebrating his upcoming marriage.[67] Assuming perhaps that Chin was Japanese, the two men blamed him for U.S. economic woes. Neither Ebens nor Nitz went to jail; each paid a fine of $3,780 for violating their victim's civil rights.

Apparently, the killers of Vincent Chin—like the creators of *Gung Ho* or those who promoted the wartime "relocation" of suspected enemy aliens—were unable or unwilling to understand the fundamental interplay between race, culture, language, citizenship, and nationality in American life. Most reprehensible about *Gung Ho* was its silent denial of the persistence of a color-caste system in American society used selectivity throughout its history to buffer what have been fundamentally class antagonisms.

SITUATING CONTRADICTIONS

The television situation comedy—like the evening news, soap operas, sports events, or talk shows—shapes paradox, conflict, and contingency into the form of a story. The story is neither neutral nor unmotivated. The form and content of the situation comedy are necessarily grounded in the society it helps to explain, legitimate, and sometimes question. In the case of postwar American society, a society that has enjoyed a high level of private consumption as serviced by the television and advertising industries, "capitalist realism" accurately describes both the aesthetic conventions and the dominant values promulgated in the sitcom.[68] Conventional wisdom maintained that postwar plentitude was to have resolved the dilemmas of class society by expanding the economic pie and making more of it available to almost everyone. By successfully "delivering the goods" to the majority of Americans, the legitimacy of the social order was to have gone unchallenged.

The decline of America as a world economic power and the slippage of its high standard of living brought to the fore innumerable equity decisions faced by the government as part of the political process. The neoconservative solution to the problem of poor economic performance was to impose "limits" on the demands placed on the government, trying to slow the rapid expansion of the state over the past forty years. While women, minorities, children, and the elderly bore the brunt of the downsizing of the American dream, corporations and individuals in the higher income brackets were the beneficiaries of regressive tax policies.

Unresolved dilemmas of liberal democratic society in the 1980s continued to make their way (often obliquely) into the situation comedy, a dramatic form constrained to admit both the topical and the contemporaneous as part of its aesthetic. Yet all too many of the situation comedies of the 1980s were noteworthy precisely for their utter lack of direct reference to the ingrained problems that plagued American life in a time of generalized economic hardship. Instead, sitcoms in the neoconservative age stood as placid preserves of democratic culture aligned against wider, disruptive external forces that threatened the collectivity.

Politics and history, the absent causes of all aesthetic constructs, provided the subtextual backdrop for sitcoms as unalike as *Alf* and *Zorro and Son*. Politics—the institutionalized means of mediating social conflict—is the *prima materia* of all drama including the situation comedy. Wedded as it is to the political economic order it helps service, the television industry as presently constituted cannot honestly confront its divided allegiance to the democratic values held by its audience and the hegemonic practices of the network oligopolies. At bottom, the situation comedy cannot directly "name" the sources of social conflict without betraying its benefactor. Hence the telling silence of television situation comedy in the neoconservative Death Valley Days of the American 1980s.

NOTES

1. Kenneth Thompson, *Beliefs and Ideology* (London and New York: Tavistock Publications, 1986), p. 103

2. Robert L. Heilbroner (1985), p. 142.

3. Peter Steinfels, *The Neoconservatives: The Men Who Are Changing America's Politics* (New York: Touchstone, 1979), pp. 53–63. Steinfel's work is at once a history and a critique. For an advocate's view, see Irving Kristol, *Reflections of a Neoconservative: Looking Back, Looking Ahead* (New York: Basic Books, Inc., 1983).

4. See Jürgen Habermas, *Legitimation Crisis* (Boston: Beacon Press, 1973).

5. Alonzo L. Hamby, *Liberalism and Its Challengers: FDR to Reagan* (New York: Oxford University Press, 1985), p. 348.

6. Morris Janowitz, *The Last Half-Century: Societal Change and Politics in America* (Chicago: University of Chicago Press, 1978), p. 339.

7. The episode of *The Facts of Life* under discussion was produced by Jerry Mayer, written by Dick Bowab, and bears the copyright date of 1980 by TAT Communications.

8. Courtland L. Boveé and William F. Arens, *Contemporary Advertising*, 2d ed. (Homewood, Ill.: Irwin, 1986), p. 442.

9. Russell L. Hanson (1985), p. 366.

10. Herbert Gans, *More Equality* (New York: Vintage Books, 1974), p. 49.

11. Stanley Aronowitz, *Food, Shelter and the American Dream* (New York: Seabury Press, 1974), p. 127.

12. Peter N. Carroll, *It Seemed Like Nothing Happened: The Tragedy and Promise of America in the 1970s* (New York: Holt, Rinehart & Winston, 1982), p. 346.

13. Fred Block et. al., *The Mean Season: The Attack on the Welfare State* (New York: Pantheon Books, 1987), p. 137.

14. Jack Nelson, "The Reagan Legacy," in *Beyond Reagan: The Politics of Upheaval,* ed. Paul Duke (New York: Warner Books, 1986), p. 107.

15. Thomas Ferguson and Joel Rogers, *Right Turn: The Decline of the Democrats and the Future of American Politics* (New York: Hill & Wang, 1986), p. 123.

16. Robert Lekachman, *Visions and Nightmares: America after Reagan* (New York: Macmillan, 1987), p. 94.

17. Lester C. Thurow, *The Zero-Sum Society: Distribution and the Possibilities for Economic Change* (New York: Penguin Books, 1981), p. 187.

18. The episode of *It's A Living* quoted was produced by Tom Whedon and Marc Sotkin, written by Robin Pennington, and directed by J. D. Lobue. The program was created by Stu Silver, Dick Clair, and Jenna, McMahon. A Witt/Thomas Production copyright 1985.

19. See Barbara Ehrenreich and Frances Fox Piven, "The Feminization of Poverty," in *Dissent*, 31 (1984): 162–170.

20. *Mama's Family* was created by Dick Clair and Jenna McMahon, and produced by Rick Hawkins. Joe Hamilton Productions.

21. This episode of *Kate & Allie* was written by Bob Randall and directed by Bill Persky, both of whom also served as producers. Produced by Mort Lachman & Associates in association with Reeves Entertainment Group.

22. Marvin Harris (1981), p. 94.

23. Janice Peskin, "Measuring Household Production for the GNP," in *Family Economics Review,* 3 (1982):25.

24. Valerie Harper was removed from the program in August of 1987 and replaced by Sandy Duncan. *Valerie* was renamed *Valerie's Family*. Miller Boyett Productions copyright 1986. Executive producers Thomas L. Miller, Robert L. Boyett, Tony Cacciotti.

25. Susan Brownmiller, *Femininity* (New York: Fawcett Columbine, 1984), p. 17.

26. *My Sister Sam* was created by Stephen Fischer and developed by Susan Beavers, produced by Karyl Miller and Korby Siamis. This episode was written by Karyl Miller. Pony Productions in association with Warner Bros. Television copyright 1987.

27. "Rise in Poverty Linked to Government Program Cuts," *Los Angeles Times,* December 8, 1986, pt. I, p. 4.

28. David Wessel, "Growing Gap: U.S. Rich and Poor Increase in Numbers; Middle Loses Ground," *The Wall Street Journal,* September 22, 1986, p. 20.

29. United Auto Workers of America, *Building America's Future* (Detroit, Mich.: United Auto Workers of America, 1985). Cited in *Dissent*, 33 (1986):439.

30. Ruth Sidel, *Women and Children Last: The Plight of Poor Women in Affluent America* (New York: Penguin Books, 1986), p. 158.

31. Brigitte Berger and Peter L. Berger, *The War Over the Family: Capturing the Middle Ground* (Garden City, N.Y.: Anchor Press/Doubleday, 1984), p. 209.

32. Todd Gitlin, *Inside Prime Time* (New York: Pantheon Books, 1983), pp. 261–262.

33. Robert Nisbet, *Conservatism: Dreams and Reality* (Milton Keynes, England: Open University Press, 1986), p. 95.

34. *Mama's Boy* was created by Bill Levinson. The debut episode was written by Don Reo and directed by J. D. Lobue. A Witt/Thomas Production, copyright 1987.

35. Samuel Bowles and Herbert Gintis, *Democracy and Capitalism: Property, Com-*

munity, and the Contradictions of Modern Social Thought (New York: Basic Books, 1986), p. 17.

36. Michael Cieply, "Thursdays Spell Trouble for the Huxtables," *The Wall Street Journal*, September 25, 1986, p. 32. Bill Cosby, who has one-half interest in the program, declined to have his show considered for the 1987 Emmy Awards.

37. Wayne Walley, "Carsey-Werner: Cosby's Co-Pilots Stay Small and Lean," *Advertising Age*, June 19, 1986, p. 38.

38. Robert E. Johnson, "TV's Top Mom and Dad: Bill Cosby, Phylicia Ayers-Allen are role model parents on award-winning television show," *Ebony*, February 1986, p. 32.

39. William Julius Wilson, *The Declining Significance of Race: Blacks and Changing American Institutions,* 2d ed. (Chicago: University of Chicago Press, 1980), p. 152.

40. *Designing Women.* Produced by Emily Marshall, created and written by Linda Bloodworth-Thompson.

41. See Joan and Stephan Baratz, "Black Culture on Black Terms: A Rejection of the Social Pathology Model," in *Rappin and Stylin Out: Communication in Urban Black America,* ed. Thomas Kochman (Urbana: University of Illinois Press, 1972), pp. 3–16.

42. The activist role of the church in the civil rights movement was documented in David J. Garrow, *Bearing the Cross: Martin Luther King, Jr., and the Southern Christian Leadership Conference* (New York: Vintage Books, 1988).

43. *Better Days,* cancelled in November of 1986, was written by Ralph Farquhar, created by Jeff Freilich, Arthur Silver, and Stuart Sheslow, produced by Ronald Rubin and Marty Nadler, directed by Stan Lathan. Magnum/Thunder Road Production in association with Lorimar Telepictures.

44. *He's the Mayor* first appeared in 1986 on ABC. Created by Winston Mass and Bob Peete, developed by Alessandro Veith, written by Terry Hart, directed by Oz Scott, executive producer Alessandro Veith, produced by Fred Rubin and Fred Fox, Jr.

45. Michael Harrington, *The New American Poverty* (New York: Penguin Books, 1984), p. 135.

46. Alan David Freeman, "Legitimizing Racial Discrimination Through Antidiscrimination Law: A Critical Review of Supreme Court Doctrine," in *Marxism and Law,* ed. Piers Beirne and Richard Quinney (New York: John Wiley & Sons, 1982), p. 229.

47. Philip Green (1981), p. 264.

48. Charles P. Alexander, "A Most Debated Issue: Illegal Workers Depress Wages But Boost Profits and Reduce Prices," *Time,* July 8, 1985, p. 75.

49. Michael Walzer, "Pluralism in Political Perspective," in *The Politics of Ethnicity,* ed. Stephen Thernstrom (Cambridge: Harvard University Press, Belknap Press, 1982), p. 8.

50. Louis Harris, *Inside America* (New York: Vintage Books, 1987), p. 419.

51. *The Facts of Life*, created by Dick Clair and Jenna McMahon, developed by Howard Leeds, Ben Starr, and Jerry Mayer, executive producer Irma Kalish. This 1986 teleplay was written by Ross Brown and Michael Poryes, story by Shirley Brown, directed by John Bowab, produced by Embassy Television. Embassy Communications is a unit of the Coca Cola Company.

52. *The Golden Girls,* created by Susan Harris. Executive producers Paul Junger Witt and Tony Thomas. A Witt Thomas Harris Production. This 1986 episode was written by Christopher Lloyd and directed by Terry Hughes.

53. See Elizabeth McLean Petras, "Towards A Theory of International Migration: The New Division of Labor," in *Sourcebook on the New Immigration: Implications for*

the United States and the International Community, ed. Roy Simón Bryce-Laporte (New Brunswick, N.J.: Transaction Books, 1980), pp. 439–449.

54. *Perfect Strangers,* created by Dale McRaven, produced by Chip Keyes and Doug Keyes. This episode was written by Chip Keyes and Doug Keyes, directed by Howard Storm.

55. *What A Country!* produced by Wendy Blair. Executive producer Martin Rips and Joseph Staretski. This 1986 episode was written by Mike Scully and Frank Mula, directed by Linda Day. Copyright 1986, Tribune Entertainment Company and Viacom International, Inc.

56. *I Married Dora,* created by Michael Leeson. Executive producer Michael Leeson, produced by Wendy Blair, Jace Richdale, Vic Rauseo, and Linda Morris, co-producer Mark Masuoka, directed by Lee Shallat. Copyright 1987, Reeves Entertainment Group.

57. Gil Loescher and John A. Scanlan, *Calculated Kindness: Refugees and America's Half-Open Door, 1945 to the Present* (New York: Free Press, 1986), p. 216.

58. Roy Hofheinz, Jr., and Kent E. Calder, *The Eastasia Edge* (New York: Basic Books, 1982), p. 171.

59. This body of literature warrants study in itself. Representative works include Ezra F. Vogel, *Japan as Number One: Lessons for America* (New York: Harper Colophon Books, 1980); William G. Ouchi, *Theory Z: How American Business Can Meet the Japanese Challenge* (New York: Avon, 1982); Richard Tanner Pascale and Anthony G. Athos, *The Art of Japanese Management: Applications for American Executives* (New York: Warner Books, 1982); John Naisbitt and Patricia Aburdene, *Re-inventing the Corporation: Transforming Your Job and Your Company for the New Informative Society* (New York: Warner, 1985).

60. Robert B. Reich, *The Next American Frontier* (New York: Penguin, 1984), pp. 140–141.

61. See Ronald T. Takagi, *Iron Cages: Race and Culture in Nineteenth-Century America* (New York: Alfred A. Knopf, 1979).

62. Michael Omi and Howard Winant, *Racial Formation in the United States: From the 1960s to the 1980s* (New York: Routledge & Kegan Paul, 1986), p. 112.

63. Morgan Gendel, "ABC Goes 'Gung Ho' Over Sitcom," *Los Angeles Times,* April 15, 1986, p. 10.

64. *Gung Ho* premiered December 5, 1986, on ABC. Produced by George Sunga. An Imagine/Four Way Production.

65. For a compelling account of life on an automobile assembly line operating under the pressures exerted by foreign competition in the early 1970s, see Stanley Aronowitz, *False Promises: The Shaping of American Working Class Consciousness* (New York: McGraw-Hill, 1974), pp. 21–50.

66. Art Pike, "Influx of Foreign Capital Stirs Backlash Across U.S., *Los Angeles Times,* June 5, 1988, pt. I, pp. 1, 28, 29.

67. Michael Moore, "Scapegoats Again." *The Progressive,* (February 1988): 25–27. According to the article, in 1986 there was a 62 percent rise in hate crimes directed against Asian Americans as reported by the U.S. Justice Department.

68. Michael Schudson, *Advertising, the Uneasy Persuasion: Its Dubious Impact on American Society* (New York: Basic Books, 1984), p. 214.

Epilogue

SITCOM AND LIBERAL DEMOCRACY

Over the course of its 40-year history, the television situation comedy has remained consistently true to its twin, often conflicting, origins in liberal democratic ideology and corporate capitalism. Through narratives that assimilate social contradictions into everyday personal experience, the situation comedy has stood as an enduring sociodramatic model that has helped "explain" American society to itself. Forming the subtext of most sitcoms has been the inherent contradiction between the affirmative aspects of liberal democratic thought and corporate capitalist social institutions that have come to dominate almost every aspect of postwar American life.

In both its ideological content and its means of reception, the situation comedy is profoundly domestic and familiar. Perhaps like the private family dwelling itself, the situation comedy has served as a symbolic refuge from what has been described as the "culture of separation," that is, a culture characterized by excessive individualism, fragmentation, privativism, incoherence, compartmentalization, and a general lack of commitment to an overarching social deal. The situation comedy, unlike most other television dramatic forms, has stood for a "culture of coherence" rooted in both a common religious heritage and political tradition that live on in vital "communities of memory."[1]

Within the situation comedy, the tradition of cultural conservatism puts into sharp relief the irrational, oppressive, hence risible aspects of American society. In the sitcom, impersonal, dehumanizing, undemocratic, and exploitative forms of social organization are always rejected over forms of sociality that foster personal autonomy, freedom, and authenticity. Big government, corporate oligopolies, bureaucratic structures, faceless authority, and the military establishment are rejected without fail in favor of family, friends, and voluntary associations. In this conservative, liberal, and socialist critiques of culture, society, and politics share interesting similarities (but significant differences) that are worthy of further discussion about the furthur democratization of American society.[2]

Even as the situation comedy has stressed the affirmative aspects of liberal democracy, it has done so only within the framework of a system of commercial television that limits the emancipatory potential of American popular culture. This curious dualism, then, allows for a situation comedy that sympathetically depicts a household of self-sufficient single women, while foregoing mention of the new female poverty, feminist politics, or other macrosocial events that would in part explain the composition of such a household. Similarly, it is no longer unusual for ethnic minority peoples to have "their own" shows, although minorities remain largely excluded from writing, producing, directing, and financially participating in most sitcoms. Perhaps the greatest failure of this dualism in situation comedy aesthetics is the depiction of average, everyday people who exercise little power of control over their lives beyond the kitchen or the living room.

CHANNELS NOT TAKEN

That the television situation comedy developed in this manner was not preordained. As early as *The George Burns Show* (October 21, 1958, to April 14, 1959), the sitcom revealed itself to be a self-consciously sophisticated television form. George Burns (as George Burns, no less) did not disguise the artificiality of the show, as he worked into the script ironic references to sponsors such as "Fab" (Colgate). Long before *It's Garry Shandling's Show,* Burns was addressing the audience and commenting on the action like a coconspirator to a foregone conclusion. It was not by chance alone that the pilot episode, "George and the Private Eye," was a satire of an exhausted aesthetic form, the detective mystery. The situation comedy itself had reached the point of exhaustion and was in need of renewal.[3]

The producer and director of *The George Burns Show*, Rod Amateau, subsequently teamed up with humorist Max Shulman to create a highly innovative self-reflexive sitcom that, because of its critical tone, was never aired.[4] *Daddy-O* ostensibly was a domestic situation comedy that self-consciously played with the clichés of the genre. Stock characters included a bumbling father, Ben Cousins (Don DeFore); a long-suffering wife, Polly (Jean Byron); and two children mildly disrespectful of parental authority. *Daddy-O*, however, was a sitcom with an ironic twist.

Daddy-O as a self-reflexive critique of the situation comedy operated on two levels—ideological and structural. This was accomplished by beginning with the premise of *Daddy-O* being a situation comedy about a situation comedy. Not only did *Daddy-O* mock the thematic and ideological conventions of the sitcom, but it did so in a way that laid bare the mechanisms of what usually passes for television realism. The ideological and structural duplicity of the situation comedy was foregrounded in the opening scene of the *Daddy-O* pilot: What at first appeared to be a quintessential sitcom moment—the gathering of the Cousins family at the dinner table—proved instead, as the camera pulled back, to be a tape being replayed on a studio monitor. In actuality, the laugh track of the scene was in the process of being "sweetened" by the cynical producer of the program, Albert Shapian (Lee Philips).[5]

Ben "Daddy-O" Cousins had difficulty allowing himself to be humiliated with pie-in-the-face humor. Cousins yearned to return to his former trade as a master carpenter so that he could once more perform work that had lasting value. His children and wife, however, had become used to the higher standard of living made possible by Ben's stardom, which made it all the more difficult for Cousins to leave the show. In these conflicting pulls of commitment and responsibility, Ben's "situation" was not unlike that of many postwar partriarchs until the mid–1960s.

Albert Shapian was especially adept in persuading Ben Cousins to stay with the show, appealing to his sense of patriotism and family. Shapian remarked that Ben possessed a "clean," "wholesome," "harmless," "safe," "warm," and most of all "pre-digested" face unlike that of professional actors. In Ben's face, Shapian observed, "you see twenty generations of nice, decent, ethical, Anglo-Saxon people who *married* each other." When all else failed, Shapian paid-off an actress to pose as an elderly woman who thanked Ben Cousins for providing her lonely existence with a sense of family. This ruse convinced Cousins that he should stay with *Daddy-O*.

The self-conscious thrust of *Daddy-O* was further made evident in a promotional trailer for the show. In it, Ben, Albert, and Polly discussed the program and its future direction. Shapian was particularly astute when it came to the exploitation of dominant themes and motifs of American culture: "You are going to remain in *Daddy-O* and continue to warm the hearts and ease the burdens of 180 million Americans—Americans of every race, creed, color and persuasion— poor Americans, rich Americans, tall Americans, short Americans, thin Americans, fat Americans—but all Americans—all living in peace and harmony and freedom under the proudest flag the world has ever known, from Valley Forge to Iwo Jima. . ."

According to Shapian, future episodes of *Daddy-O* would treat domestic themes such as "homemaking," "child rearing," "domestic bliss," "domestic strife," "civic virtue," and "adolescent love." Unlike other sitcoms, however, the program would include "inside stuff" about Ben's show business life complete with behind-the-scenes looks at writers' conferences, laugh track sessions, music scoring, special effects, agency conferences, and other activities related to producing a sitcom. Having finished his spiel, Albert stated that all that remained was to find "some patriotic American sponsor to buy the show." But neither in fact nor fiction was it to be; *Daddy-O* never made it on the air.

One of the more obvious reasons why *Daddy-O* never progressed beyond the pilot stage was that it was too critical of the commercial system upon which it depended. Even then, as a self-mocking, satirical metacommentary on both the business and the art of television, *Daddy-O* probably would have been within the range of acceptability for its audience. But by its merciless lampoon of the family, American society, and its dominant cultural beliefs, *Daddy-O* precluded the possibility of connecting with its prospective audience.

A less obvious reason for the failure of *Daddy-O* had more to do with the real-life politics of producing television shows. As writer Max Shulman explained it, James Aubrey, at the time president of CBS television, had Shulman and Amateau develop both *Daddy-O* and a spin-off from *The Many Loves of Dobie Gillis* to be called *Zelda*. Shulman later found out that Aubrey had no intention of buying either program. For one, financing the two pilot episodes had the effect of preventing Shulman and Amateau from shopping their wares to the two other competing networks. Second, although *The Many Loves of Dobie Gillis* was a good lead-in to *The Beverly Hillbillies* and *The Dick Van Dyke Show*, CBS television had no direct financial participation in *The Many Loves of Dobie Gillis*, all the more reason to let it flounder from neglect.[6]

The case of the ill-fated sitcom *Daddy-O* serves to illustrate the limitations imposed by the commercial structure of network television. Moreover, the failure of the show also helps indentify the ideological boundaries in which the situation comedy has continued to function almost thirty years later. But rather than understand *Daddy-O* as simply another casualty in the battle between commerce and art, the program points out the untapped potential of television to reveal truths about American culture, society, and politics no matter how painful they may be. That *Daddy-O* was even produced holds out the possibility for the retrieval of democracy not only as it pertains to the commercial system of television and its many forms, but for American society at large.

IN TELEVISION BEGIN RESPONSIBILITIES

A symposium held in 1959 cosponsored by the Tamiment Institute and *Daedalus,* the Journal of the American Academy of Arts and Sciences, featured many of the luminaries who have made important contributions to the "mass culture" debate. In many important ways, the insights and observations that came out of the symposium helped to shape the contours of criticism and thought on the mass media for the subsequent three decades. Lone among symposium participants—most of whom were academics, critics, writers, or otherwise engaged in intellectual activity—was Frank Stanton, then president of CBS. His contribution to the symposium, "Parallel Paths," contained arguments that have often been used in reaffirming the legitimacy of network dominance.

"Parallel Paths" was noteworthy for the way in which it falsely pitted the need of a large and demographically diverse public to be informed and entertained against the presumably antidemocratic tendencies of intellectuals, most of whom expressed disatisfaction with the mass media. According to Stanton, "some sort of hostility on the part of intellectuals toward the mass media is inevitable," because as a minority they were "not really reconciled to some basic features of democratic life."[7]

Stanton was correct in assessing the democratic possibilities of television. Perhaps he was even correct in arguing against the elitist prejudices held at that time by many mass media critics, but he was mistaken in accusing critics of hostility toward democracy on the basis of their refusal to abide by the law of large numbers. The stoicism of the viewing public, born of forced choice, could hardly be confused with the democratic process.

On the contrary, the capture of a large viewing public and resulting high profits were made possible by virtue of monopoly conditions enjoyed by the networks.[8] The mass defection of viewers from network television in 1988 for alternative sources of domestic entertainment—prerecorded videocassettes, cable programing, independent "networks" such as Fox Broadcasting—demonstrated that the networks for forty years had held a captive market largely by default.[9] The democratic processes and procedures extolled by Stanton had little to do with accounting for network dominance.

The current proliferation of new information and communications technologies makes it all the more urgent for responsible social actors to oversee the development of democratic television. The democratization of the television industry and the positive influence this will exert on its various aesthetic forms can proceed only to the extent that American society at large becomes more fully democratized. Democratization will not proceed in a predetermined, teleological fashion, but fitfully and perhaps incompletely.

It is clear that the democratization of television and its forms will require fuller participation of all segments of society in every area of the industry. Among those who work in television a greater degree of control over production processes, active involvement with decisions concerning the deployment of resources, and a scaling down of inflated corporate managerial salaries would do much to ease the pressure of meeting unrealistic profit plans. This is not a question of private versus public enterprise. Nor is it even necessary that the network oligopolies be replaced by state-run institutions that might prove equally as repressive. "The answer is not elimination of private enterprise in the media," writes Ben Bagdikian. "The answer is the same for other central institutions of a democratic society—equitable distribution of power."[10]

A practical (but far from comprehensive) five-point agenda that could begin to move television in the direction of greater democracy might include the following items:

1. Affirmative action hiring practices in all areas of the television industry is imperative. For example, a 1987 report commissioned by the Writers Guild of America, west, indicates that women, ethnic minorities, and older writers suffer serious disadvantages of employment and in matters of pay equity.[11] Affirmative action will not degrade

program quality, as has been asserted. Indeed, much of the success of MTM Productions can be attributed to the infusion of female writing talent which brought fresh insights to the art of sitcom writing.[12]

2. If select colleges and universities are to continue as state-sponsored training centers for aspiring industry workers, then admission to communications and media production programs should be opened to include a more diverse pool of applicants. Curricula for such academic programs should maintain an emphasis on a traditional liberal arts curriculum, rather than narrow vocationalism, to include a study of world history and comparative culture.

3. In addition to staff, support personnel, and certain highly visible on-air talent, independent stations and networks must begin to reflect the diversity of American society in future hiring at the mid- and upper-levels of management.

4. A "mixed system" comprising for-profit and public television already exists in the United States, but not on an equal basis.[13] Direct government subsidy of public television programing would relieve ordinary pressures of the marketplace and correct the imbalance that results from the indirect government subsidy of the for-profit system.

5. The "land-grant" system established by the Morrill College Land Grant Act of 1862 was used to finance and encourage the development of democratizing institutions such as state colleges and universities. Similarr legislation might allow for the sale and federal regulation of the public airwaves to commercial broadcasters, which could in turn help subsidize public sector television.

In fulfilling its public mandate, it would seem that the commercial system of television must begin to more closely conform to the image of the "commons" as opposed to that of the "market." As in the case of other social resources held in common, the airwaves are too precious to be squandered by an elite that is allowed to render monumental decisions in undemocratic settings on behalf of the public. The possibility for substantive change exists, for although the values of the marketplace have been central to the functioning of American society, so too have democratic and egalitarian values. It will be a test of political will to determine which values will ultimately guide the television of the future.

Since the time of the New Deal, the divisions, dilemmas, and contradictions within liberal democratic thought and society have supplied the conflicts that give rise to situation comedy humor. Even as comedic humor disrupts ordinary language, perception, and order, it gives voice to otherwise ineffable social truths. Just as the irrepressibility of truth is manifested in dreams, slips of the tongue, parapraxes, and spoonerisms, the humor of the situation comedy resists repression and censorship. Laughter is the material expression of the collision between truth and falsehood.

Throughout the postwar era, however, the full expression and realization of liberal democratic values—both in society and in its popular art—has been muted by the undemocratic character of key social institutions such as the media oligopolies. While no society is ever fully free of its internal contradictions and conflicts, until such a time that a greater degree of democratic control is exercised over economic production and the distributive activity of the state, the television situation comedy will not cease to evoke a large amount of nervous laughter.

NOTES

1. Robert N. Bellah et al., *Habits of the Heart: Individualism and Commitment in American Life* (Berkeley: University of California Press, 1985), pp. 277–281.

2. See Peter Clecak, *Crooked Paths: Reflections on Socialism, Conservatism, and the Welfare State* (New York: Harper & Row, 1977).

3. The first episode of *The George Burns Show*, "George and the Private Eye," was filmed on August 22, 1958 and aired October 24, 1958. This particular script went through eight revisions before reaching its final form. Written by Norman Paul, Keith Fowler, Harvey Helm, and William Burns. Produced and directed by Rod Amateau.

4. Rod Amateau, interview at Burbank Studios. Burbank, California, July 17, 1981.

5. *Daddy-O*, created and written by Max Shulman. Produced and directed by Rod Amateau. A Selby-Lake–Cottage Industries, Production. "Father Strikes Back" bears the production number 4300–1. The final draft of the script bears the date October 10, 1960. Filming dates are noted as 12/28, 12/29, 12/30, 1960.

6. Max Shulman, interview, Los Angeles, California, June 13, 1988. Shulman died of cancer shortly after this interview on August 28, 1988.

7. Frank Stanton, "Parallel Paths," in *Culture for the Millions? Mass Media in Modern Society,* ed. Norman Jacobs (Boston: Beacon Press, 1964), p. 90.

8. See Alan Pearce, "The Economic and Political Strength of the Television Networks," in *Network Television and the Public Interest*, ed. Michael Botein and David M. Rice (Lexington, Mass.: D. C. Heath & Co., 1980), pp. 3–24.

9. All three networks failed to reach even half (49%) of the viewing audience during the week of the Democratic National Convention in July 1988. This is the worst ever record of viewership since the Nielsen ratings began. See Ray Richmond, "Network Viewership Reaches a New Low," *The Orange County Register*, July 27, 1988, pp. L1, L10. The erosion of broadcast network audiences is also seen in the 24 percent increase of cable network advertising billings over 1987, exceeding $1 billion dollars in revenue for the first time. By contrast, ABC, CBS, and NBC fell 15 percent over the same period. See Wayne Walley, "Cable Steals Upfront Show From TV Nets," *Advertising Age,* June 13, 1988, pp. 1, 70. Bickering over substantially lower audience estimates broke out between the networks, advertisers, and the A. C. Nielsen Company, which replaced its diary system with the "people meter." Lower television ratings compelled advertisers to try to negotiate lower rates with the networks. See Peter Barnes and Joanne Lipman, "Networks and Ad Agencies Battle Over Estimates of TV Viewership," *The Wall Street Journal,* 7 January 1987, p. 25.

10. Ben H. Bagdikian, *The Media Monopoly* (Boston: Beacon Press, 1983), p. 226.

11. William T. Bielby and Denise D. Bielby, *The 1987 Hollywood Writers' Report: A Survey of Ethnic, Gender and Age Employment Practices* (Los Angeles: Writers Guild of America, west, 1987).

12. Vince Waldron, p. 130.

13. See Martin Esslin, *The Age of Television* (San Francisco: W. H. Freeman & Co., 1982), pp. 108–113.

Selected Bibliography

Adler, Richard P., ed. *All in the Family: A Critical Appraisal*. New York: Praeger, 1979.

Alperovitz, Gar, and Jeff Faux. *Rebuilding America*. New York: Pantheon Books, 1984.

Andrews, Bart. *The "I Love Lucy" Book*. Garden City, N.Y.: Doubleday, 1985.

Applebaum, Irwyn. *The World According to Beaver*. New York: Bantam Books, 1984.

Aronowitz, Stanley. *False Promises: The Shaping of American Working Class Consciousness*. New York: McGraw-Hill, 1974.

————. *Food, Shelter and the American Dream*. New York: Seabury Press, 1974.

Bagdikian, Ben H. *The Media Monopoly*. Boston: Beacon Press, 1983.

Bakhtin, M. M., and P. N. Medvedev. *The Formal Method in Literary Scholarship: A Critical Introduction to Sociological Poetics*. Translated by Albert J. Wehrle. Cambridge: Harvard University Press, 1986.

Banfield, Edward C. *The Unheavenly City Revisited*. Boston: Little, Brown & Co., 1974.

Baran, Paul A., and Paul M. Sweezy. *Monopoly Capital: An Essay on the American Economic and Social Order*. New York: Modern Reader Paperbacks, 1966.

Barnouw, Erik. *Tube of Plenty: The Evolution of American Television*. Rev. ed. New York: Oxford University Press, 1982.

Barthes, Roland. *Elements of Semiology*. Translated by Annette Lavers and Colin Smith. New York: Hill & Wang, 1968.

————. *Mythologies*. Translated by Annette Lavers. New York: Hill & Wang, 1972.

Beirne, Piers, and Richard Quinney, eds. *Marxism and Law*. New York: John Wiley & Sons, 1982.

Bell, Daniel. *The End of Ideology: On the Exhaustion of Political Ideas in the Fifties*. Rev. ed. New York: Free Press, 1962.

————. *The Cultural Contradictions of Capitalism*. New York: Basic Books, 1978.

Bellah, Robert N., Richard Madsen, William M. Sullivan, Ann Swidler, and Steven M. Tipton. *Habits of the Heart: Individualism and Commitment in American Life*. Berkeley: University of California Press, 1985.

Bennett, Tony. *Formalism and Marxism*. London and New York: Methuen, 1979.

Bennett, Tony, Susan Boyd-Bowman, Colin Mercer, and Janet Woollacott, eds. *Popular Television and Film*. London: British Film Institute, 1981.

Bensman, Joseph, and Arthur J. Vidich. *American Society: The Welfare State and Beyond*. Rev. ed. South Hadley, Massachusetts: Bergin & Garvey, 1987.

Berger, Brigitte, and Peter L. Berger. *The War Over the Family: Capturing the Middle Ground*. Garden City, N.Y.: Anchor Press/Doubleday, 1984.

Bensen, Stanley M., Thomas G. Krattenmaker, A. Richard Metzger, Jr., and John R. Woodbury. *Misregulating Television: Network Dominance and the FCC*. Chicago: University of Chicago Press, 1984.

Bielby, William T., and Denise D. Bielby. *The 1987 Hollywood Writers' Report: A Survey of Ethnic, Gender and Age Employment Practices*. Los Angeles: Writers Guild of America, west, 1987.

Block, Fred, Richard A. Cloward, Barbara Ehrenreich, and Frances Fox Piven. *The Mean Season: The Attack on the Welfare State*. New York: Pantheon Books, 1987.

Blum, Richard A., and Richard D. Lindheim. *Primetime: Network Television Programming*. Boston: Focal Press, 1987.

Blumberg, Paul. *Inequality in an Age of Decline*. New York: Oxford University Press, 1980.

Boggs, Carl. *Social Movements and Political Power: Emerging Forms of Radicalism in the West*. Philadelphia: Temple University Press, 1986.

Bonacich, Edna, and John Modell. *The Economic Basis of Ethic Solidarity: Small Business in the Japanese American Community*. Berkeley: University of California Press, 1980.

Boorstin, Daniel J. *The Americans: The Democratic Experience*. New York: Vintage Books, 1974.

Botein, Michael, and David M. Rice, eds. *Network Television and the Public Interest: A Preliminary Inquiry*. Lexington, Mass.: D. C. Heath & Co., 1980.

Bottomore, T. B. *Classes in Modern Society*. New York: Vintage Books, 1966.

Bovée, Courtland L., and William F. Arens. *Contemporary Advertising*. 2d ed. Homewood, Ill.: Irwin, 1986.

Bower, Robert T. *Television and the Public*. New York: Holt, Rinehart & Winston, 1973.

Bowles, Samuel, and Herbert Gintis. *Schooling in Capitalist America*. New York: Basic Books, 1976.

———. *Democracy and Capitalism: Property, Community, and the Contradictions of Modern Social Thought*. New York: Basic Books, 1986.

Bowles, Samuel, David M. Gordon, and Thomas E. Weisskopf. *Beyond the Waste Land: A Democratic Alternative to Economic Decline*. Garden City, N.Y.: Anchor Press/Doubleday, 1983.

Braestrup, Peter. *Big Story: How the American Press and Television Reported and Interpreted the Crisis of Tet in Vietnam and Washington*. Garden City, N.Y.: Anchor Books, 1978.

Brantlinger, Patrick. *Bread and Circuses: Theories of Mass Culture as Social Decay*. Ithaca, N.Y.: Cornell University Press, 1983.

Braverman, Harry. *Labor and Monopoly Capital: The Degradation of Work in the Twentieth Century*. New York: Monthly Review Press, 1974.

Brown, Les. *Television: The Business Behind the Box.* New York: Harcourt Brace Jovanovich, 1971.

Brownmiller, Susan. *Femininity.* New York: Fawcett Columbine, 1984.

Bryce-Laporte, Roy Simón, ed. *Sourcebook on the New Immigration: Implications for the United States and the International Community.* New Brunswick, N.J.: Transaction Books, 1980.

Carroll, Peter N. *It Seemed Like Nothing Happened: The Tragedy and Promise of America in the 1970s.* New York: Holt, Rinehart & Winston, 1982.

Carter, Paul A. *Another Part of the Fifties.* New York: Columbia University Press, 1983.

Chafe, William H., and Harvard Sitkoff, eds. *A History of Our Times: Readings on Postwar America.* New York: Oxford University Press, 1983.

Cheng, Lucie, and Edna Bonacich, eds. *Labor Immigration Under Capitalism: Asian Workers in the United States Before World War II.* Berkeley: University of California Press, 1984.

Clark, Kenneth B. *Dark Ghetto: Dilemmas of Social Power.* New York: Harper & Row, 1967.

Clecak, Peter. *Crooked Paths: Reflections on Socialism, Conservatism, and the Welfare State.* New York: Harper & Row, 1977.

————. *America's Quest for the Ideal Self: Dissent and Fulfillment in the 60s and 70s.* New York: Oxford University Press, 1983.

Cogley, John. *Report on Blacklisting, II: Radio-Television.* New York: Fund for the Republic, 1956.

Cohen, Joshua, and Joel Rogers. *On Democracy: Toward a Transformation of American Society.* New York: Penguin Books, 1983.

Comstock, George, Steven Chaffee, Natan Katzman, Maxwell McCombs, and Donald Roberts. *Television and Human Behavior.* New York: Columbia University Press, 1978.

Connolly, William, ed. *Legitimacy and the State.* New York: New York University Press, 1984.

Cox, Andrew, Paul Furlong, and Edward Page. *Power in Capitalist Societies: Theory, Explanation and Cases.* Brighton, England: Wheatsheaf Books, 1985.

Cripps, Thomas. *Slow Fade to Black: The Negro in American Film, 1900–1942.* New York: Oxford University Press, 1977.

Cunningham, Frank. *Democratic Theory and Socialism.* Cambridge: Cambridge University Press, 1987.

Daniels, Roger, and Harry H. L. Kitano. *American Racism: Exploration of the Nature of Prejudice.* Englewood Cliffs, N.J.: Prentice-Hall, 1970.

Denisoff, R. Serge. *Solid Gold: The Popular Record Industry.* New Brunswick, N.J.: Transaction Books, 1975.

Dickstein, Morris. *Gates of Eden: American Culture in the Sixties.* New York: Basic Books, 1977.

Dolbeare, Kenneth M., and Patricia Dolbeare. *American Ideologies: The Competing Political Beliefs of the 1970s.* 3rd ed. Boston: Houghton Mifflin Co., 1976.

Duke, Paul, ed. *Beyond Reagan: The Politics of Upheaval.* New York: Warner Books, 1986.

Dunning, John. *Tune in Yesterday: The Ultimate Encyclopedia of Old-Time Radio 1925–1976.* Englewood Cliffs, N.J.: Prentice-Hall, 1976.

Dworkin, Ronald. *A Matter of Principle.* Cambridge: Harvard University Press, 1985.

Eagleton, Terry. *Literary Theory: An Introduction*. Minneapolis: University of Minnesota Press, 1983.

Ehrenreich, Barbara. *The Hearts of Men: American Dreams and the Flight from Commitment*. Garden City, N.Y.: Anchor Press/Doubleday, 1983.

Eisenstein, Zillah R. *The Radical Future of Liberal Feminism*. New York: Longman, 1981.

Eliot, Marc. *Television: One Season in American Television*. New York: St. Martin's Press, 1983.

Ellis, John. *Visible Fictions: Cinema, Television, Video*. London: Routledge & Kegan Paul, 1982.

Essien-Udon, E. U. *Black Nationalism: A Search for an Identity in America*. New York: Dell, 1964.

Esslin, Martin. *The Age of Television*. San Francisco: W. H. Freeman & Co., 1982.

Evans, Sara. *Personal Politics: The Roots of Women's Liberation in the Civil Rights Movement of the New Left*. New York: Vintage Books, 1980.

Feagin, Joe R. *Subordinating the Poor*. Englewood Cliffs, N.J.: Prentice-Hall, 1975.

Ferguson, Thomas, and Joel Rogers. *Right Turn: The Decline of the Democrats and the Future of American Politics*. New York: Hill & Wang, 1986.

Feuer, Jane, Paul Kerr, and Tise Vahimagi, eds. *MTM "Quality Television."* London: BFI Publishing, 1984.

Fiske, John. *Television Culture*. New York: Methuen, 1987.

Friedan, Betty. *The Feminine Mystique*. New York: Dell, 1963.

Frith, Simon. *Sound Effects: Youth, Leisure, and the Politics of Rock 'n' Roll*. New York: Pantheon Books, 1981.

Galbraith, John Kenneth. *The New Industrial State*. 2d ed. Boston: Houghton Mifflin Co. 1971.

———. *Economics in Perspective: A Critical History*. Boston: Houghton Mifflin Co., 1987.

Gans, Herbert. *More Equality*. New York: Vintage Books, 1974.

Garrow, David J. *Bearing the Cross: Martin Luther King, Jr., and the Southern Christian Leadership Conference*. New York: Vintage Books, 1988.

Gilbert, James. *Another Chance: Postwar America, 1945–1985*. 2d ed. Chicago: Dorsey Press, 1986.

Gillett, Charlie. *The Sound of the City: The Rise of Rock 'n' Roll*. New York: Dell, 1972.

Gitlin, Todd. *The Whole World Is Watching: Mass Media in the Making and Unmaking of the New Left*. Berkeley: University of California Press, 1980.

———. *Inside Prime Time*. New York: Pantheon Books, 1983.

———. *The Sixties: Years of Hope, Days of Rage*. New York: Bantam Books, 1987.

Gordon, Milton. *Assimilation in American Life: The Role of Race, Religion, and National Origins*. New York: Oxford University Press, 1964.

Green, Joey. *The Unofficial Gilligan's Island Handbook: A Castaway's Companion to the Longest-Running Shipwreck in Television History*. New York: Warner Books, 1988.

Green, Philip. *The Pursuit of Inequality*. New York: Pantheon Books, 1981.

Greenberg, Bradley S., and Brenda Dervin. *Use of the Mass Media by the Urban Poor: Findings of Three Research Projects, with an Annotated Bibliography*. New York: Praeger, 1970.

Habermas, Jürgen. *Legitimation Crisis*. Boston: Beacon Press, 1973.

Halberstam, David. *The Powers That Be*. New York: Alfred A. Knopf, 1979.

Hamby, Alonzo L. *Liberalism and Its Challengers: FDR to Reagan*. New York: Oxford University Press, 1985.

Hanhardt, John, ed. *Video Culture: A Critical Investigation*. New York: Visual Studies Workshop Press, 1986.

Hanson, Russell L. *The Democratic Imagination in America: Conversations with Our Past*. Princeton, N.J.: Princeton University Press, 1985.

Harrington, Michael. *The Other America: Poverty in the United States*. Baltimore: Penguin Books, 1971.

——. *The Twilight of Capitalism*. New York: Touchstone, 1976.

——. *The New American Poverty*. New York: Penguin Books, 1984.

Harris, Jay S., ed. *TV Guide: The First 25 Years*. New York: New American Liberary, 1980.

Harris, Louis. *Inside America*. New York: Vintage Books, 1987.

Harris, Marvin. *America Now: The Anthropology of a Changing Culture*. New York: Touchstone, 1981.

Harrison, Bennett. *Education, Training, and the Urban Ghetto*. Baltimore: Johns Hopkins University Press, 1972.

Hastings, Max. *The Fire This Time: America's Year of Crisis*. New York: Taplinger, 1969.

Hawkes, Terence. *Structuralism and Semiotics*. Berkeley and Los Angeles: University of California Press, 1977.

Heath, Jim F. *Decade of Disillusionment: The Kennedy-Johnson Years*. Bloomington and London: Indiana University Press, 1975.

Heilbroner, Robert. *The Nature and Logic of Capitalism*. New York: W. W. Norton, 1985.

Heller, Celia S., ed. *Structured Social Inequality*. New York: Macmillan, 1969.

Henry, Jules. *Culture Against Man*. New York: Vintage Books, 1965.

Higham, John. *Send These to Me: Jews and Other Immigrants in Urban America*. New York: Atheneum, 1975.

Hobsbawm, E. J. *Industry and Empire: From 1750 to the Present Day*. New York: Penguin Books, 1969.

Hodgson, Godfrey. *America in Our Time*. Garden City, N.Y.: Doubleday, 1976.

Hofheinz, Roy, Jr., and Kent E. Calder. *The Eastasia Edge*. New York: Basic Books, 1982.

Hofstadter, Richard. *Anti-Intellectualism in American Life*. New York: Vintage Books, 1963.

Hook, Sidney. *Political Power and Personal Freedom: Critical Studies in Democracy, Communism, and Civil Rights*. New York: Criterion Books, 1958.

Horowitz, Irving Louis. *Ideology and Utopia in the United States: 1956–1976*. New York: Oxford University Press, 1977.

Howe, Irving. *World of Our Fathers: The Journey of the East European Jews to America and the Life They Found and Made*. New York: Touchstone, 1976.

——. *Socialism and America*. New York: Harcourt Brace Jovanovich, 1985.

Hunt, E. K. *History of Economic Thought: A Critical Perspective*. Belmont, Calif.: Wadsworth, 1979.

Huntington, Samuel P. *American Politics: The Promise of Disharmony*. Cambridge: Harvard University Press, Belknap Press, 1981.

Issel, William. *Social Change in the United States, 1945–1983*. New York: Schocken Books, 1987.

Jackson, Kenneth T. *Crabgrass Frontier: The Suburbanization of the United States*. New York: Oxford University Press, 1985.

Jacobs, Norman, ed. *Culture for the Millions? Mass Media in Modern Society*. Boston: Beacon Press, 1964.

Jameson, Frederic. *The Political Unconscious: Narrative as a Socially Symbolic Act*. Ithaca, N.Y.: Cornell University Press, 1981.

Janowitz, Morris. *The Last Half-Century: Societal Change and Politics in America*. Chicago: University of Chicago Press, 1978.

Jay, Martin. *The Dialectical Imagination: A History of the Frankfurt School and the Institute of Social Research 1923–1950*. Boston: Little, Brown & Co., 1973.

Jezer, Marty. *The Dark Ages: Life in the United States 1945–1960*. Boston: South End Press, 1982.

Jones, Jacqueline. *Labor of Love, Labor of Sorrow: Black Women, Work, and the Family from Slavery to the Present*. New York: Vintage Books, 1986.

Jones, Landon Y. *Great Expectations: America and the Baby Boom Generation*. New York: Coward, McCann & Geoghegan, 1980.

Jorgensen, Joseph G. *The Sun Dance Religion: Power for the Powerless*. Chicago: University of Chicago Press, 1972.

Kairys, David, ed. *The Politics of Law: A Progressive Critique*. New York: Pantheon Books, 1982.

Kaplan, H. Roy, ed. *American Minorities and Economic Opportunity*. Itasca, Ill.: F. E. Peacock, 1977.

Kaplan, Marshall, and Peggy L. Cuciti, eds. *The Great Society and Its Legacy: Twenty Years of U.S. Social Policy*. Durham: Duke University Press, 1986.

Kelly, Richard. *The Andy Griffith Show*. Winston-Salem, N.C.: John R. Blair, 1984.

Kochman, Thomas, ed. *Rappin' and Stylin' Out: Communication in Urban Black America*. Urbana: University of Illinois Press, 1972.

Kotkin, Joel, and Paul Grabowicz. *California, Inc*. New York: Avon Books, 1982.

Kristol, Irving. *Reflections of a Neoconservative: Looking Back, Looking Ahead*. New York: Basic Books, 1983.

Lasch, Christopher. *Haven in a Heartless World: The Family Besieged*. New York: Basic Books, 1979.

———. *The Culture of Narcissism: American Life in an Age of Diminishing Expectations*. New York: W. W. Norton & Co., 1979.

Lekachman, Robert. *Visions and Nightmares: America after Reagan*. New York: Macmillan, 1987.

Leuchtenburg, William E. *A Troubled Feast: American Society Since 1945*. Boston: Little, Brown & Co., 1973.

Lévi-Strauss, Claude. *Structural Anthropology*. Translated by Claire Jacobson and Brooke Grundfest Schoepf. New York: Basic Books, 1963.

———. *Tristes Tropiques*. Translated by John Russell. New York: Atheneum, 1971.

Lodziak, Conrad. *The Power of Television: A Critical Appraisal*. London: Frances Pinter, 1986.

Loescher, Gil, and John A. Scanlan. *Calculated Kindness: Refugees and America's Half-Open Door, 1945 to the Present*. New York: Free Press, 1986.

Lowery, Shearon, and Melvin L. DeFleur. *Milestones in Mass Communication Research: Media Effects*. New York: Longman, 1983.

MacDonald, J. Fred. *Don't Touch That Dial! Radio Programming in American Life From 1920 to 1960*. Chicago: Nelson-Hall, 1979.

———. *Blacks and White TV: Afro-Americans in Television since 1948*. Chicago: Nelson-Hall, 1983.

———. *Television and the Red Menace: The Video Road to Vietnam*. New York: Praeger, 1985.

———. *Who Shot the Sheriff? The Rise and Fall of the Television Western*. New York: Praeger, 1987.

McCrohan, Donna. *The Honeymooner's Companion: The Kramdens and the Nortons Revisited*. New York: Workman, 1978.

Marc, David. *Demographic Vistas: Television in American Culture*. Philadelphia: University of Pennsylvania Press, 1984.

Mayer, Martin. *About Television*. New York: Harper & Row, 1972.

Mead, Margaret. *Culture and Commitment: The New Relationship Between Generations in the 1970s*. Rev. ed. Garden City, N.Y.: Anchor Books, 1978.

Melman, Seymour. *The Permanent War Economy: American Capitalism in Decline*. New York: Simon & Schuster, 1974.

Metz, Robert. *CBS: Reflections in a Bloodshot Eye*. New York: Signet, 1976.

Miliband, Ralph. *The State in Capitalist Society: An Analysis of the Western System of Power*. New York: Basic Books, 1969.

Miller, Jim, ed. *The Rolling Stone Illustrated History of Rock and Roll*. New York: Rolling Stone/Random House, 1976.

Miller, Merle. *The Judges and the Judged*. Garden City, N.Y.: Doubleday, 1952.

Minow, Newton N. *The Private Broadcaster and the Public Interest*. Edited by Lawrence Laurent. New York: Atheneum, 1964.

Monaco, James. *Media Culture: Television, Radio, Records, Books, Magazines, Newspapers, Movies*. New York: Dell, 1978.

Montagu, Ashley. *Man's Most Dangerous Myth: The Fallacy of Race*. 5th ed. New York: Oxford University Press, 1974.

Morgan, Robin. *Going Too Far: The Personal Chronicle of a Feminist*. New York: Vintage Books, 1978.

Morris, Charles R. *A Time of Passion: America 1960–1980*. New York: Penguin Books, 1986.

Moynihan, Daniel P. *Maximum Feasible Misunderstanding: Community Action in the War on Poverty*. New York: Free Press, 1969.

Murray, Charles. *Losing Ground: American Social Policy 1950–1980*. New York: Basic Books, 1984.

Myrdal, Gunnar. *An American Dilemma: The Negro Problem and Modern Democracy*. New York: Harper & Row, 1944.

Newcomb, Horace, ed. *Television: The Critical View*. 4th ed. New York: Oxford University Press, 1987.

Nisbet, Robert. *Conservatism: Dreams and Reality*. Milton Keynes, England: Open University Press, 1986.

Norback, Craig T., Peter G. Norback, and the editors of *TV Guide* Magazine, *TV Guide Almanac*. New York: Ballantine Books, 1980.

O'Connor, John E., ed. *American History/American Television: Interpreting the Video Past*. New York: Frederick Ungar, 1983.

Omi, Michael, and Howard Winant. *Racial Formation in the United States: From the 1960s to the 1980s*. New York: Routledge & Kegan Paul, 1986.

O'Neill, William L. *Coming Apart: An Informal History of American in the 1960s*. New York: Quadrangle Books, 1971.

Palmer, Robert. *Deep Blues*. New York: Penguin Books, 1982.

Peterson, William. *Japanese Americans: Oppression and Success*. New York: Random House, 1971.

Pines, Burton Yale. *Back to Basics: The Traditionalist Movement That is Sweeping Grass-Roots America*. New York: William Morrow & Co., 1982.

Piven, Frances Fox, and Richard A. Cloward. *Regulating the Poor: The Functions of Public Welfare*. New York: Vintage Books, 1971.

———. *The New Class War: Reagan's Attack on the Welfare State and Its Consequences*. New York: Pantheon Books, 1982.

Poster, Mark. *Critical Theory of the Family*. New York: Seabury Press, 1978.

Potter, David M. *People of Plenty: Economic Abundance and the American Character*. Chicago: University of Chicago Press, 1954.

Poulantzas, Nicos. *Political Power and Social Classes*. Translated by Timothy O'Hagan. London: Verso Editions, 1978.

Reel, A. Frank. *The Networks: How They Stole the Show*. New York: Charles Scribner's Sons, 1979.

Reich, Robert B. *The Next American Frontier*. New York: Penguin Books, 1984.

Riesman, David, in collaboration with Revel Denney and Nathan Glazer. *The Lonely Crowd: A Study of the Changing American Character*. Abridged ed. New Haven, Conn.: Yale University Press, 1961.

Roszak, Theodore. *The Making of a Counter Culture: Reflections of the Technocratic Society and Its Youthful Opposition*. Garden City, N.Y.: Doubleday, 1969.

Rowe, Mike. *Chicago Breakdown*. London: Edison Press, 1973.

Schiller, Herbert I. *Information and the Crisis Economy*. New York: Oxford University Press, 1986.

Schrag, Peter. *The Decline of the WASP*. New York: Simon & Schuster, 1971.

Schudson, Michael. *Advertising, the Uneasy Persuasion: Its Dubious Impact on American Society*. New York: Basic Books, 1984.

Seiden, Martin H. *Who Controls the Mass Media? Popular Myths and Economic Realities*. New York: Basic Books, 1974.

Sennett, Richard. *Authority*. New York: Alfred A. Knopf, 1980.

Shames, Laurence. *The Big Time: The Harvard Business School's Most Successful Class— And How It Shaped America*. New York: Harper & Row, 1986.

Shorter, Edward. *The Making of the Modern Family*. New York: Basic Books, 1975.

Sidel, Ruth. *Women and Children Last: The Plight of Poor Women in Affluent America*. New York: Penguin Books, 1986.

Siegel, Frederick F. *Troubled Journey: From Pearl Harbor to Ronald Reagan*. New York: Hill & Wang, 1984.

Sklar, Robert. *Movie-Made America: A Cultural History of American Movies*. New York: Vintage Books, 1975.

Smith, Russell, E., and Dorothy Zietz. *American Social Welfare Institutions*. New York: John Wiley & Sons, 1970.

Sontag, Susan. *Against Interpretation: And Other Essays*. New York: Dell, 1966.

Sowell, Thomas. *Ethnic America: A History*. New York: Basic Books, 1981.

————. ed. *Essays and Data on American Ethnic Groups*. Washington, D.C.: Urban Institute, 1978.

Steiner, Gary A. *The People Look at Television: A Study of Audience Attitudes*. New York: Alfred A. Knopf, 1963.

Steinfels, Peter. *The Neoconservatives: The Men Who Are Changing America's Politics*. New York: Touchstone, 1979.

Szatmary, David P. *Rockin' in Time: A Social History of Rock and Roll*. Englewood Cliffs, N.J.: Prentice-Hall, 1987.

Takagi, Ronald T. *Iron Cages: Race and Culture in Nineteenth-Century America*. New York: Alfred A. Knopf, 1979.

Thernstrom, Stephen, ed. *The Politics of Ethnicity*. Cambridge: Press, Belknap Press, 1982.

Thompson, Kenneth. *Beliefs and Ideology*. London and New York: Tavistock, Publications, 1986.

Thurow, Lester C. *The Zero-Sum Society: Distribution and the Possibilities for Economic Change*. New York: Penguin Books, 1981.

Todorov, Tzvetan. *The Fantastic: A Structural Approach to a Literary Genre*. Translated by Richard Howard. Ithaca, N.Y.: Cornell University Press, 1973.

————. *Mikhail Bakhtin: The Dialogical Principle*. Translated by Wlad Godzich. Minneapolis: University of Minnesota Press, 1984.

Tuchman, Gaye, Arlene Kaplan Daniels, and James Benet, eds. *Hearth and Home: Images of Women in the Mass Media*. New York: Oxford University Press, 1978.

Turner, Bryan. *Equality*. New York: Tavistock Publications, 1986.

Turner, Jonathan H., and David Musick. *American Dilemmas: A Sociological Interpretation of Enduring Social Issues*. New York: Columbia University Press, 1985.

U.S. Commission on Civil Rights. *Window Dressing on the Set: Women and Minorities in Television*. Washington, D.C.: Report of the United States Commission on Civil Rights, 1977.

U.S. National Advisory Commission on Civil Disorders. *Report of the National Advisory Commission on Civil Disorders*. Washington, D.C.: U.S. Government Printing Office, 1968.

Waldron, Vince. *Classic Sitcoms: A Celebration of the Best Prime-Time Comedy*. New York: Collier Books, 1987.

Walzer, Michael. *Radical Principles: Reflections of an Unreconstructed Democrat*. New York: Basic Books, 1980.

Ward, Ed, Geoffrey Stokes, and Ken Tucker. *Rock of Ages: The Rolling Stone History of Rock and Roll*. New York: Rolling Stone Press/Summit Books, 1986.

Wertheim, Arthur Frank. *Radio Comedy*. New York: Oxford University Press, 1979.

Wilk, Max. *The Golden Age of Television: Notes from the Survivors*. New York: Dell, 1976.

Williams, William Appleman. *America in a Changing World: A History of the United States in the Twentieth Century*. New York: Harper & Row, 1978.

Wilson, William Julius. *The Declining Significance of Race: Blacks and Changing American Institutions*. 2d ed. Chicago: University of Chicago Press, 1980.

Winston, Brian. *Misunderstanding Media*. Cambridge: Harvard University Press, 1986.

Wyllie, Irvin G. *The Self-Made Man in America: The Myth of Rags to Riches*. New York: Free Press, 1966.

Zaretsky, Eli. *Capitalism, the Family and Personal Life*. New York: Harper & Row, 1976.

Index

About the Author

DARRELL Y. HAMAMOTO is a professor of sociology at National University and serves as program coordinator for the School of Arts and Sciences. Professor Hamamoto holds a Ph.D. in Comparative Culture from the University of California, Irvine, and an M.A. in Popular Culture Studies from Bowling Green State University, Ohio. He received his B.A. in political science from California State University, Long Beach. Dr. Hamamoto pursues an active career in journalism having written extensively in the areas of popular culture and mass media. He is arts and entertainment editor for *Random Lengths,* an independently owned alternative newspaper in the Los Angeles/Long Beach area. His critical pieces and photographs have appeared in *Rock and Roll Confidential, Pulse!, Film Quarterly, Guitar Player, L.A. Weekly, The Orange County Register,* and *The Journal of Popular Film and Television.* Hamamoto also heads the group Double Veteran, a studio group that produces "post-modern dance music for monads."